W9-BTP-372

INSPIRE / PLAN / DISCOVER / EXPERIENCE

MEXICO

DK EYEWITNESS

MEXICO

CONTENTS

DISCOVER 6

EXPERIENCE MEXICO CITY 64

EXPERIENCE MEXICO 134

NEED TO KNOW 310

Left: Ceramic skulls at a market stall
Previous page: Temple overlooking the beach, Tulum
Front cover: The colorful cityscape of Guanajuato

DISCOVER

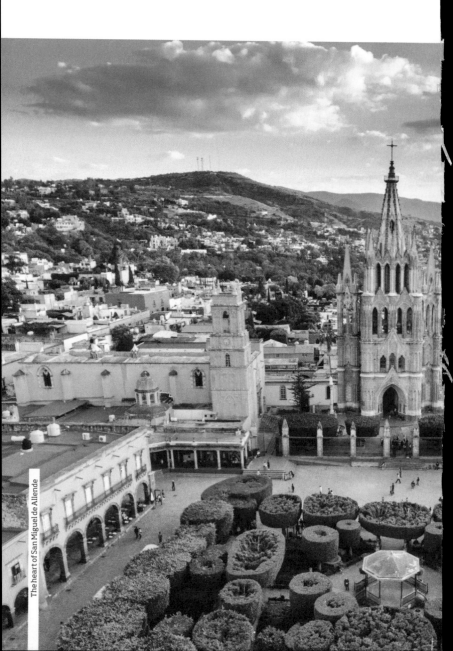

The heart of San Miguel de Allende

WELCOME TO
MEXICO

Bold Rivera murals in the city and ancient Maya ruins in the jungle. Tranquil deserts, pristine beaches, vast canyons, and snow-capped volcanoes. Spicy salsas followed up with fiery tequila. Whatever your dream trip to Mexico includes, this DK Eyewitness travel guide is the perfect companion.

1 Soft-tortilla tacos.

2 *Papel-picado* hanging over a street in San Miguel de Allende.

3 A mariachi musician.

4 Popocatépetl volcano and Cholula's hilltop Nuestra Señora de los Remedios.

Some people picture Mexico as a vast, cacti-studded desert – and while that reflects the landscape just south of the US border, a little exploring will turn up so much more. Farther inland, great mountains and volcanoes dominate the landscape, while the jungles of the south harbor tropical wildlife and the crumbling Mesoamerican ruins. All around the country, Mexico's beaches are a major draw, from the wildlife-rich waters of Baja California, to the wild, surf-rich stretches in the states of Chiapas and Oaxaca – not to mention the balmy, Caribbean coast of the Riviera Maya.

When it comes to urban pleasures, few places in the world can match Mexico City, with its teeming markets, vibrant galleries, and enthusiastic sports scene. Cities such as Guanajuato and San Miguel de Allende are beautiful bastions of old New Spain, while Monterrey and Tijuana are hubs of modern Mexican culture and entertainment. In the south, Oaxaca and San Cristóbal offer a very different vibe, immersed in rich indigenous culture and culinary traditions.

From the western Baja California border to the curving Yucatán peninsula and everything in between, we've broken the country down into easily navigable chapters, with detailed itineraries, expert local knowledge, and comprehensive maps. So whether you're hunting down unique regional dishes, a fun local festival, or stunning views of weathered pyramids, this Eyewitness travel guide will ensure that you have everything you need to plan the perfect adventure. Enjoy the book, and enjoy Mexico.

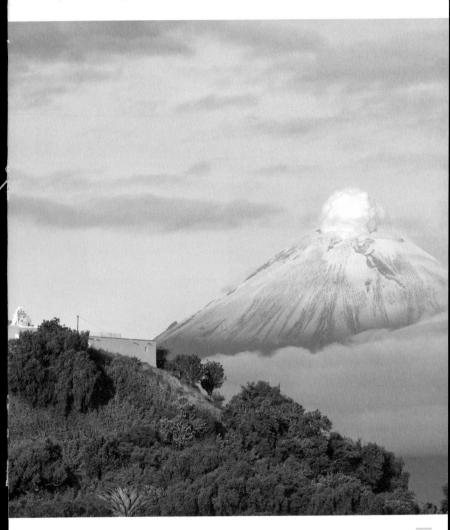

REASONS TO LOVE
MEXICO

With such rich and varied cultural traditions, regional foods, and natural beauty, there's no such thing as "typical" here – instead you'll find hundreds of different things to discover and love. Here are just some of our favorites.

1 FIESTA CULTURE

From party-hard Carnival to the traditional Day of the Dead festivities – not to mention regional events up and down the country – there's always something going on (p54).

MESOAMERICAN CITIES 2

Mexico is studded with monumental pre-Hispanic remains. Scale the Pyramid of the Sun, hike the jungle paths of Palenque, and admire the murals at Bonampak.

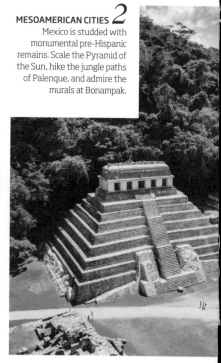

3 MEXICAN FLAVORS

There's more to Mexican cuisine than its famous street food. Try the fragrant Veracruz-style red snapper, enjoy small-batch tequila, and indulge at gourmet restaurants (p52).

THE SILVER ROAD 4

Follow this old route *(p26)* that once linked the capital and the country's silver mines, to discover all the beautifully preserved towns between Zacatecas and Mexico City.

VIBRANT ART 5

Aztec serpents and Spanish conquistadors share space with priests and Pancho Villa in bold murals, while folk-art-inspired paintings by Frida Kahlo capture the spirit of Mexico *(p38)*.

"EL CHEPE" RAILROAD 6

This scenic route cuts through vast, gold and rust-red canyons. The region is rich in natural beauty, making it perfect terrain for one of the world's great train journeys *(p180)*.

OAXACA CITY 7
Mexico's most exciting colonial-era city is crammed with attractions: Zapotec markets, culinary hot spots, art museums, cultural festivals, and ancient Monte Albán (p234).

SWIMMING IN CENOTES 8
Giant limestone caverns open up like underground cathedrals beneath the Yucatán region. Crystal-clear swimming pools fill the sinkholes, perfect for a refreshing dip (p281).

9 MUSEO NACIONAL DE ANTROPOLOGÍA
Spanning over 3,000 years of Mexican history, the nation's finest museum explores the country's incredible past with staggering exhibits of statuary and reconstructed tombs (p100).

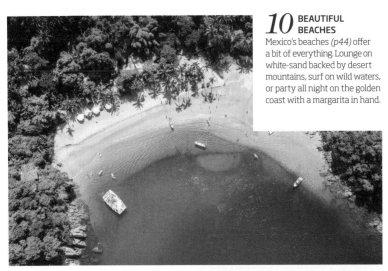

10 BEAUTIFUL BEACHES

Mexico's beaches *(p44)* offer a bit of everything. Lounge on white-sand backed by desert mountains, surf on wild waters, or party all night on the golden coast with a margarita in hand.

11 TRADITIONAL CRAFTS

Crafts in Mexico are an essential part of ceremonial and daily life. Head to a *mercado* (market) to hunt down local treasures like woven *huarache* sandals or Taxco silverwork.

12 MARIACHI MUSIC

Beginning with guitars, trumpets, and a harmonized chorus, mariachi bands grow in number as the day goes on, enticing dancers to fill the city plazas *(p32)*.

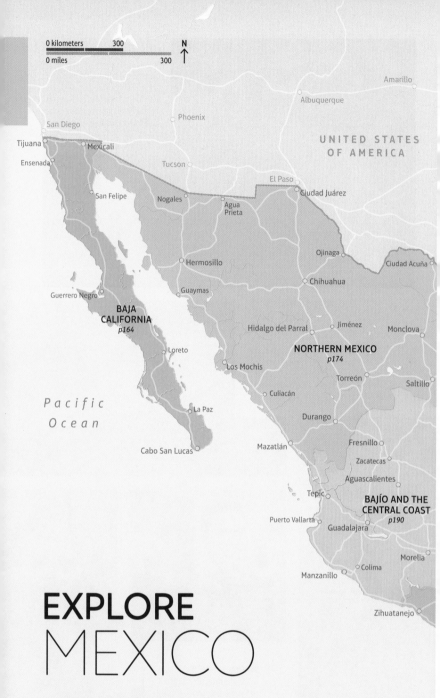

BAJA
CALIFORNIA
p164

NORTHERN MEXICO
p174

BAJÍO AND THE
CENTRAL COAST
p190

Pacific
Ocean

UNITED STATES
OF AMERICA

EXPLORE
MEXICO

This guide divides Mexico into eight color-
coded sightseeing areas, as shown on this
map. Find out more about each area on the
following pages.

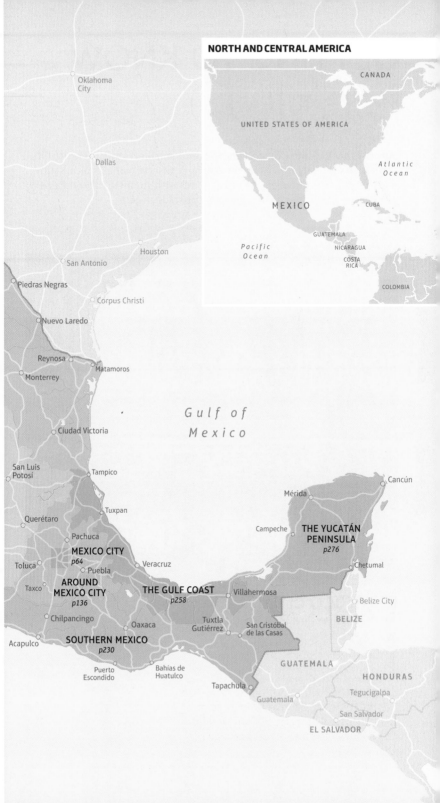

GETTING TO KNOW
MEXICO

Mexico is divided into 32 states and the autonomous district of Mexico City, the nation's capital *(p64)*. From the northern deserts to the tropical south and everything in between, Mexico abounds with stunning natural scenery, a rich history, delicious dishes, and plenty of hidden gems.

PAGE 64

MEXICO CITY

Teeming craft markets, massive Diego Rivera murals, the wafting aromas of street food, and the invigorating sounds of marimba and mariachi – Mexico City has it all. It's a sprawling metropolis of distinct neighborhoods, where you'll find high-end boutiques and hip bars in Polanco, colonial-era monasteries and Aztec ruins in the Historic Center, and tranquil suburban enclaves in San Ángel and Coyoacán. The city also boasts some of Latin America's best restaurants, museums, performing arts, and sporting events, so get ready for non-stop excitement in this high-energy capital.

Best for
Museums, art, architecture, dining, and nightlife

Home to
Catedral Metropolitana, Templo Mayor, Palacio de Bellas Artes, Palacio Nacional, Museo Nacional de Antropología, Museo Frida Kahlo, and Xochimilco

Experience
Listening to live mariachi bands in Plaza Garibaldi

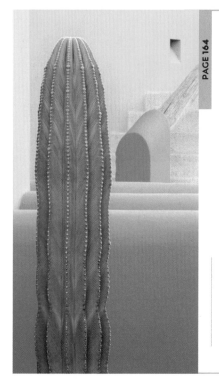

PAGE 136

AROUND MEXICO CITY

The patchwork of small, densely populated mountain states around the capital are a treasure trove of Mexican history and culture. Indigenous civilizations created the pyramids of Tula and Teotihuacán, the latter being Mexico's most famous pre-Hispanic site. From the 16th century, the Spanish founded their own towns, such as Pachuca and Mineral del Monte, that are now picturesque spots full of pretty Spanish Colonial architecture. The western part of the region has cool forests and scenic lakes, while to the south, warmer weather attracts visitors to busy Cuernavaca and beautiful Taxco.

Best for
Ancient ruins and Spanish Colonial architecture

Home to
Teotihuacán, Museo Nacional del Virreinato, and Puebla

Experience
Scaling the Pyramid of the Sun to survey the ruins of the great Mesoamerican city of Teotihuacán

PAGE 164

BAJA CALIFORNIA

A long, thin peninsula surrounded by sub-tropical waters, Baja California is a land of giant cacti, golden deserts, and tranquil, untouched beaches. Sparsely populated, it's a favorite of North American snowbirds who migrate south on the Transpeninsular Highway every year. Its mix of wild landscapes, remote communities, and tourist fame means there's a diverse blend of experiences for travelers to discover here: the party-hard vibe of Tijuana, whale-watching at Guerrero Negro, ancient cave paintings in the wilderness, and pristine beaches enclaves of Los Cabos.

Best for
Beaches, nightlife, and watersports

Home to
Cabo San Lucas, Tijuana, and la Paz

Experience
Strolling along the seaside promenade in Ensenada then stopping for lunch to savor the town's famous fish tacos

→

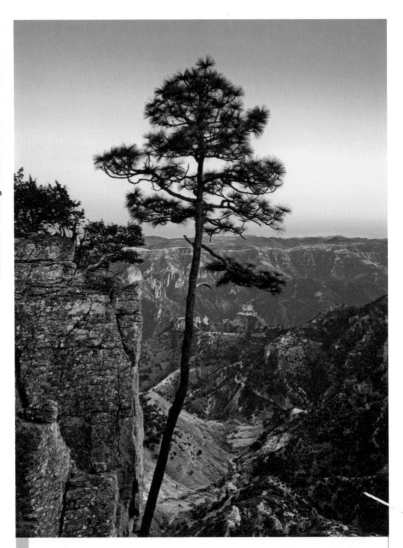

PAGE 174

NORTHERN MEXICO

This is the home of the cacti-strewn deserts that most people picture when they think of Mexico. Those who yearn for adventure will find the empty miles and wild landscapes that provide some of Mexico's most memorable moments. There are vast deserts, old-fashioned beach resorts, wild frontier towns, and modern cities – all inhabited by communities deeply rooted in tradition and ranching culture. Of course, there are plenty of great experiences that are easy to access without heading out by car: riding the magnificent Copper Canyon railroad, discovering energetic and cosmopolitan Monterrey, and walking the streets of western film sets near Durango.

Best for
Colonial-era history, culture, and natural beauty

Home to
Paquimé and the Copper Canyon

Experience
Riding on the El Chepe Railroad in Copper Canyon for incredible views of the Sierra Tarahumara

BAJÍO AND
THE CENTRAL COAST

Mexico's Pacific Coast is a sunseeker's paradise, dotted with beautiful resorts for those who want some serious leisure time. But most of the major highlights of the region are in the small states that make up Mexico's heartland – known as Bajío – which offers up a blend of gorgeous colonial-era silver mining towns, rolling mountain scenery, and indigenous cultures. The region has given the world quintessential Mexican exports such as tequila, mariachi music, and Diego Rivera, but it's also full of lesser-known indigenous traditions – the colorful yarn paintings of the Wixáritari people, and the festivals of the Lake Pátzcuaro area, deeply rooted in the heartland's traditional cultures.

Best for
Beaches, indigenous culture, architecture, and festivals

Home to
Guadalajara, Guanajuato, Zacatecas, Querétaro, and Morelia

Experience
Enjoying the concerts and art exhibitions at the Feria de San Marcos in Aguascalientes

$\rightarrow$

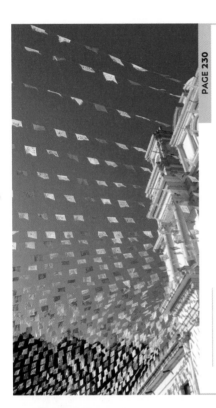

PAGE 230

SOUTHERN MEXICO

The southern states are blanketed with some of Mexico's most impressive backdrops, from spectacular mountain peaks to waterfall-streaked valleys. The Pacific coast is a major draw for many visitors, some of whom come for resorts such as Acapulco. Others seek the surfers' paradise of Puerto Escondido, or the wild beaches of Chiapas. One of the most fascinating things about the region, though, is that it's the meeting place of so many different cultures and communities, each of which has helped shape the way of life here. Even for Mexico, where several dozen indigenous languages are still in use, this southern region is particularly diverse.

Best for
Indigenous culture, natural beauty, Mesoamerican ruins, and Mexican cuisine

Home to
Oaxaca, Monte Albán, Acapulco, and Palenque

Experience
Taking a foodie tour of Oaxaca city

PAGE 258

THE GULF COAST

While this region is little more than a thin slip of land, the Gulf Coast is still bursting with attractions both old and new. The cooler, mountainous interior is perfect for active travellers looking for some outdoor thrills, while El Tajín's ruins and Xalapa's anthropology museum offer up plenty of fun for history lovers. Meanwhile, the port of Veracruz is an interesting blend of cultures: traditional Mexican music drifts down streets lined with Spanish Colonial architecture, while the beach resort atmosphere and coffee culture are a taste of the ultra-modern.

Best for
History and outdoor adventures

Home to
El Tajín and the Museo de Antropología de Xalapa

Experience
Taking a temazcal in Catemaco – a sauna, followed by a massage or mud bath

PAGE 276

THE YUCATÁN PENINSULA

The Yucatán Peninsula is Mexico's holiday haven. Visitors from around the world flock to the stunning Caribbean beaches and diving hotspots of the Riviera Maya, sandwiched between the super-resort of Cancún and the Maya ruins of Chichén Itzá. Further inland, the peninsula is covered in a vast, flat swathe of jungle, its limestone surface riddled with cenotes (sinkholes), and sprinkled with pristine towns that look almost no different than they did in the days when Mexico was known as New Spain.

Best for
Beaches, diving, Mayan ruins, and nightlife

Home to
Riviera Maya, Uxmal, Tulum, Mérida, and Chichén Itzá

Experience
A refreshing dip in a crystal-clear cenote, keeping an eye out for the colorful marine life

←

1 Palacio de Bellas Artes.

2 A colorful *trajinera* on the canals of Xochimilco.

3 Sugar-dusted churros with chocolate sauce.

4 A performance of the Ballet Folklórico de México.

Mexico is bursting at the seams with unique cultural experiences, diverse cuisines, and truly magnificent natural scenery. These itineraries will help you make the most of your visit to this fascinating country.

3 DAYS
in Mexico City

Day 1

Morning Start with an indulgent breakfast of churros and chocolate at El Moro (*www. elmoro.mx*). After, stroll north up Cárdenas to the Torre Latinoamericana (*p88*) which has a spectacular observation deck.

Afternoon Walk along pedestrianized Madero, the city center's premier shopping strip, and you'll reach the city's traditional heart: the grand plaza known as the Zócalo (*p92*). Sit back and relax with lunch on the plaza – a perfect spot to people watch – then tour the famous sights on the plaza, including the Palacio Nacional (*p82*) and the Catedral Metropolitana (*p76*).

Evening Enjoy a dinner of fajitas at the elegant La Ópera Bar (*p87*) then head to Plaza Garibaldi (*p83*), where you'll be serenaded by mariachi bands over cocktails in one of the plaza's many bars.

Day 2

Morning Start the day at Museo Frida Kahlo (*p116*). Here you'll find artwork by Kahlo and mementos of her turbulent life.

Afternoon For lunch, head to Plaza Hidalgo in the tranquil Coyoacán district and choose from street food such as sizzling quesadillas or bubbling *pozole* (stew) at the stalls in Mercado de Antojitos (*Higuera 10*). Next stop is a visit to the canal-side neighborhood of Xochimilco (*p128*) to hire a traditional boat for a cruise through the famous floating gardens.

Evening Linger in Xochimilco to experience one of its many *pulquerias* (traditional bars). Pulqueria El Templo de Diana (*Av. 5 de Mayo 65*) is one of the oldest, evocative of the 1950s.

Day 3

Morning Journey out of the city to see the spellbinding Mesoamerican ruins at Teotihuacán (*p140*). From the Pyramid of the Sun, head down the main avenue to the Citadel, where the Temple of Quetzalcoatl is the star attraction. Stop off at the on-site museum before heading back to Mexico City for lunch.

Afternoon Make for the Museo Nacional de Antropología (*p98*), Mexico's greatest museum. With such an abundance of fascinating exhibits, such as giant Olmec heads and replicas of ancient tombs, you can spend the whole afternoon here.

Evening Book dinner at Pujol (*www.pujol. com.mx*), a swanky restaurant from celebrity chef Enrique Olvera in the upscale Polanco district. For a spectacular finale to your Mexico City stay, reserve tickets to see the Ballet Folklórico de México at the Palacio de Bellas Artes (*p78*).

6 DAYS

in Baja California

Day 1

The western peninsula of Baja California is the perfect place for a road trip. Long stretches of highway wind through wild desert or stretch out beside vivid blue coastlines, all broken up with interesting towns, hidden gems, and tasty regional dishes to discover along the way. Begin your journey in the northern town of Ensenada *(p168)*. Take in the scene along the seafront promenade then peruse the exhibits on the peoples and cultures of Baja California at the Museo de Historia *(www.museoens.com)*. Sample Ensenada's famed fish tacos at the Mercado de Mariscos, then get a taste of Baja's famous wines at the Bodegas de Santo Tomás *(www.santo-tomas.com)*. End the day at Hussong's *(www.cantinahussongs. com/inicio.html)*, which serves tasty tacos and the original margarita.

Day 2

South of Ensenada, the Transpeninsular Highway cuts through arid mountain chains and heavily farmed plains. On the three-and-a-half hour journey from Ensenada to El Rosario, stop and take a break at San Quintín to sample the local oysters served at La Ostionera de Bahía Falsa *(www.laostionera.com)*. Finish up the drive in El Rosario, a quintessential rural Baja California town. Have dinner at Mama Espinosa's *(616 165 87 70)* in the middle of town, famed for its lobster burritos.

Day 3

Get an early start for the 575 km (360 mile) journey to Santa Rosalía. Allow nine hours for the drive, plus time for breaks, such as a seafood lunch at Malarrimo *(www.malarrimo.com)* in Guerrero Negro. Stop for a while in San Ignacio *(p170)* in the late afternoon to stretch your legs on a walk to the pretty central Plaza Ecoturismo. If you have time to spare, head to the Museo de las Pinturas Rupestres de San Ignacio to learn more about the ancient artwork that has been discovered in Baja California *(p170)*. Reaching Santa Rosalía *(p170)* before dark, take an early evening ramble to view the Gustav Eiffel-designed Iglesia de Santa Bárbara.

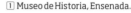

1 Museo de Historia, Ensenada.

2 Freshly baked treats at Panadería El Boleo, Santa Rosalía.

3 The Transpeninsular Highway.

4 Nuestra Señora de Loreto, Baja California's first mission church.

5 Waterfront in Cabo San Lucas.

Day 4

Try the French-style pastries at Panadería El Boleo (*Obregón 30*), before a short drive to Mulegé (*p171*). Visit the hilltop church and see prehistoric artifacts in the Museo Mulegé, before lunch at Los Equipales (*Moctezuma 70*). Loreto (*p171*) is two-and-a-half hours south, but you'll want to pause at one or two of Bahía Concepción's mesmerizing beaches en route for some sunbathing and a dip in the beautiful waters of this inland bay. Tonight, enjoy more of Baja's exquisite seafood at El Caloron (*López Mateos 2*), which has stellar views across the Gulf of California.

Day 5

Spend the morning taking a walk to explore Loreto's enigmatic mission church, the first to be established in Baja. Have an early lunch at Mi Loreto (*Salvatierra 50*), a colorful local restaurant known for its mole sauces, then continue your road trip with a four-hour drive to La Paz (*p172*). Enjoy a leisurely promenade along the city's famously scenic *malecón*, then indulge in a dinner of lobster and tacos at Mariscos Bismarkcito (*Paseo Alvaro Obregon*), finishing up with cocktails at Cervecería La México (*Obregón 1665*).

Day 6

Start with artisanal coffee and pastries at Doce Cuarenta (*Madero 1240*) near the central Plaza Constitución. View the local history exhibits at the Museo Regional de Antropología e Historia before lunch at Rancho Viejo (*Márquez de León 228*) – a popular spot renowned for its steak tacos. Hop back in the car for an hour's drive to Todos Santos (*p173*), where you can easily spend a couple of hours wandering the town's charming streets. Stop for a coffee at the Hotel California (*www.hotelcalifornia baja.com*), then take a stroll to the lovely, palm-fringed plaza in the heart of town, surrounded by the humble church and elegant theater. One last hour on the road will get you to your final destination: Cabo San Lucas (*p172*). Embrace the town's free-wheeling spirit at one of the bars on Playa El Médano and enjoy the views of the stone arch known as El Arco, a jagged rocky archway, on Lovers' Beach.

6 DAYS
on the Ruta de Plata

Day 1

The silver route takes in several of Mexico's iconic colonial-era towns, following the former silver transport trails used by the Spanish. This tour begins in the elegant city of Querétaro (p206). For an idea of what life was like for local elites in the 18th century, amble south to the Museo Casa de la Zacatecana, which is decorated with original furnishings. At lunchtime, try a *torta* (Mexican sandwich) at Las Tortugas (Andador 5 de Mayo 27). After, take a stroll through town to the Mirador de los Arcos, which provides spellbinding views of the city's historic aqueduct. Sample the creative Mexican dishes at Chinicuil (Pasteur Sur 52), then head to Alquimia (5 de Mayo 71) – a sophisticated, dimly lit bodega – for cocktails.

Day 2

A couple of hours by bus will take you to the city of Dolores Hidalgo (p220). The town's top sights are clustered around Plaza Principal, beginning with the church where Father Hidalgo issued the declaration that started Mexico's War of Independence in 1810. Make sure you stop and sample the town's famously inventive ice-cream flavors, such as cactus and shrimp, that are sold around the main plaza. After a 45-minute bus ride, finish the day at San Miguel de Allende (p224), and while away the evening at La Azotea (Umarán 6), the town's coolest rooftop bar.

Day 3

Stay in San Miguel Allende and spend the whole day exploring this beautifully preserved colonial-era town. Start with a stroll around El Jardín Principal, admiring the sights on this charming plaza. Follow this up with lunch at La Alborada (Sollano 11), famed for its traditional soups and stews. Stop at Plaza Cívica to see its two colonial-era churches – Templo de Nuestra Señora de la Salud with its unusual concave facade, and San Felipe Neri for its stunning oil paintings. Afterward, peruse Mexican folk art, pottery, and souvenirs at the Mercado de Artesanías. For dinner, try the excellent Peruvian restaurant La Parada (www.laparadasma.com).-

① Statue overlooking the aqueduct in Querétaro City.

② A colorful street in Guanajuato.

③ Cable car in Zacatecas.

④ A *gordita*-style corn taco.

⑤ Ice-cream vendor in the town of Dolores Hidalgo.

Day 4

An hour and a half by bus will take you to the gorgeous city of Guanajuato *(p196)*. Start by taking the funicular up to the Monumento al Pipila – a statue of a local independence hero – where you can enjoy spectacular views of the city. Descend on foot to Jardín de la Unión, the main plaza, then treat yourself to a delicious lunch of Mexican street food from Mercado Hidalgo. Head north to Museo Regional de Guanajuato and spend the afternoon learning more about Mexico's War of Independence *(p59)*. Enjoy a dinner of classic Spanish dishes at Tasca de la Paz *(Plaza de la Paz 28)*, before joining a traditional *callejóneadas*, a street tour conducted in Spanish by students dressed as medieval minstrels *(p198)*.

Day 5

Take the bus to Aguascalientes *(p224)*, and spend the late morning wandering around Plaza de la Patria. Have lunch at Mercado Juárez, where stalls serve *bírria* (goat or mutton stew). It's a short stroll to the fascinating Museo Nacional de la Muerte, which examines Mexico's preoccupation with images of death. This evening, take a taxi to experience the hot springs that gave Aguascalientes its name – the Baños Termales de Ojocaliente *(www.banos termalesojocaliente.mx)*. For dinner, sample traditional Mexican dishes at Restaurante Mitla's buffet *(Maduro 220)*.

Day 6

After the two-hour bus ride to Zacatecas *(p202)*, head straight to the cathedral in Plaza de Armas. From here you can make a loop through the heart of the old city, exploring its narrow, arcaded streets, and grand churches and mansions. Head over to Gorditas Doña Julia *(Hidalgo 409)* for lunch at this locally famous chain known for its *gorditas* (stuffed corn pastries). Take a guided tour of Mina El Edén, a preserved silver mine deep in the hillside. For dinner, splurge on the restaurant inside the fabulous Quinta Real hotel *(www. quintareal.com)*, before heading to La Mina Club *(www.minaeleden.com.mx/ minaclub/index.htm)*, a dance club and bar inside the Edén mine.

←

1 Mole ingredients for sale in Mercado Benito Juárez.

2 A craftsman weaving in Teotitlàn del Valle.

3 Ruins at Monte Albán.

4 Paper in Taller Leñateros, San Cristóbal de las Casas.

5 DAYS

in Southern Mexico

Day 1

Starting in the city of Oaxaca (p234), wander north on Macedonio Alcalá, browsing the craft shops along this pedestrianized shopping street. For lunch, visit Casa Oaxaca (www.casa oaxacaelrestaurante.com) to try mole – a traditional marinade and sauce dish that comes in many varieties and flavors. In the afternoon, explore the Museo de las Culturas de Oaxaca, a regional history museum with a fine collection of Mixtec jewelry and gold. For dinner, Los Danzantes (www.losdanzantes.com) offers innovative Oaxacan dishes such as barbecue chicken with fried cactus and chocolate.

Day 2

There are enough fascinating markets in Oaxaca to take up the whole morning. The vast food market of Mercado Benito Juárez is filled with the wafting scent of fresh produce, mole powder, and chilli peppers, while Mercado de Artesanías is the place for Zapotec handicrafts. Make sure you end at the sprawling Mercado de Abastos, where there are plenty of choices for lunch. After, admire Mesoamerican art at Museo de Arte Prehispánico de México. For dinner, splurge at Zandunga (www. zandungasabor.com), which serves 60 types of mezcal plus regional specialties.

Day 3

You'll need to rent a car for some adventures farther afield today. Leave early and spend the morning at the famously scenic ruins at Monte Albán (p240). Head to Santa María del Tule for lunch at the food stalls at Mercado el

Tule, then drive to Teotitlán del Valle, home to more ancient ruins and Zapotec arts-and-crafts stalls, famous for their fine rugs. Enjoy some tasty moles, tamales, and enchiladas at Teotitlán's Comedor Conchita's (Juárez 104) before driving back to Oaxaca. Here you'll need to switch to a bus for the overnight trip to San Cristóbal de las Casas (p249).

Day 4

Ease into San Cristóbal life with coffee at El Kiosco (Plaza 31 de Marzo). Afterwards, check out Museo de San Cristóbal, the stately former city hall converted into a local history museum. After lunch, walk north up Andador Eclesiástico to Santo Domingo. The plaza here, filled with craft stalls, is the best place to buy souvenirs. Next door is the fascinating Museo Centro Cultural de los Altos, which focuses on local indigenous cultures, with an especially rich textile display. For dinner, try Spanish tapas at La Viña de Bacco (Real de Guadalupe 7).

Day 5

Take a guided tour of the contemporary Tzotzil Maya villages of San Juan Chamula and San Lorenzo de Zinacantán, where the people are known for maintaining their cultural traditions. You can book through your hotel, or via Jalapeño Tours (www.jalapenotours.com). Afterward, make for Taller Leñateros (www.tallerlenateros. com), a paper-making shop that uses traditional Maya techniques. For a dinner of innovative, contemporary Chiapas food, snag a table at El Secreto (16 de Septiembre 24).

1

5 DAYS
in the Yucatán Peninsula

Day 1

Start your tour of the peninsula in Campeche *(p300)* with a hearty breakfast at El Bastión *(www.elbastion.mx/restaurante. html)*, which overlooks the central plaza. Check out the grand cathedral followed by the Museo de la Arquitectura Maya, which contains Maya monuments and sculpture, and also provides access to the old city walls. Just beyond the walls, the city market is worth a browse for its stalls of colorful fruit and produce. It's also surrounded by restaurants where you can stop for lunch. Drive out to the archaeo-logical museum in Fuerte de San Miguel, home to an impressive cache of pre-Hispanic gold and the first mummified body to be found in Mesoamerica. The *paradores de cockteleros* (seafood and cocktail stalls) on the coast are perfect for dinner as you watch the sun go down.

Day 2

It's just over two hours by car to the ancient Maya city of Uxmal *(p284)*, famed for its elaborately decorated buildings. After a couple of hours exploring the site,

drive on to Mérida *(p290)*. Grab a seafood lunch at El Marlin Azul *(Calle 62 No. 488)*, before setting off to explore the town. Check out the beautifully restored Museo Casa Montejo – a 16th-century palace – as well as the vast Modernist murals by Fernando Castro Pacheco in the Palacio de Gobierno. You can then spend several happy hours admiring the handicrafts in the Casa de Artesanías *(Calle 63)* which sells traditional products made by local artisans; the hammocks you'll see here are a particular specialty. Sample the innovative Mexican fusion cuisine at Rosas and Xocolate *(www.rosasandxocolate.com)* for dinner, and then catch a classical performance at the Teatro Peón.

Day 3

Drive to the iconic Maya ruins at Chichén Itzá *(p294)*, aiming to arrive early so you can miss the busy late morning rush. Allow about three hours to explore; start with the pyramids in the area known as Chichén Nuevo on the north side of the site, then tackle the Chichén Viejo ruins to the south, where fewer visitors go. For

① The Baroque cathedral on Plaza de la Independencia, Campeche. ↑

② Uxmal's Pyramid of the Magician.

③ Climbing the ruins of Cobá.

④ Archaeological site of Tulum overlooking the sandy beach.

⑤ A diver in Gran Cenote.

lunch, try the excellent Yucatecan buffet (roast pork to fresh seafood) at Hacienda Selva Maya (www.mesondelmarques.com/hacienda-selva-maya), a short drive away in Valladolid (p306). One hour's drive from here is the Maya city of Cobá (p304), where you can spend a couple of hours exploring huge pyramids soaring high above the jungle. In the evening, have a modern Mexican dinner at Hartwood (www.hartwoodtulum.com) on Tulum beach, where all the cooking is done by open fire.

Day 4

The Tulum ruins are a collection of Maya pyramids and structures sitting above the Caribbean (p288). The site itself takes only an hour or so to explore but it's best to arrive early to avoid the crowds. After Tulum, head to Gran Cenote, one of the area's best cenotes – a naturally forming sinkhole in the limestone, filled with crystal-clear water. Lucky visitors may even spot turtles here – make sure to keep your distance if you do. After a swim, head back into Tulum town for lunch; try

the tasty tacos and moles at El Tacoqueto (Av. Tulum at Acuario). Decamp to the beach – Tulum has one of the best in the area. There are several public access points, but you can also try one of the beach clubs where you pay for lounge chairs and drinks (your hotel may have its own operation). For something special tonight, try The Dining Experience (www.thediningexperience.rocks), a seven-course dinner party with a local host and Maya drinking ceremony.

Day 5

Drive north up the stunning Riviera Maya (p282), stopping at Akumal (p283) for a refreshing swim in Cenote Azul. Aim to reach the Cancún (p282) beach strip for a late seafood lunch at El Fish Fritanga (p283). The best thing about Cancún is the beach, so dedicate a whole afternoon to enjoying the sun, sea, and sand. For a tranquil spot away from the busy Hotel Zone, head to the north-facing beaches on Boulevard Kukulcan. Finish the day with a lavish meal at Restaurante Careyes (www.oasishoteles.com/es/restaurantes/careyes).

The Fiesta Sound

Mexico's rich music and dance culture is the focal point of several major festivals, giving you a great chance to immerse yourself in the sights and sounds of lively musical traditions. Some of the best options are Día de Santa Cecilia on November 22nd – when the patron saint of musicians is feted with gusto across the country – or Guadalajara's Encuentro Internacional del Mariachi y la Charrería in late August, celebrating both mariachi music and *charrería*, the Mexican art of horsemanship. Many other fiestas include music and dance as part of their festivities – such as Guelaguetza *(p48)* and Día de Santa Cecilia *(p55)*.

$\rightarrow$

Dancers performing at the Encuentro Internacional del Mariachi y la Charrería

MEXICO FOR
MUSIC AND DANCE

Fed by its cultural diversity, Mexico's traditional music and dance scene is fantastically rich and exciting, and with so many street performers and fiestas around, it's easy to lose yourself to the country's rhythms.

Regional Traditions

Mexico has a vast range of dances performed only by specific communities or in certain regions. Some hark back to pre-Hispanic times and ancient rituals, while others were introduced by Spanish friars and show European influences. During Carnival in Tlaxcala *(p159)*, for example, dancers wear elaborate, sequined garments and carved wooden masks with pale skin tones, to parody their ancient oppressors. In Mexico City, the *concheros* dance has evolved over the centuries from different spiritual traditions, both indigenous and Spanish. You can find performers at the main plaza *(p94)* – just keep your ears out for the tell-tale rattle that comes from the seed pods worn on the dancers' ankles.

$\leftarrow$

Conchero dancers performing for a crowd in Mexico City

African Roots

The Afro-Mexican community has had a big influence on the country's music and dance scene since colonial times. The Gulf and Pacific coasts, with their large Afro-Mexican populations, are particularly rich in dance: look out for the *danza de los diablos* (dance of the devils), for example, which is often performed in Oaxaca and Guerrero states during the Day of the Dead and other festivities. The city of Veracruz *(p268)*, meanwhile, is a great place to hear the Afro-Mexican branch of *son mexicano* folk music known as *son jarocho*, with performances on Friday and Saturday nights in the Plazuela de Campaná.

←

Danza de los diablos dancers wearing sutis and masks for an event

Mariachi Beats

Mariachi music boomed in the 1950s with a string of films that made stars of Mariachi Vargas – considered the best mariachi band of all time. Today, you'll hear it all over Mexico, especially in its birthplace of Guadalajara *(p194)*. Typical bands comprise guitars, violin, trumpet, and singer, but drummers and other musicians may join in to create bigger, more complex bands, especially around popular spots like Plaza Garibaldi *(p85)*, where a band can grow as the night goes on and create an impromptu party atmosphere that lasts until the early hours.

549
—
The number of musicians in the largest mariachi band ever.

Mariachis in traditional attire playing at Plaza Garibaldi, Mexico City ↑

▷ Tropic Jungles

A rich array of wildlife roams through the jungles in the south of Mexico. All kinds of magical sights are hidden away amid the lush growth, so a trip out to these verdant landscapes is worth it not just for the beautiful scenery but also to stumble on enigmatic sights like the Garden of Eden at Las Pozas *(p218)* or the ruins of the Maya site of Palenque *(p244)*.

◁ Mexico from the Movies

Deserts really do smother northern Mexico and Baja California, with the vast Chihuahuan desert being the largest in North America. To see this stunning landscape of cacti-studded hills, bright sunshine, and dried riverbeds, hit the Transpeninsular Highway for a road trip *(p24)*, or stay in a Baja oasis town such as Mulegé *(p171)*.

MEXICO FOR
NATURAL
BEAUTY

Beyond the dusty deserts of Mexico's northern border, an incredible mixture of landscapes decorate the country, from soaring, snow-fringed volcanoes to golden coastlines hugging sapphire blue oceans.

◁ Snorkeling the Cenotes

Some of the most enticing snorkeling spots in Mexico are actually found inland, across the Yucatán Peninsula. Thanks to the Yucatán's unique geology – riddled with limestone caverns and underground rivers – giant sinkholes known as cenotes pockmark the peninsula *(p281)*. The natural holes are filled with crystal-clear water, and many – such as the beautiful Cenote Azul (p300) – provide great opportunities for cave diving, snorkeling, or just a leisurely dip.

△ Mountains and Canyons
More than half the country is over 1,000 m (3,200 ft) above sea level, making Mexico a true land of mountains. See the soaring heights and plunging depths at the epic, lake-filled Sumidero Canyon *(p252)*, and the stunning gorges of the Copper Canyon system *(p180)*, which dwarfs the Grand Canyon in the US.

▷ Rich Wetlands
Birdwatchers should always have their binoculars at the ready in the Yucatán. Mangroves along the coastline provide a habitat for a plethora of wading birds, while the marshlands of the Sian Ka'an Biosphere Reserve *(p309)* attract even rarer birds. But the highlight of the region is the phenomenal sight of vast colonies of coral pink flamingos that inhabit the lagoons *(p303)*.

◁ Smoking Giants
Central Mexico is peppered with volcanic mountains, from the mighty Pico de Orizaba *(p270)* – the nation's highest peak – to the more humble cinder cone volcano of Paricutín *(p214)*. There are also some active volcanoes, such as the Volcán de Fuego; hike up to the summit of nearby Nevado de Colima *(p216)* to see its smoky top from a safe distance.

Did You Know?
Popocatépetl volcano became active in 1994 and has been erupting at irregular intervals ever since.

Magnificent Muralists

Mexican artists have been creating colorful murals since pre-Hispanic times, as seen in the vibrant friezes found in Teotihuacán *(p140)* and Bonampak *(p248)*. The art form exploded onto the scene again after the 1910 Mexican Revolution, with huge murals promoting a sense of national identity. Visit universities and city halls across the country to get a look at these dramatic tableaux, proudly preserved as national cultural treasures. Of course, Mexico City has a plethora of examples, by leading artists of the mural movement such as José Clemente Orozco, David Alfaro Siqueiros, and Diego Rivera.

MEXICO FOR
ART LOVERS

From mysterious Maya glyphs to modern murals emblazoned with symbolism, Mexican art is at once familiar and yet startling. Day of the Dead skulls and Frida Kahlo's self-portraits have become global pop icons, but there are plenty of lesser-known works just waiting to be discovered.

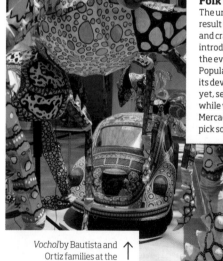

Folk Crafts

The unique vitality of Mexican folk art is a result of the fusion of traditional Mexican arts and crafts with technologies and themes introduced after the Spanish Conquest. See the evolution of folk art at the Museo de Arte Popular *(p87)*, where curated collections trace its development throughout history. Better yet, see traditional arts and crafts in person while wandering through a market like Mercado de Abastos *(p237)* where you can pick something up as an authentic souvenir.

Vochol by Bautista and Ortiz families at the Museo de Arte Popular ↑

Did You Know?
—
On the last Wednesday of each month, many museums stay open till late in the evening.

INSIDER TIP
ArtWalk

The town of Puerto Vallarta *(p225)* is a major arts center. Get a taste of its flourishing contemporary art scene on the weekly Wednesday ArtWalk, held from late October to late May *(www. puertovallartaart walk.com)*. During the event, some 16 galleries open their doors until 10pm and people.

←

Rivera's *The History of Mexico* (1935) in the Palacio Nacional

A Mexican Icon

Known for her bold, Surrealist self-portraits, Frida Kahlo is one of the most instantly recognizable artists in the world. Kahlo didn't start painting seriously until she was 18, inspired by folk art, politics, and even the chronic pain she suffered throughout her life. Kahlo's paintings can be seen in galleries all over Mexico but the best place to start is her former home, the Casa Azul in Mexico City *(p116)*.

←

A photograph of iconc Mexican artist Frida Kahlo

Modern Mexico

Today, murals and folk art have been exchanged for digital works and urban street art. At the same time, many Mexican artists are rediscovering their indigenous roots, freeing themselves from European and US influences. Discover Mexico's latest artistic movements in modern galleries such as the Museo Jumex *(www.fundacionjumex.org)* and the Museo de Arte Indígena Contemporáneo *(p157)*, which explores contemporary indigenous art.

→

Museo Jumex on Plaza Cars, surrounded by chic modern architecture

Sun, Sea, and Sand

Mexico's coasts offer plenty of ways to enjoy some quality family time, whether you're playing on the sandy beach, snorkeling among tropical fish, or chowing down on freshly cut coconuts. Isla Mujeres (p280) features the most kid-friendly beaches in Mexico, while older children can try surfing in Oaxaca or exploring the wilder beaches in Baja California.

→

Surfing practice in the tropical waters of the Riviera Maya

MEXICO FOR
FAMILIES

With so many colorful fiestas, fascinating facts, and amazing flavors, Mexico is a big hit with the kids. Family is central to Mexican society and traveling with children is common practice, so you'll find plenty to occupy excited kids wherever you go, as well as the facilities to make it easy.

SHOP

Mercado De Artesanías La Ciudadela

This market is full of colorful handicrafts, jewelry, hammocks, and traditional artwork. It's a great spot for the whole family: an exciting place for the kids to explore, and full of authentic Mexican souvenirs for adults to peruse.

🅐H4 🚇 Avenida Balderas and Plaza de la Ciudadela, Mexico City
🕙 10am-7pm Mon-Sat (to 6pm Sun)
🌐 laciudadela.com.mx

Adventure Time

Mexico's ancient ruins are a great adventure for the whole family. All the stuffiness of history falls away when you're setting foot in real Mesoamerican city, hearing stories of the ritualistic ballgame at Chichén Itzá (p294) or scaling the Pyramid of the Sun (p140). The fabulous Museo Nacional de Antropología is also fascinating enough to keep the attention of energetic kids, with its reconstructions of creepy old tombs.

→

Setting off for the Pyramid of the Sun, Teotihuacán

Theme-Park Fun

When it comes to letting off steam (and cooling down), resorts like Cancún *(p283)* and Acapulco *(p242)* boast numerous water parks. And just outside Mexico City, serious thrills are delivered at the Six Flags México theme park – Latin America's most popular – where you can tackle the world's first boomerang coaster and rides themed around DC superheroes.

INSIDER TIP
Ice Cream for the Bold

In Dolores Hidalgo *(p220)* ice cream has evolved into something extra special. Come here to brave bizarre flavors such as mole, avocado, and even shrimp.

↑ A kid-friendly roller-coaster at the popular Six Flags México

Fiesta Fever

Raucous parades, vibrant costumes, pounding drums, and folk dancers – Mexican festivals are sure to be a thrill for young visitors *(p54)*. Fiestas almost always include special events to get children involved and active, as well as temporary funfairs. For sheer spectacle, it's hard to beat the Guelaguetza cultural festival, or Carnival, which is at its most flamboyant in La Paz *(p172)* and Veracruz *(p268)*.

←

Dressing up at Oaxaca's Guelaguetza, a festival celebrating indigenous culture

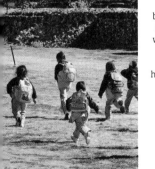

Wild Mexico

You don't need zoos to get a glimpse of the wildlife in Mexico. Whale-watching is common all along the Pacific coast, but especially in Baja California *(p173)*. Bring your binoculars to spy the animals out at sea, or take a boat tour with Baja Expeditions *(www.bajaex.com)* to catch a closer look. The Yucatán is also home to the awesome sight of a flamboyance of flamingos at Celestún *(p303)* and Río Lagartos *(p307)*.

→

A whale leaping up from the inland Sea of Cortez in Baja California

Lace Up Your Boots

The national parks, mountain ranges, and snow-capped volcanoes of Mexico are all laced with fantastic hiking trails, so whether you're looking for a casual walk or an epic challenge, there's plenty to enjoy. Grades of difficulty vary as much as the landscapes, from the gentle lakeside walks of Valle de Bravo *(p155)*, to the climb up Pico de Orizaba *(p270)*, which requires crampons and an ice axe. The awe-inspiring Copper Canyon *(p180)* is a popular hiking area, with trekking trails plus dramatic gorges for more adrenaline-fueled activities like abseiling.

$\rightarrow$

Mountain climbers resting atop Pico de Orizaba, the highest peak in Mexico

MEXICO FOR
OUTDOOR ADVENTURES

Rafting the white-water rapids of the Río Filobobos, horseback riding in the rugged homeland of the Rarámuri, hiking the blackened slopes of dormant volcanoes – Mexico's enormously varied landscapes provide enticing settings for all kinds of action-packed adventures.

Annual Adventures

The Mexican calendar is peppered with events that make the perfect focal point for an adrenaline-fueled trip. For the Baja 1000 *(p168)*, hundreds of vehicles compete in a grueling off-road race in Baja California. For sports-fishing fans, there's a cash prize to be won at the Black and Blue Marlin Tournament in Cabo San Lucas *(p172)*.

$\leftarrow$

Racing in the Baja 1000, held every November

TOP 4 GOLF COURSES IN MEXICO

Cabo del Sol
W cabodelsol.com
Luxury resort in Cabo San Lucas.

Cozumel Country Club
W clubcorp.com
An 18-hole course on the Riviera Maya.

El Camaléon
W mayakobagolf.com
The only Mexican stop on the PGA Tour.

Riviera Maya Golf Club
W rivieramaya-golfclub.com
Incorporating jungle, cenotes, and lakes.

Roving Riders

Mexico is a land of cowboys, which makes a tour on horseback a truly traditional way to experience the country's exciting landscapes. Ride the flower-filled trails of Valle de Bravo *(p155)*, the volcanic slopes of Paricutín *(p214)*, or the rustic byways of the Sierra Chincua Monarch Butterfly Sanctuary. Always be sure to find a reputable company for your tour and don't ride in the midday sun, for the safety of yourself and the horses.

← Horseback riders exploring the area around Cabo San Lucas

Mexico's Waterways

Expert thrill-seekers and casual explorers alike can enjoy seeing Mexico by boat. Mountain torrents tumble out of the Sierras, offering thrilling adventures like rafting the rapids on the Río Filolobos *(p265)*. For more tranquil exploration, many hotels on the Riviera Maya *(p280)* offer kayaks for trips through the mangroves toward Ascension Bay, or around the exquisite lake at Bacalar. There are also plenty of ways to get out and enjoy Mexico's fabulous coastal waters *(p44)*.

→ Whitewater rafting near Huasteca in San Luis Potosí

◁ The Colonial Era

From tiny hamlets to the biggest cities, colonial-era churches abound in Mexico. With missionaries as architects and indigenous craftsmen adding the details, the result was a blend of styles that add unique and eclectic facades to the nation's townscapes. Follow the Convent Route from Maní *(p307)* for a string of examples.

▷ Modernist Marvels

The functional, clean lines of Modernism transformed the Mexican architectural scene after World War II. Luis Barragán (1902–98) designed everything from urban sculptures – such as the Torres de Satélite in Mexico City – to housing projects and gardens. A tall, slim skyscraper, the Torre Latinoamericana *(p90)*, was the pinnacle of the 1950s Modernist style in Mexico.

MEXICO FOR
ARCHITECTURE

From towering Maya pyramids to Modernist innovations, Mexico is crammed with architectural wonders. Today, a new generation of Mexican architects continues to transform the country with exciting, contemporary designs.

▷ Mesoamerican Masterpieces

The distinctive pyramids and geometric designs of Mexico's early civilizations are not just ruins – they've influenced modern architects such as Frank Lloyd Wright and the whole Art Deco movement. The Zapotec site of Mitla *(p252)* is especially well known for its intricate mosaic fretwork.

◁ Bringing the Baroque

The Spanish brought many styles to Mexico, but it was Baroque – and its flamboyant offshoot, Churrigueresque – that made the most impact. Puebla *(p148)* is especially rich in Baroque architecture, its skyline dotted with tangerine cupolas, pale yellow bell towers, and Talavera-tiled mansions.

◁ The Porfiriato

In the 19th century, a newly independent Mexico was eager to impress the world, and President Porfirio Díaz did it with buildings. There's the wonderful Art Nouveau Palacio de Bellas Artes *(p78)*, and the Teatro Juárez *(p196)*, which combines Neo-Classicism with lavish French styles of decoration. Much of the investment went into public buildings; Mexico City's Correo Mayor (Main Post Office) is a particularly grand example.

TOP 3 MODERN MEXICAN ARCHITECTS

Tatiana Bilbao (b. 1972)
An architect with a diverse range of projects from gardens to sustainable housing.

Frida Escobedo (b. 1979)
A Mexican artist who specializes in designing and restoring different urban spaces.

Michel Rojkind (b. 1969)
Responsible for innovative designs such as the Nestlé Chocolate Museum.

△ Contemporary Mexico

While historic highlights dominate the average sightseeing checklist, there's nothing quite like taking a stroll in the city and stumbling upon an extravagant 21st-century masterpiece. There are magical modern wonders to discover everywhere, such as the snake-like Nestlé Chocolate Museum near Toluca *(p160)* or the fabulous, glittering Museo Soumaya *(p133)*.

Beach Life

Sure, Mexico's coastlines provide plenty of adventures – but there's nothing quite like lazing in a deck chair, sipping margaritas under the palm trees while you watch jewel-blue waves lapping at the sand. Whether you're looking for a secluded spot or a luxury resort, sunseekers will be spoiled for choice all across Mexico. For some serious R&R, head to one of the big resort beaches around Cancún *(p282)*, Cabo San Lucas *(p172)*, or Acapulco *(p242)*. Each one offers watersports and swimming for when you're feeling active, as well as cocktails on the sand or spa facilities when you need a break.

→

Puerto Vallarta, a port city on the popular Pacific resort of Banderas Bay

MEXICO FOR
INCREDIBLE
COASTS

Mexico has an epic 9,330 km (5,800 miles) of coastline, so whether you're after a quiet place to relax and sunbathe, some prime coral reefs for scuba diving, or serious surf spots, you'll find the perfect niche carved out for you somewhere on the country's coast.

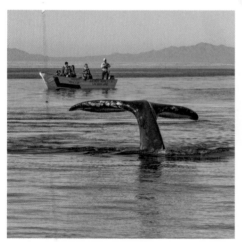

Eco-Friendly Wildlife Tours

Baja California is famous for the rare marine animals that can be seen here, in the Sea of Cortez to the east and the tranquil lagoons dotting the west coasts. Baja Expeditions *(www.bajaex.com)* and Cabo Expeditions *(www. caboexpeditions.com.mx)* are two reputable tour operators, both of which visit Isla Espíritu Santo – a protected reserve where the number of visitors is carefully managed at all times to enforce sustainable wildlife tourism.

←

The tail of a humpback whale off Baja California

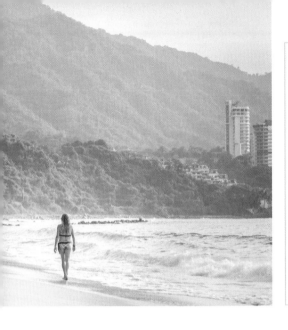

STAY

The Beach
Tulum Hotel

This luxurious hotel has rooms that open up right on the beach. Enjoy lavish four-poster beds, outdoor tubs, a stylish pool, and free yoga classes.

🅰G4 🏠Carr. Tulum-Boca Paila Km 7, Tulum Beach 🆆thebeach-tulum.com

$$$

Under the Sea

The Great Maya Reef is one of the world's largest coral reef systems. The reef is an endangered ecosystem, so it's best to book a trip to a protected area, such as the Sian Ka'an Biosphere Reserve *(p309)*, which can help to regulate guests and their impact on the reef. Snorkeling is an easy alternative, and off Cozumel *(p280)* – where reefs come close inshore – you can often see as much with a snorkel as with scuba tanks.

←

A scuba diver observing a French Angelfish in the waters off Cozumel

Surf's Up

A perfect match to all Mexico's inland action *(p40)*, the Pacific coast is prime surf territory for travelers looking for a fun-fueled day at the beach. Puerto Escondido *(p254)* is the most popular surfing hotspot, with many local operators offering lessons and board rentals for first-timers and casual surfers. Those with more experience can head for the wild, undeveloped beaches of Baja California.

→

Surfing in Puerto Escondido, in the state of Oaxaca

¡Viva la Revolución!

Bring history to life by following the life and times of some of the best-known figures in Mexican history – radical revolutionaries Emiliano Zapata *(p62)* and Pancho Villa *(p184)*. Trace Zapata's footsteps along the Ruta Zapata – a network of historic towns in the state of Morelos. For the life of Pancho Villa, visit Museo Histórico de la Revolución *(p184)*, his former house in Chihuahua.

←

A mural depicting Pancho Villa, in the Museo de la Revolución

MEXICO FOR
HISTORY BUFFS

With its roots in ancient civilizations stretching back over 20,000 years, Mexico draws on a long and rich cultural heritage. From majestic ancient pyramids to dazzling futuristic museums and galleries, it's easy to immerse yourself in the history that echoes all around you.

The Time of New Spain

The legacy of the Spanish rule is best seen through a stroll in one of the well-preserved towns that date from this period (1521–1821). Urban planning was strictly controlled, and towns were modeled on the capital. Straight streets led to a large *plaza mayor* (main plaza) with civic buildings and churches, plus *portales* (arcades) for the merchants. Mérida *(p290)* and San Cristóbal de las Casas *(p249)* are perfect examples, with fine central plazas that reflect the old colonial era.

→

Church towers rising above the trees on Mérida's *plaza mayor*

Did You Know?

The town of Valladolid was renamed Morelia in 1828 in honor of its most famous citizen.

National Heroes

No history tour would be complete without discovering the stories of Miguel Hidalgo and José María Morelos: two of Mexico's greatest heroes *(p59)*. There are museums in each of their birth places, Guanajuato *(p196)* and Morelia *(p208)* respectively, but the best way to experience their legacy is to hit the streets and join the crowds of patriots celebrating Independence Day on September 16.

→

A parade commemorating Independence Day

Archaeological Wonders

Some of Mexico's ancient cities and enigmatic pyramids are world-famous sights, such as Teotihuacán *(p140)* and Chichén Itzá *(p294)*. Other lesser-known spots, however, reveal unique art and majestic architecture of their own. The walls of Mitla *(p252)* are covered with magnificent geometric mosaics; the vibrant Maya murals at Bonampak *(p248)* are amazingly preserved; and excavations at Sayil *(p302)* uncovered intriguing details of how ordinary Maya once lived in a sacred ceremonial center.

←

The incredible Maya murals at Bonampak dating from around AD 790

Remains to be Seen

Despite the ravages of time and forces of nature, Mexico has preserved an incredible archive of archaeological treasures. While many sites have kept their most precious artifacts in situ at on-site museums, there are also some magnificent collections to visit, particularly Xalapa's Museo de Antropología *(p264)*, one of the country's finest.

→

A reconstructed facade at the Museo Nacional de Antropología

Cultural Festivals

There's no better place to immerse yourself in Mexican culture than one of its fantastic fiestas, where you can often see performers from local communities displaying their traditional dances and attire. Oaxaca's Guelaguetza in July is the perfect choice, a dedicated indigenous cultural festival with dances, food stands, and crafts by communities from around Oaxaca. Be aware that some Mexicans don't appreciate having tourists at this festival, so be respectful and considerate if attending.

$\rightarrow$

A folk dance group at Oaxaca's Guelaguetza cultural festival

MEXICO FOR
INDIGENOUS CULTURE

Descendants of Mexico's ancient civilizations and a number of other indigenous peoples still live all over the country, preserving their heritage in contemporary Mexico through traditional customs and creative works.

Trading Places

Markets are part of everyday life for indigenous Mexicans, as much a social hub as a place to sell their produce. For visitors, these markets are a fantastic cultural showcase of food, arts, and crafts. Some of the best markets include the Mercado de Abastos (p236) and Tlacolula Sunday market in Oaxaca state, and Mexico City's sprawling Mercado de La Merced (p132), on the site of an old Aztec market.

$\leftarrow$

Fresh produce on sale at the food stalls in Tlacolula's Sunday market

Learning Firsthand

Organizations and activities run by indigenous people help to share the community's history, customs, and daily life. The Na Bolom foundation (p249) has a museum and guesthouse and plans expeditions with the Lacandón Maya, while Kiichpam Kaax (www.sumak-travel.org) shows visitors traditional activities, from beekeeping to rubber-tree tapping.

$\longrightarrow$

The Na Bolom headquarters in San Cristóbal de las Casas

Artisan Crafts

Indigenous handicrafts range from delicate jewelry to massive sculptures. This rich artistic heritage dates back to the earliest civilizations, with modern artisans adapting to today's changing fashions. The best place to see modern crafts is in markets, like those in Tequisquiapan (p216) and Izamal (p305), where you can buy items from the makers.

$\longleftarrow$

Embroidering a *huipil*, a common style of traditional dress from the Yucatán Peninsula

Timeless Towns

Sleepy plazas shaded by palms. Shoe-shine stalls and sugarcane juice sellers. Cobbled streets and weathered Baroque churches built by the Spanish. Mexico is rich with lesser-known towns and villages dripping with charm and history. Santa Rosalía's *(p170)* mining roots are clear from the old installations still scattered around, while Batopilas *(p183)* is so remote it feels untouched by the modern world.

$\rightarrow$

The colorful veranda of the Riverside Lodge, in Batopilas

MEXICO
OFF THE BEATEN PATH

Step off the regular tourist trail and you'll discover intriguing surprises all across Mexico. You might stumble upon isolated jungle ruins, a colonial-era town seemingly frozen in time, or a trendy new winery.

Quirky Festivals

While it's no secret that the Mexican calendar is full of great events, even well-known dates can offer up surprises, like the fascinating regional variations you'll see at Easter *(p185)*. Sometimes, you may even stumble on a truly unique event, like Oaxaca's *Noche de los Rábanos* (Night of the Radishes) in December *(p254)*.

$\uparrow$ Night of the Radishes, when locals compete in radish carving

Lost Missions of Mexico

Some of the most haunting sights in Mexico are its isolated mission churches from the time of New Spain. The Misión San Francisco Javier de Viggé-Biaundó *(p171)* is an enigmatic memorial to the Cochimí people, while the "lost" Satevó Mission *(p182)* lies in a remote valley in the Copper Canyon.

→

A Franciscan mission built by the local Xi'iuy people in the Sierra Gorda

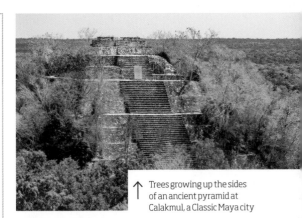

Craft Beer and Boutique Wine

Large breweries have dominated production for years in Mexico, but times are changing. The craft beer scene is growing steadily, with companies like Baja Brewing *(www.baja brewingcompany.com)* creating high-quality beers you can try at its own tap rooms. Meanwhile, the wines of Valle de Guadalupe *(p168)* continue to gain international renown, led by the likes of Casa de Piedra winery.

←

Wine tasting in Mexico's finest wine region, Guadalupe Valley in Baja California

---

TOP 4 BAJA VINEYARDS

Adobe Guadalupe
 adobeguadalupe.com
Famous for its 55 per cent Merlot, Gabriel.

Monte Xanic
w montexanic.com.mx
Try its exquisite Gran Ricardo Bordeaux blend.

Château Camou
w chateau-camou.com.mx
Its specialty is Viñas de Camou, a Cabernet Sauvignon, Cabernet Franc, and Merlot blend.

L.A. Cetto
w lacetto.mx
Known for Reserva Privada, made from an Italian red grape.

↑ Trees growing up the sides of an ancient pyramid at Calakmul, a Classic Maya city

Mighty Mesoamerica

Mexico is dotted with the ruins of historic Mesoamerican civilizations, and while there are plenty on the tourist map, others are empty, remote spots perfect for adventurous travelers. The Río Bec sites *(p308)*, for example, are extremely isolated and rarely visited. Deep in the jungle, the once great city of Calakmul *(p309)* is never busy, despite boasting one of the largest Maya pyramids.

Street Food

The Mexican foods most foreigners are familiar with are known as *antojitos* (light courses or appetizers), best experienced at street stalls and food markets in places like Oaxaca *(p234)*, Ensenada *(p168)*, and Mexico City. Tortillas are a staple element of *antojitos*, used for tacos (filled with meat or veggies), enchiladas (similar to tacos but rolled and baked), chilaquiles (ripped up tortillas cooked with meat and sauce), and gorditas (stuffed corn tortillas, baked or fried).

→
A street food stall in Oaxaca, one of Mexico's greatest foodie spots

MEXICO FOR
FOODIES

The dishes you'll find here bear little resemblance to the typical meals made elsewhere in the world in the name of Mexico. The country's real cuisine blends ingredients and recipes that have developed through Aztec, Spanish and modern eras, creating a sophisticated menu of delicious flavors.

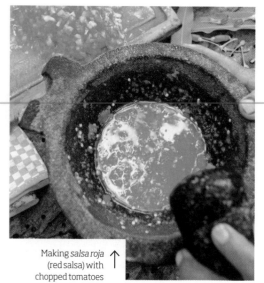

Making *salsa roja* ↑
(red salsa) with
chopped tomatoes

Spicy Salsas

The spicy heat of Mexican dishes comes from red and green salsas. From celebrity chefs to street stall owners, everyone takes pride in their recipes, though all use the same basic ingredients, including tomato, onion, and chili. Taquería Hermanos González in La Paz *(p172)*, offers some tasty examples.

Did You Know?

Mexico is home to at least 150 different varieties of chili pepper.

THE SPIRIT OF MEXICO

A potent distilled spirit made from the agave plant, mezcal has been made in Mexico since roughly the 16th century. Tequila is a type of mezcal, albeit one that must use only blue agave and is produced mainly in the state of Jalisco. Aficionados always sip tequila straight, never in cocktails.

Celebrity Chefs

Mexico's temples of haute cuisine are a world away from its street food stalls. Leading the pack is Pujol in Mexico City (www.pujol.com.mx), the flagship of Enrique Olvera, the country's best-known culinary maestro. In Ensenada, Benito Molina cooks up fresh seafood at Manzanilla (www.rmanzanilla.com), while Elena Reygadas helms Rosetta in Mexico City (www.rosetta.com.mx).

Camaron y jicama, a shrimp and yam bean dish made by Estanis Carenzo, a visiting chef at Pujol

Taste the Regions

Across Mexico you'll discover regional dishes that take pride of place on the menu in each state. Baja California is famous for fish tacos, while Central Mexico is the home of guacamole. Some towns even have their own specialty, so keep an eye out for local favorites or ask for recommendations. In Monterrey (p187) they'll suggest the *cabrito asado* (roast goat), while Puebla (p148) is known for *mole poblano*, a blend of chilis and chocolate.

A chef from Oaxaca state's El Sabor Zapoteco Cooking School making tamales

A YEAR IN
MEXICO

JANUARY

△ **Día de los Santos Reyes** *(Jan 6)*. Throughout Mexico, street stalls, parties, and gift exchanges are held in honor of the biblical Three Wise Men.

Festival Alfonso Ortiz Tirado *(late Jan)*. Álamos hosts the second biggest music festival in Mexico, with nine days of concerts.

FEBRUARY

Día de la Bandera *(Feb 24)*. Day of tribute to the Mexican national flag, celebrated with military parades, patriotic songs, and speeches.

△ **Carnival** *(Feb/Mar)*. Colorful parades, gigs, and dances are held over five days leading up to Ash Wednesday, with particularly lively celebrations in Veracruz and Mazatlán.

MAY

Día del Trabajo *(May 1)*. Labor Day public holiday with parades held in Mexico City and other large cities.

△ **Corpus Christi** *(May/Jun)*. Masses are held across the country on this important date in the Catholic calendar, 60 days after Easter.

JUNE

Día de la Marina *(Jun 1)*. Battle reenactments and torchlit processions honoring the navy and fishing industry, particularly popular in Guaymas, Sonora.

△ **Mexico City Gay Pride** *(late Jun)*. Around one million people attend this Pride parade from the city's main LGBT+ district, Zona Rosa.

SEPTEMBER

Día del Charro *(Sep 14)*. This hugely popular event is held nationwide in tribute to Mexico's cowboys and cowgirls – *los charros* – with horseback displays, rodeos, and parades.

△ **Día de la Independencia** *(Sep 16)*. The most patriotic event in the Mexican calendar, particularly important in Dolores Hidalgo where independence was proclaimed.

OCTOBER

△ **Festival Internacional Cervantino** *(throughout)*. A diverse arts festival, with performances of Cervantes plays on the streets of Guanajuato.

Día de la Raza *(Oct 12)*. Originally the celebration of Christopher Columbus's arrival in the Americas, this day now focuses on celebrating Mexico's ethnic diversity.

MARCH

△ **Vive Latino** *(mid-Mar)*. A huge Latino rock festival in Mexico City, attracting top international Hispanic stars.

Natalicio de Benito Juárez *(Mar 21)*. The revered 19th-century president is celebrated with flag displays and floral tributes, notably in his birthplace of San Pablo Guelatao, in Oaxaca state.

APRIL

△ **Semana Santa** *(Easter)*. Starting on Palm Sunday, a week of parades and passion plays, with some regions such as the Copper Canyon blending Catholic and indigenous rituals.

Regata del Sol al Sol *(late Apr)*. Fireworks, a basketball match, and parties mark the end of this international yacht race from St. Petersburg, Florida, to Isla Mujeres off the coast near Cancún.

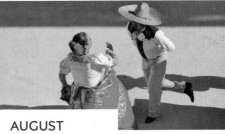

JULY

△ **Festival Internacional de Guitarra de México** *(mid-Jul)*. Celebrating string instrument music of all kinds – from Baroque lute to tango guitar – Saltillo hosts orchestral concerts and recitals across the city, with leading international musicians.

Día de Santiago *(Jul 25)*. Horseback processions for the patron saint of Spain, with particularly festive events held in many villages in Chiapas state.

AUGUST

△ **Festival Zacatecas del Folclor Internacional** *(early Aug)*. This festival of traditional music and dance in Zacatecas is one of the best of its kind in the country.

Dia de la Asunción *(Aug 15)*. Parades and processions commemorating the Virgin Mary's ascent to heaven, with the most famous celebrations held in the states of Aguascalientes, Jalisco, and Tabasco.

NOVEMBER

△ **Día de Muertos** *(Nov 1–2)*. Mexico's most famous festival, when families commemorate their deceased loved ones. Celebrated with multicolored papier-mâché skeletons, food, and drink. Pátzcuaro has particularly atmospheric festivities.

Día de Santa Cecilia *(Nov 22)*. Concerts throughout the country to honor the patron saint of music; particularly popular with mariachi bands in Mexico City and Guanajuato.

DECEMBER

△ **Día de la Virgen de Guadalupe** *(Dec 12)*. Millions of devotees of Mexico's patron saint join an annual pilgrimage to the Basilica of Guadalupe in Mexico City.

Dia de la Navidad *(Dec 25)*. Mexicans celebrate Christmas Day with particular zeal and elaborate Nativity scenes.

A BRIEF
HISTORY

Mexico's history spans the rise and fall of ancient civilizations, the Spanish crown, short-lived emperors, famous revolutionaries, and political leaders. Today, Mexico continues to forge its own modern identity while still bearing the influence of these historic eras and cultures.

Earliest Settlers

By 8000 BC, Mexico's early hunter-gatherer population had begun settling in villages and farming the land. Around 1500 BC, the Olmec culture arose on the Gulf Coast, resulting in great ceremonial centers – but during the first millennium BC, the Olmecs declined, for reasons unknown.

Classic Cultures

One of Central America's most advanced civilizations – the Maya – originated in southern Mexico. The Maya Classic Period peaked from AD 200 to 800, with numerous city-states based around

Did You Know?

The name Mexico is derived from the alternative word for the Toltec culture: the Mexica.

Timeline of events

20000 BC

Hunter-gatherer migrants cross from Asia into the Americas and gradually spread south to the Valley of Mexico.

c 1500 BC

First Olmec settlements established on the Gulf Coast.

c 200 BC

Founding of the city of Teotihuacán.

c 8000 BC

Development of agriculture, with the cultivation of corn, chili peppers, and beans.

c AD 800

Collapse of the Classic Maya civilization. Monte Albán abandoned at around the same time.

elaborate temples. The Classic Maya were sophisticated artists and their complex "Long Count" calendar showed remarkable mathematical and astronomical knowledge. Nevertheless, by around AD 900, the Maya culture had collapsed, unable to sustain its growing population. Further north, meanwhile, a great city-state was emerging in the Valley of Mexico. Teotihuacán was built and abandoned by unknown founders before rising once again from AD 100 to 650. During the 7th century, however, Teotihuacán waned, weakened by attacks, poverty, and internal dissent.

Warring Rivals and Invaders

Teotihuacán's fall led to the rise of militarized successor states, most notably the Toltecs, who settled in the Valley of Mexico during the 10th century. After their capital at Tula was overrun by rival groups, the Aztecs emerged as Central America's last great empire. When Spanish conquistador Hernán Cortés landed in Mexico in 1519, he and his men marched on the Aztec capital, Tenochtitlán. By now, the Aztecs faced overpopulation, internal dissidence, and resistance from outlying states. Joining forces with one such state, Cortés took on the Aztec army and, after a destructive siege, Tenochtitlán was conquered.

1 A map of Nueva Galicia, a kingdom of New Spain on Mexico's central coast.

2 A giant Olmec head at the Parque-Museo de la Venta, in Villahermosa.

3 Detailed stonework in the Hall of the Columns, in the Zapotec city of Mitla.

4 A meeting between Cortés and Moctezuma II, the Aztec ruler.

909

Last recorded inscriptions of the Classic Maya, found at Toniná in Chiapas state.

1519

Cortés lands on the coast of Veracruz, with a force of 450 conquistadors.

1521

The Aztecs surrender to the Spanish at Tenochtitlán and the Aztec Empire falls.

c 1325

The Aztecs establish their capital Tenochtitlán (modern Mexico City) on an island in Lake Texcoco.

Colonial-Era Mexico

Within three years of the Aztecs' defeat, the Spanish had subjugated most of present-day Mexico, which was renamed "New Spain." Huge quantities of bullion were remitted to its European ruler, and as the colonial economy grew, New Spain relied heavily upon the free labor of enslaved Africans. By the early 1600s, Mexico had the largest African slave population in the Americas. Meanwhile, the mixing of Spanish-born settlers with other ethnic groups led to intermediate castes and a new Creole elite in addition to the wealthy, white European immigrants, who spent their time financing grandiose residences and lavish churches. Indigenous peoples and Africans were at the bottom of New Spain's social hierarchy, and became the focus of much attention by Franciscan and Dominican friars who tirelessly preached to, converted, and baptized them.

Rising Discontent

Being a vast colony far away from the seat of the Spanish crown, and with a new elite growing rich and powerful from the treasures and land of New Spain, Mexico enjoyed partial autonomy

ENCOMIENDAS

The Spanish Crown granted conquistadors *encomiendas*: parcels of land with their own indigenous workers. *Encomendero* landlords were expected to protect and convert their charges who, in return, provided tribute with labor, produce, and resources such as metals. In practice, the *encomienda* system became a brutal form of slavery, and it was abolished in 1542.

Timeline of events

1531
An apparition in Tepeyac, north of Mexico City, initiates the cult of the Virgin of Guadalupe, the patron saint of Mexico.

1546
Zacatecas city is founded, following the discovery of silver deposits.

1692
Anti-government riots by indigenous protestors in Mexico City, triggered by food shortages and ethnic tensions.

1765
Bourbon reforms tighten Spain's hold on Mexico.

compared to other colonies. In the 18th century, however, the new Bourbon dynasty in Spain sought to claw back control Royal power was centralized, weakening the Church, and relations between Spain and Mexico worsened as the Creole community resented the interference of Spanish officials, while the lower castes suffered from rising taxes and shortages of basic goods. The old alliance between Crown and Church was further undermined when, in 1767, the Jesuits were expelled for their perceived excessive power and influence.

The War of Independence

Responding to the tensions, and exploiting Spain's distraction with the Napoleonic Wars, Mexican independence campaigners acted. On September 16, 1810, a parish priest, Miguel Hidalgo, gave his famous call to arms, *El Grito* (The Cry). The revolt failed, however, and Hidalgo was executed. Another revolt in 1814, led by priest José María Morelos, was also crushed. Guerrilla resistance continued and, in 1821, Mexico's Creole elite proclaimed independence. Spain lacked the ability to fight on, and its main American colony became the independent nation of Mexico.

1 Zacatecas, a colonial-era silver-mining town.

2 A hacienda built by Spanish settlers.

3 Plaza Mayor, Mexico City, in 1692.

4 José María Morelos.

Did You Know?

Mexico's African population outnumbered the white Europeans during the colonial era.

1810
Miguel Hidalgo launches a popular revolt against Spanish rule, sparking the War of Independence.

1821
End of the war of Independence; Agustín de Iturbide becomes president.

1767
Expulsion of the Jesuits from Mexico, in a purge in Europe and its colonies.

1814
José María Morelos leads a second attempt at Mexican independence. He is captured and executed in 1815.

The New Nation

After a brief imperial interlude – when Agustín de Iturbide made himself emperor (1821–3) – Mexico became a republic. The newly independent country was split between Liberals and Conservatives. Liberal intellectuals, supported by indigenous workers, favored a progressive, free-trading secular society. Elite Conservatives preferred a centralized state, backed by Church and army. Administrations came and went: 30 presidents governed in the 50 years following Mexican independence. The army also generated a host of *caudillos* (military leaders) who built up their retinues and contested for political power.

Disastrous Wars

The most prominent *caudillo* was Antonio López de Santa Anna. He attained the presidency 11 times, but led the country to a crushing defeat in the 1836 war with Texas – then part of Mexico, but home to a large population of US immigrants. Ten years later, Texas joined the US, sparking a war between the two countries. Mexico's defeat resulted in the loss of nearly half its territory to the US, in the Treaty of Guadalupe.

1 Emperor Agustín I.

2 Monument honoring heroes of the Mexican-American War.

3 The death of Emperor Maximilian I.

4 Castillo de Chapultepec.

Did You Know?

The era under president Porfirio Díaz is known as the *Porfiriato*.

Timeline of events

1824
Mexico becomes a federal republic.

1836
Texas Revolution; General Santa Anna is victorious at the Alamo but defeated at San Jacinto.

1846
The start of the Mexican-American War.

1848
The war ends; Mexico loses much of its territory to the US.

1858–61
War of the Reform; Liberal victory under Benito Juárez.

4

The Reform

Provoked by its defeat, Mexico's Liberal government, led by Benito Juárez, advocated radical reforms. Its 1854 program known as *La Reforma* (The Reform) would separate Church and State, and make all citizens equal. The Church and the army resisted, but in the ensuing War of the Reform (1858–61) the Liberals were victorious. In 1864, however, the Conservatives sought support from Napoleon III, and declared Maximilian of the Hapsburg Emperor of Mexico. The Liberals fought back and Maximilian was executed. Mexico's last monarchy had fallen, and the republic, under Juárez, was restored.

From Dictatorship to Revolution

Four years after the death of Juárez in 1872, general Porfirio Díaz seized power, ruling as an authoritarian president for over three decades. During this time, cities expanded and communications improved but, by the 1900s, Díaz had impoverished the rural workers and exasperated the middle classes with his authoritarian control. Mexico yearned for real democracy, setting the scene for revolution.

VICENTE GUERRERO

Mexico's second president, Vicente Guerrero, was of Afro-Mestizo descent, according to the colonial caste system - making him America's first black president. Guerrero became president after serving as a general in the War of Independence. Among other liberal orders, he called for the immediate abolition of slavery on September 16, 1829.

1862

Mexican forces defeat French invaders at Puebla.

1863

French forces enter and successfully capture Mexico City.

1864–7

French occupation under Emperor Maximilian.

1867

On June 19, Maximilian is executed by firing squad at Querétaro.

1876–1911

Porfirio Díaz is president of Mexico.

1

A Decade of Revolution

The Mexican Revolution began in 1910, initially in opposition to Diaz's dictatorial regime. Although Diaz was succeeded by Francisco Madero, Madero failed to unify the country and was assassinated by the military. Another war broke out when revolutionary leaders Emiliano Zapata and Pancho Villa joined together against the subsequent regime of General Victoriano Huerta. Despite their victory against Huerta, disagreements over authority broke out between opposing revolutionary groups, prompting a final civil war. Venustiano Carranza's defeat of Villa in 1917 led to a radical new constitution and Carranza's rise to presidency. By the end of the revolution, violent conflict had touched almost every part of Mexico. Over a million people had died or left the country, the currency had collapsed, and Mexico's infrastructure was in tatters.

The Aftermath

Carranza was eventually ousted by his former general, Álvaro Obregón, in 1920. In the following years, the new regime battled to appease the Church and the US, which disapproved of its

↑ Venustiano Carranza, a key leader of the Mexican Revolution

---

Timeline of events

1910
The Mexican Revolution is launched by Francisco Madero.

1917
Mexico's liberal, revolutionary constitution is passed.

1941–5
Mexico joins with the Allies during World War II.

1929
Partido Nacional Revolucionario (PNR) is formed.

1957
Death of Diego Rivera, one of the founding members of Mexican mural movement.

expropriation of foreign-owned businesses and land. In 1928, Obregón was assassinated, causing further instability.

Toward the New Millennium

The 1950s and 1960s saw an "economic miracle," powered by the private sector. Later, the discovery of offshore oil led the government to borrow and spend extravagantly. Inflation rose, the economy slumped, and recession continued despite the 1993 North American Free Trade Agreement. However, social reform was on the rise. In 1992, Mexico launched the Third Root Project, acknowledging African presence and influence in Mexico. And in 1994, indigenous peoples in Chiapas united in rebellion against the government demanding political representation.

Mexico Today

The early 21st century has been turbulent for Mexico: the division of wealth is wide and drug gang violence, corruption, and migration are key concerns for the government. However, tourism is booming, as people around the world continue to be drawn to this beautiful and fascinating country.

1 Pancho Villa in 1914.

2 Chihuahua in the 1960s.

3 Leaders gather in 1993.

4 Ancient sights such as Teotihuacán draw visitors to present-day Mexico.

Did You Know?

The capital of Mexico City is the most populous urban area in North America.

1985

An earthquake hits Mexico City, killing an estimated 9,000 people.

2015

"Afro-Mexicano" is included as an ethnicity option in a census for the first time.

2019

Alfonso Cuarón's *Roma* wins Mexico's first Best Foreign-Language Film Oscar.

1968

Olympic Games in Mexico City; a student protest is repressed, resulting in many deaths.

2007

Chichén Itzá is named one of the New Seven Wonders of the World.

EXPERIENCE
MEXICO CITY

Shops and cafés in the Coyoacán district

EXPLORE
MEXICO
CITY

This section divides Mexico City into three sightseeing areas, as shown on this map, plus an area beyond the city center. Find out more about each area on the following pages.

Museo Nacional de Antropología

AROUND PASEO DE LA REFORMA
p96

Museo de Arte Moderno

AV. CHAPULTEPEC

Bosque de Chapultepec

LOMAS

AV. CONSTITUYENTES

TACUBAYA

PERIFÉRICO

CIRCUITO INTERIOR

AVENIDA INSURGENTES SUR

DEL VALLE

SANTA FE

MIXCOAC

AVENIDA SANTA LUCIA

LAS AGUILAS

PERIFÉRICO

SAN ÁNGEL AND COYOACÁN
p112

SAN ÁNGEL

COYOACÁN

Plaza San Jacinto

PROGRESO

0 kilometers — 2
0 miles — 2

N ↑

GETTING TO KNOW
MEXICO CITY

Mexico City is the fiesta-fueled, football-loving, political, economic, and cultural heart of the nation. We've broken the city down into three main areas that contain all the must-see highlights, plus a wider area beyond the center reaching out towards the fringes of this vast metropolis.

THE HISTORIC CENTER

PAGE 72

The Aztec Empire may be long gone, but its former capital, Tenochtitlan, is now the beating heart of Mexico City. The Spanish colonizers began building their own city over the remains of Tenochtitlan in the 16th century, and now the Historic Center is so named for the many important buildings that stand here. Today the area is one of the best places to see the many faces of Mexico all in one place: priests and nuns mingle with shoe-shiners and taco-vendors, and mariachi blares from shop windows while patrons linger over *café de olla* in cool, colonial-era cafés.

Best for
Architecture, history, and culture

Home to
Catedral Metropolitana, Palacio de Bellas Artes, Templo Mayor, and Palacio Nacional

Experience
Catching a live performance of Mexican folk dances at the Ballet Folklórico

AROUND PASEO DE LA REFORMA

Running through the heart of the city, the Paseo de la Reforma is a magnificent avenue modeled after those in European capitals. Clustered along the edges are the skyscrapers of the nation's financial center, and on the outskirts there are plenty of cool districts to discover. The Zona Rosa is Mexico's most popular LGBT+ scene, while affluent Polanco is home to posh boutiques, superb restaurants, and the e-scooters favored by young professionals. At the southern end of the Paseo lies Mexico's most beautiful urban park, Bosque de Chapultepec, replete with bike trails, gardens, and a castle.

Best for
Museums, nightlife, and parks

Home to
Museo Nacional de Antropología

Experience
Staying up all night in the Zona Rosa, hopping between its many restaurants, bars, and nightclubs

$\rightarrow$

SAN ÁNGEL AND COYOACÁN

In this sprawling metropolis, San Ángel and Coyoacán stand out as especially enticing suburbs, perfect for those seeking out an authentic local atmosphere. Stroll the tranquil, cobbled streets and you'll be rewarded with chic cafés, interesting boutiques, aging churches, picturesque canals, and the vestiges of the old Aztec city. This is also where you'll find the homes and studios of Frida Kahlo and Diego Rivera, as well as the last home of Leon Trotsky – all of which are now fascinating museums.

Best for
Art, history, and strolling

Home to
Museo Frida Kahlo

Experience
Having brunch at the San Ángel Inn before perusing the local Saturday craft market

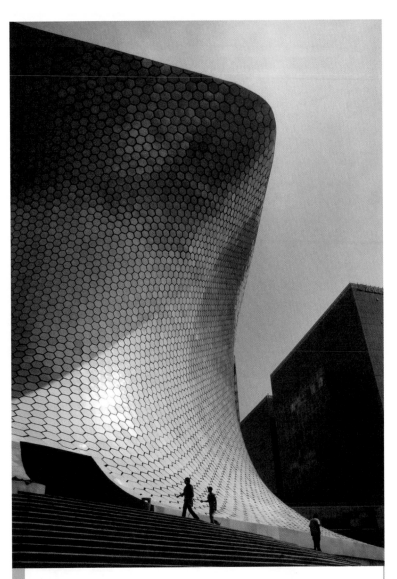

BEYOND THE CENTER

Mexico City has expanded into the valleys and high plateaus far beyond its traditional center, and is full of diverse neighborhoods, from shantytowns to posh suburbs. Dotted all around are interesting spots that are well worth the trip beyond the more famous central districts. Tour the canals of Xochimilco, join the locals at the home of Mexican soccer, wander through the city's biggest market, and visit some of the city's most exciting art museums and modern architectural marvels.

Best for
Traditional culture and modern architecture

Home to
Xochimilco

Experience
Hopping aboard a boat in Xochimilco for a cruise through its ancient waterways and floating gardens

THE HISTORIC CENTER

Mexico City's Historic Center lies on what was once the ceremonial heart of Tenochtitlán, the Aztec capital. When Hernán Cortés led his army into the city in 1521, it stood on an island in Lake Texcoco. After conquering the city, the Spanish razed it to the ground, reusing much of the stonework in their own constructions, and gradually filling in the lake.

Today the district retains an elegant feel, its narrow streets lined with old-fashioned cafés and shops, and its mansions converted into offices, banks, and museums. Most of the buildings here date from the colonial and post-independence eras. In a patchwork of architectural styles, they range from Spanish Colonial to Art Deco.

THE HISTORIC CENTER

Must Sees

1. Catedral Metropolitana
2. Palacio de Bellas Artes
3. Templo Mayor
4. Palacio Nacional

Experience More

5. Secretaría de Educación Pública
6. Antiguo Colegio de San Ildefonso
7. Templo de la Enseñanza
8. Plaza Garibaldi
9. Iglesia de la Santísima Trinidad
10. Museo José Luis Cuevas
11. Museo de la Ciudad de México
12. Museo de Arte Popular
13. Museo Mural Diego Rivera
14. Laboratorio Arte Alameda
15. Casa de los Azulejos
16. Museo Nacional de Arte
17. Palacio de Cultura Citibanamex
18. Museo de la Caricatura
19. Museo Nacional de la Estampa
20. Torre Latinoamericana
21. Plaza de Santo Domingo
22. Museo Franz Mayer
23. Palacio de la Escuela de Medicina

Eat

1. Café de Bellas Artes
2. El Caguamo
3. Tortas Been
4. Tacos El Huequito

Drink

5. La Opera Bar
6. Café Tacuba
7. Terazza Gran Hotel

AROUND PASEO DE LA REFORMA p96

❶

CATEDRAL METROPOLITANA

⊙ K3 **⊕** Zócalo **Ⓜ** Zócalo **⊙** Choir: 10am–3pm daily; sacristy: 11am–2pm daily; bell tower: 10:30am–6pm daily **Ⓦ** catedralmetropolitana.org

Dominating the Zócalo plaza, the Metropolitan Cathedral is built atop the ruins of a former Aztec ceremonial center. The ornate facade bristles with Churrigueresque sculptures, while its interior dazzles with gilded altars, and unadorned white columns supporting a soaring ceiling.

One of the biggest churches in Latin America, Mexico City's cathedral is at the heart of the world's largest Catholic diocese. It took almost three centuries – from 1525 to 1788 – to complete. This long period is reflected in the multiple styles of its architecture and internal decoration, ranging from Classical through Baroque and Churrigueresque to Neo-Classical. It has five principal altars, and 16 side chapels containing a valuable collection of paintings, sculpture, and church furniture.

The two oil paintings on the Baroque Altar de los Reyes are the Adoration of the Kings *and the* Assumption of the Virgin, *both by Juan Rodríguez Juárez.*

The sacristy contains 17th-century paintings and items of carved furniture, including a decorated cabinet.

→
Illustration of Catedral Metropolitana

The sculptures on the Altar de los Reyes are of canonized kings and queens.

Side entrance

The high altar is a block of white marble carved with images of saints.

Capilla de San José is one of 16 side chapels dedicated to saints and manifestations of the Virgin, all exquisitely decorated.

←
The imposing facade of the massive Catedral Metropolitana

Spanish Colonial

Work began in 1573. The basic plan of three huge vaulted naves was the work of Claudio de Arciniega. Much of the first walls were built by Juan Miguel de Agüero.

Churrigueresque

▽ Built between 1710 and 1737, the *estípites* (square-sided relief columns) are a hallmark of the Churrigueresque style. The foremost example is the Sagrario Metropolitano's facade, built by Lorenzo Rodríguez.

Baroque

▲ Most of the cathedral was built in the mid-17th century, the oldest sections in the restrained Spanish Baroque style known as Plateresque. The three portals of the main facade, from 1670–90, are grander.

Neo-Classical

The bell towers and upper stories were added in the 1780s. Manuel Tolsá added the clock tower and rebuilt the dome in an austere Neo-Classical style.

Attached to the east side of the cathedral is the Sagrario, built in the mid-18th century as the parish church. It has a high Baroque facade adorned with sculpted saints.

The clock tower is decorated with statues of Faith, Hope, and Charity.

The facade is divided into three and flanked by monumental bell towers.

Main entrance

With its gold-alloy choir-rail imported from Macao, superbly carved stalls, and two magnificent organs, the choir is one of the highlights of the cathedral.

> 💬 **INSIDER TIP**
> ### Subsidence
>
> Over time, the cathedral began sinking into the soft clay on which it was built, causing its floor to slope. After a devastating earthquake in 1985, the structure was stabilized.

2 ⬡ ⬡ ⬡ ⬡

PALACIO DE BELLAS ARTES

📍 J3 🔲 Eje Central & Avenida Juárez 🅼 Bellas Artes 🕐 10am–5:45pm Tue–Sun 🖥 museopalaciodebellasartes.gob.mx

This magnificent monument houses a prestigious collection of Mexican muralist art, and its theater hosts traditional folk-dance performances and live classical concerts by world-leading orchestras and artists.

Arguably the most beautiful building in the Historic Center, the Palacio de Bellas Artes was conceived in 1905 as a new national theater. Italian architect Adamo Boari designed an innovative building around a steel frame, incorporating Neo-Classical and Art Nouveau elements together with pre-Hispanic decorative details. The exterior of the building is clad in Italian marble and its cupolas are covered in tiles. The largest, central dome is surmounted by a Mexican eagle surrounded by figures representing the dramatic arts. Interrupted by the revolution, the work was completed by Federico Mariscal in 1934. This accounts for the contrasting Art Deco interior, with its geometric shapes in colored marble and eye-catching illumination, especially the vertical lamps flanking the entrance to the auditorium.

Outside the Palacio de Bellas Artes, its dome a major landmark in the Historic Center ↑

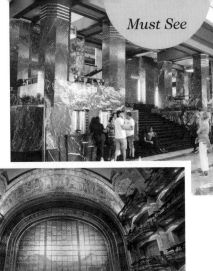

→ The Art Deco entrance hall, clad in cream and gold-colored marble

EAT

Café de Bellas Artes
Whether you're seeking a mid-concert cocktail, or a hearty meal after browsing the galleries, this little café is the ideal place for a break, with a great menu and a convenient location inside the Palacio. Dishes include Mexican classics such as *chiles en nogada* (stuffed chiles in walnut sauce).

🏠 Avenida Juarez s/no and corner of Eje Central Lazaro Cardenas
📞 5512-2593

⑂⑂⑂

↑ A stunning glass mosaic curtain, which was made by Tiffany Studios of New York

TOP 4 **HIGHLIGHTS OF THE PALACIO**

Murals
17 artworks by Mexico's foremost muralists, including Rivera, Orozco, and Siqueiros.

Theater Curtain
Made of a million pieces of glass by Tiffany Studios, the curtain depicts the iconic Popocatépetl and Iztaccíhuatl volcanoes.

Museo Nacional de Arquitectura
Contemporary architecture from around the world is displayed.

Facade
The Art Nouveau exterior features Carrara Italian marble columns, topped by golden domes of Marotti glass and ironwork.

③ 🗡 Ⓜ 🛍

TEMPLO MAYOR

📍K3 🚇Seminario Ⓜ Zócalo ⏰9am–5pm Tue–Sun
🌐 templomayor.inah.gob.mx

Although in ruins and surrounded by modern buildings, the remains of the Great Temple still convey the grandeur of the former Aztec city, Tenochtitlán. The museum houses a scale model of the original complex and the giant carved monolith of the goddess Coyolxauhqui.

This temple once stood at the heart of the Aztec city of Tenochtitlán. The Aztecs chose this spot for their most important religious building to fulfil a prophecy, having been advised by their god, Huitzilopochtli, to pitch their tents where they saw an eagle perched on a cactus, devouring a snake.

The first temple was built some time after 1325, but it was enlarged many times over the course of the next two centuries. The complex was almost completely destroyed by the Spanish after their conquest of the Aztec capital in the early 1500s. The chance discovery of the extraordinary Coyolxauhqui carving in 1978 prompted excavations that uncovered the remains of superimposed temples denoted by their stages of construction.

A museum attached to the archaeological site contains eight rooms of impressive Aztec exhibits, with some of the items having been discovered here at Templo Mayor. These include the Eagle Knights, two identical life-size clay statues of elite Aztec warriors in feathered costumes.

The layout of the ruin complex can be confusing. Authorized tours are recommended, as are audio guides, both of which are available from the museum.

↑ Stones carved by the Aztecs uncovered at the site, now displayed in the museum

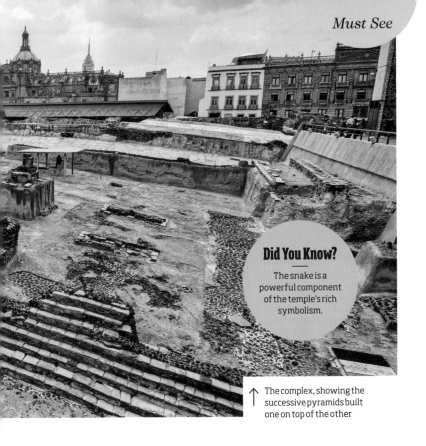

Did You Know?

The snake is a powerful component of the temple's rich symbolism.

↑ The complex, showing the successive pyramids built one on top of the other

Present-day buildings are shown here to give an idea of the scale of the pyramid.

Temple of Tlaloc

Temple of Huitzilopochtli

North Room

Museum

Two snake heads guard the foot of the main staircase.

Sacrificial victims were tied to this stone block before being killed with an obsidian knife.

Reconstruction of ↑ Templo Mayor

A carved round stone shows the dismembered body of Coyolxauhqui.

After sacrifice the body of the victim would be thrown down the staircase.

PALACIO NACIONAL

📍K3 🏠Plaza de la Constitución s/n 📞(55) 36 88 12 55
Ⓜ Zócalo 🕐9am-5pm Tue-Sun

The National Palace has been the seat of government since 1562. Its distinguished facade reflects the history of the presidents who have lived and worked here, as depicted by Rivera's murals.

Filling the east side of the Zócalo, this imposing building occupies the former site of the palace of Aztec emperor Moctezuma, and later the home of the conquistador Hernán Cortés. The present palace was begun in 1562 in an austere Baroque style typical of Spanish architecture of the time. It has had an eventful history, and was attacked by rebels in 1624 and 1692. After independence in 1821, it became the residence of the presidents of Mexico, and the offices used by President Juárez in the 1860s are open to the public. In the 1920s a third story was added, in harmony with the original style. While Rivera's murals are the undoubted highlight of the palace, the former Chamber of Deputies, Benito Juarez's rooms, and the history museum are all worth seeing.

Rivera Murals

These extraordinary murals around the staircase of the main patio were painted by Diego Rivera from 1929 to 1935. The main murals above the great staircase present a dynamic panorama of Mexican history. On the right-hand wall is an idealized vision of ancient Mexico before the arrival of the Spanish. Filling the bottom of the central panel are the bloody battles of the Conquest, while independence forms the centerpiece of the main panel. Foreign invasions – by the United States in 1847 and France in the 1860s – are shown in the far right and left panels of the main wall. The inner right panel refers to Juárez's Reform Laws of 1857, and the 1910 revolution appears on the upper left. On the left wall is the astonishing *Mexico Today and Tomorrow*, an exuberant portrayal of the promise of the revolution.

> Filling the east side of the Zócalo, this imposing building occupies the former site of the palace of Aztec emperor Moctezuma.

↑ Interior detail showcasing the building's Spanish Baroque style

← Exterior of the Palacio Nacional, beguiling when illuminated at night

↑ Visitors pausing on the staircase to admire the Rivera murals

Murals

Wrapped around the staircase of the main patio, Rivera's murals depict Mexican history, enlivened by the artist's distinctive characterization.

Botanical Garden

▽ These little gardens of Mexican flora occupy a tranquil courtyard next to the Royal Chapel. They contain hundreds of native species.

Palacio Highlights

Juárez Museum

△ Benito Juárez spent the last five years of his life in the palace. This museum has his possessions, including a letter to Abraham Lincoln.

History Museum

The six rooms of this museum cover some 600 years of Mexican history, including Hernán Cortés, the Spanish viceroys, and the Bourbon era.

Main Balcony

△ Home of the bell rung by Miguel Hidalgo in 1810, and where the president makes the "Grito" before Independence Day on September 16.

⑤

Secretaría de Educación Pública

📍 K3 🏛 República de Argentina 28 Ⓜ Zócalo, Allende 🕐 9am–5pm Mon-Fri 🌐 sep.gob.mx

This former convent building, dating from 1639, is renowned for its large series of murals by prominent Mexican painter Diego Rivera. Painted between 1923 and 1928, they reflect Rivera's diverse influences: Italian frescoes, French Cubists, and pre-Hispanic Mexico. Visitors will need to bring photo ID to enter the site.

The ground floor of the first patio is dedicated to the glorification of labor. On the staircase is a series of Mexican landscapes, while on the third floor, in a panel called *The Painter, The Sculptor and the Architect*, is a well-known self-portrait. The first-floor walls contain *grisailles* (monochromatic paintings) depicting scientific, artistic, and intellectual labor, and on the top floor are portraits of workers' heroes, such as Zapata (*p62*). The second patio, on the ground floor, features panels of fiestas.

The third floor draws on revolutionary songs *(corridos)* for its subject matter and includes a panel, *The Arsenal*, in which the artist Frida Kahlo (p116) hands out guns to gathered revolutionaries.

In stark contrast to the style of Rivera is a striking mural by David Alfaro Siqueiros, *Patriots and Parricides*. This is located on the staircase in a part of the building which used to be a customs house (the Ex-Aduana), near the República de Brasil entrance.

---

⑥

Antiguo Colegio de San Ildefonso

📍 K3 🏛 Justo Sierra 16 Ⓜ Zócalo, Allende 🕐 10am–6pm Tue-Sun 🌐 sanildefonso.org.mx

This 16th-century building, originally a Jesuit seminary, is an outstanding example of Mexican civil architecture from the colonial era. It was remodeled in the 18th century, but the Baroque- and Neo-Classical-inspired facade on Calle San Ildefonso is original.

Today the building belongs to the national university and

🔍 HIDDEN GEM
Palacio Postal

A 15-minute walk from the Antiguo Colegia, the Main Post Office reveals a fabulously ornate wrought-iron and marble interior behind its somber stone facade. It still functions as a post office and has a small postal museum.

serves as a museum. Its star attraction is the collection of murals from the earliest years of the Mexican muralist movement (1920s–70s) – in fact, San Ildefonso is considered to be the birthplace of the movement.

The first murals commissioned included those of Siqueiros, who, in 1922–4, painted four works around the stairwell of the Colegio Chico, the oldest of the three patios which make up the San Ildefonso complex. At around the same time, Orozco was painting a series of murals on the north wall of the Patio Grande with equally universal themes – among them motherhood, freedom, and justice and the law. These

↑ Mariachi musicians playing for diners seated outside on Plaza Garibaldi

include *Revolutionary Trinity* and *The Strike*. Arguably the most dramatic piece, however, is *The Trench*.

The Orozco works to be found on the staircase – including a nude study of Cortés and his mistress La Malinche – relate mostly to the theme of *mestizaje*, or the mixing of the races that formed the Mexican nation. The Anfiteatro Simón Bolívar contains an early work by Diego Rivera, *The Creation*. The other murals in this hall were painted by Fernando Leal between 1930 and 1942.

The conference room to the north of the Patio Grande, known as El Generalito, is furnished with 17th-century carved wooden choir stalls.

Templo de la Enseñanza

📍 K3 🏛 Donceles 102
📞 (55) 57 02 18 43
Ⓜ Allende, Zócalo
🕐 9:30am-7pm Mon-Sat, 11am-2pm Sun

One of the most remarkable churches in Mexico City, the Templo de la Enseñanza has

Diego Rivera murals at the Secretaría de Educación Pública

an extremely narrow and ornate facade sloping backward slightly from ground level. The atrium is tiny and the interior decoration the height of late-18th-century "ultra-Baroque."

Built as a convent church, La Enseñanza was vacated by the nuns as a result of the anti-clerical Reform laws of the 19th-century. It was later used by various government bodies, including the Ministry of Education.

The dazzling gold main altarpiece is studded with sculpted figures of saints. It rises up to the roof of the church, flanked by huge paintings, its height enhancing its vertical dimensions. The vault above is adorned with a fresco of the Virgin of El Pilar, to whom the church is dedicated.

In the lower choir, situated to either side of the altar, are lattice work screens intended

to hide the nuns from the gaze of other worshippers in the church.

Plaza Garibaldi

📍 J2 🏛 N of the Alameda, off Avenida Lázaro Cárdenas

Plaza Garibaldi is the home of mariachi music in Mexico City. Dressed in their iconic costumes, the musicians can be seen scouting for work along the nearby Avenida Lázaro Cárdenas.

Mariachi music was born in the area around Guadalajara in Jalisco (*p194*). In the early 20th century there was heavy migration from Jalisco to the capital, and Plaza Garibaldi became the mariachis' home.

Today the area abounds with bars and restaurants serving a staple fare of tacos and tequila. Mariachi bands can be hired per song or by the hour, and rates vary depending on the size of the band and its musical prowess.

The plaza also has a modern cultural space, MUTEM Garibaldi, which houses **El Museo del Tequila y el Mezcal**, where visitors can learn about the two spirits and have a taste.

El Museo del Tequila y el Mezcal

🏛 Plaza Garibaldi s/n
🕐 1-10pm daily (to midnight Thu-Sat) 🌐 mutem garibaldi.mx

LUCHA LIBRE IN THE CAPITAL

Lucha libre (wrestling) is massively popular in Mexico City. In the freestyle acrobatic bouts, competing *luchadores* (wrestlers) often wear masks and costumes to create superhero-like personalities. Bouts take place several times a week at the two wrestling arenas close to the historic center: Arena México (*Dr Lavista 189*) and Arena Coliseo (*República de Peru 77*).

The intricate facade of the Iglesia de la Santísima Trinidad ↑

INSIDER TIP
Late-Night Museums

Museums in Mexico City stay open until late on the last Wednesday of the month, and some also offer guided tours, concerts, workshops, film screenings, and other activities.

19th century and declared a national monument in 1932. Since 1988 it has housed an art gallery reflecting the personal tastes of Mexican painter and sculptor José Luis Cuevas (1934–2017).

The exquisite patio is dominated by the massive bronze sculpture of *La Giganta (The Giantess)*, which Cuevas created specifically for this space. A number of smaller bronzes by the artist are dotted around the ground floor. The galleries contain paintings by Cuevas and other Mexican artists, including a number of portraits of him and his wife Bertha. There are also temporary exhibits by international artists.

At the entrance to a small "dark room" dedicated to Cuevas' works of erotica, visitors are warned, tongue-in-cheek, of the dangers they

9
Iglesia de la Santísima Trinidad

📍L3 🏛️Emiliano Zapata 60 Ⓜ️Zócalo 📞(55) 55 22 22 15 🕐10am–2pm & 4–8pm Tue–Sat, 10am–2pm Sun

Formerly a hospice, the 18th-century Church of the Holy Trinity is only a few blocks from the Zócalo (p94) but is easily overlooked amid the bustle of the surrounding streets. It has an intricate Churrigueresque facade, with finely worked tapered columns and sculpted figures.

The interior is simpler, but it's still worth entering the church to see the paintings of the martyrs in the nave, the two wooden sculptures representing the Trinity, and the crucifix inlaid with bone and precious woods. The wooden screen in the entrance to the church and the choir balustrade is also impressively carved.

10
Museo José Luis Cuevas

📍L3 🏛️Academia 13 Ⓜ️Zócalo 🕐9:30am–5:30pm Tue–Sun 🌐museo joseluiscuevas.com.mx

Formerly the cloisters of the Santa Inés convent, this 17th-century jewel was converted to private dwellings in the

→
Jose Louis Cuevas'
La Giganta (1991) at the
Museo José Luis Cuevas

pose to those who have had a puritan upbringing.

On your way out of the museum, take a moment to admire the entrance of the church of Santa Inés next door. The doors are carved with reliefs showing scenes from the life of St. Inés, and portraits of the founders of the convent kneeling in prayer.

Museo de la Ciudad de México

⑪ K4 ◆ Pino Suárez 30, corner of República del Salvador ☎ (55) 55 22 99 36 Ⓜ Zócalo ⏰ 10am–6pm Tue–Sun

The palace of the counts of Santiago de Calimaya, long renowned for their ostentatious lifestyle, is regarded as one of the most outstanding 18th-century buildings in the city. Built in 1781, the palace is faced with red volcanic *tezontle* stone. Its Baroque portal and magnificent carved wooden doors convey the social standing of its former inhabitants. At the foot of the southwest corner, the builders incorporated a stone serpent's head, which was taken from a wall made up of similar heads that surrounded the Aztecs' ceremonial center.

The first courtyard is noteworthy for the fountain with its carving of a mermaid holding a guitar, and for the trilobate arches near the staircase. Also outstanding is the richly carved stone doorway to the first-floor chapel.

In the early 20th century, the building was home to the painter and political activist Joaquín Clausell (1866–1935). The walls of his studio, on the third floor, are covered with an unusual mural, consisting

of a collage-like set of scenes influenced by the Impressionists that Clausell met when he was in France.

The building has been occupied by the Museum of Mexico City since the 1960s. The collection displays furniture and carriages associated with the house, as well as temporary exhibits.

Museo de Arte Popular

⑫ H3 ◆ Revillagigedo 11 Ⓜ Juárez ⏰ 10am–6pm Tue–Sun (to 9pm Wed) 🖥 map. cdmx.gob.mx

Located inside an Art Deco building, the Museum of Folk Art brings together traditional works from all over Mexico. Its collection of more than 3,000 objects includes contemporary and traditional pieces made from many different materials, such as wood, ceramics, glass, metal, paper, and textiles. Colorful indigenous costumes and religious art are especially well represented.

EAT

El Caguamo
One of the city's most famous seafood stalls.

⑨ J4 ◆ Corner of Ayuntamiento 18 and Lopez Ayuntamiento 18

$ $ $

Tortas Been
This tiny joint is worth tracking down for its amazing *torta* sandwiches.

⑨ L4 ◆ Off República del Salvador 152 ☎ (55) 55 12 30 20

$ $ $

Tacos El Huequito
This hole-in-the-wall, no-frills takeaway serves up superb tacos.

⑨ J3 ◆ Ayuntamiento 21

$ $ $

→ A boy studies folk art exhibits at the Museo de Arte Popular

Museo Mural Diego Rivera

📍H3 ⚐Corner of Colón and Plaza Solidaridad Ⓜ Hidalgo, Juárez 🕐10am–6pm Tue–Sun 🌐museomuraldiegorivera.bellasartes.gob.mx

This gallery is built around one of muralist Diego Rivera's masterpieces: *Dream of a Sunday Afternoon in Alameda Park*. Painted in 1947 for the dining room of the Hotel Prado, it combines Mexico's history with the dreams of its protagonists and the recollections of the artist. He includes two self-portraits, and an image of his wife, the famous artist Frida Kahlo (p116).

Did You Know?

One of the Historic Center's subway statons, Pino Suarez, contains an Aztec pyramid.

The three-sectioned painting caused a stir when first unveiled. The phrase "God does not exist" was removed by Rivera after a Christian group defaced the mural.

Laboratorio Arte Alameda

📍H3 ⚐Doctor Mora 7 Ⓜ Hidalgo 🕐9am–5pm Tue–Fri & Sun, 10am–2pm Sat 🌐artealameda.bellasartes.gob.mx

This museum of contemporary art is located in the former convent and church of San Diego de Alcalá, built in the 16th century. From 1964 to 1999, the building housed the Pinacoteca Virreinal, a collection of religious art now displayed in the Museo Nacional de Arte. In 2000 the doors opened to the Laboratorio Arte Alameda. This art space is dedicated to showing major works by Mexican and international artists, and focusing on transdisciplinary, temporary exhibits and events. With its cutting-edge shows, it hopes to interest new audiences in contemporary art and to raise the profile of Mexican artists.

Casa de los Azulejos

📍J3 ⚐Francisco I Madero 4 📞(55) 55 12 78 24 Ⓜ Bellas Artes, Allende 🕐8am–10pm daily

The 16th-century "House of Tiles" was originally the palace of the counts of Orizaba. The blue-and-white tiled exterior is attributed to a 1737 remodeling by the 5th countess, who is said to have imported the style from the city of Puebla, where she had been living previously. Now occupied by the Sanborns store and restaurant chain, the lovingly restored building conserves much of its original Mudéjar interior. The main staircase is decorated with waist-high tiling, and there is a mural on the first floor landing by José Clemente Orozco, entitled *Omniscience*, which was painted in 1925. On the upper floor it is worth

Diego Rivera's *Dream of a Sunday Afternoon in Alameda Park* (1947) ↑

↑ The restaurant at the Casa de los Azulejos, or "House of the Tiles"

taking note of the mirrors surrounded by elaborate gold frames that contain the figures of angels and cherubs.

Museo Nacional de Arte

📍 J3 🚇 Tacuba 8 Ⓜ Allende 🕐 10am–6pm Tue–Sun 🌐 munal.com.mx

Created in 1982, the National Art Museum is worth a visit for the building alone. An imposing, Neo-Classical piece of architecture, it was completed in 1911 as the Ministry of Communications and Public Works. Its double staircase, in bronze and marble, is enclosed by a semi-circular window three stories high. The interior, with its intricate ironwork and many candelabra, is sumptuous.

The museum's galleries encompass Mexican art from the 16th century to 1954. The collection includes commercial engravings, political cartoons, and folk art, as well as paintings. Much of the collection of religious art from the 16th to early 19th century resulted from confiscations following anti-clerical Reform laws in the 1800s. As well as works by the great muralists – Rivera, David Alfaro Siqueiros, and Orozco – the outstanding pieces include a series of landscapes by 19th-century painter José María Velasco. One room is devoted to portraits, including a depiction of the art-lover María Asúnsolo by Siqueiros.

Right in front of the museum is the Plaza Manuel Tolsá, centering on one of the city's favorite monuments – *El Caballito* (The Little Horse), which is a massive equestrian statue of Carlos IV of Spain by Manuel Tolsá (1802).

Palacio de Cultura Citibanamex

📍 J3 🚇 Madero 17 Ⓜ Allende 🕐 10am–7pm Mon–Fri 🌐 fomento culturalbanamex.org

This magnificent 18th-century residence was the home of Agustín de Itúrbide during his reign as the first Emperor of Mexico (1821–23). The elaborate, Churrigueresque facade had wrought-iron balconies and fortified towers. It now houses a cultural center with a museum of antiquities and an art gallery that displays temporary exhibitions in its spectacular central courtyard.

Museo de la Caricatura

📍 K3 🚇 Donceles 99 Ⓜ Zócalo 🕐 10am–6pm daily 🌐 museodela caricatura.org

With its intricate and finely preserved Baroque facade, the former Colegio de Cristo is one of the best examples in Mexico City of an upper-class 18th-century dwelling. Originally conceived in 1610 as an educational foundation for poor students, it was rebuilt in the 1740s, and later became a private house. The tiny patio and the broad staircase with its low, stone archway are some of the architectural highlights.

In the 1980s, the building was restored to house the collection of the Mexican Society of Cartoonists. This includes contemporary cartoons and works by the influential political satirist and engraver José Guadalupe Posada (1852–1913).

19

Museo Nacional de la Estampa

J3 **Avenida Hidalgo 39** **Bellas Artes** **10am-6pm Tue-Sun** **museo nacionaldelaestampa. bellasartes.gob.mx**

The Museum of Graphic Arts (also known as MUNAE) has an extensive collection of pre-colonial and contemporary prints, only part of which is on show at any one time.

Probably the best-known artist on display is José Guadalupe Posada (1852–1913). Posada's work featured in the satirical newspapers of his day, and his enduring image of *La Calavera Catrina* – a well-dressed skeleton woman – is among the most familiar symbols of the nation's fascination with death.

In the Sala de Técnicas is a range of works illustrating the different techniques used by print artists. The building itself has a 1986 stained-glass skylight by Salvador Pinoncelly.

20

Torre Latinoamericana

J3 **Eje Central Lázaro Cárdenas and Francisco I Madero** **Bellas Artes** **9am-10pm daily** **torrelatino.com**

This skyscraper rises 44 floors and has the best view of the city – weather permitting. Completed in 1956, it has survived a number of earthquakes, notably that of 1985. In 30 seconds, its express elevators whisk visitors to the 37th floor. On the 38th floor is an exhibition devoted to the history of the tower. Two floors down, the Museo del Bicentenario covers post-colonial Mexico. A second elevator rises to a 44th-floor viewing platform and a café.

From here a spiral staircase leads to the open-air cage below the TV mast.

21

Plaza de Santo Domingo

K3 **Allende**

Second only in importance to the Zócalo *(p94)*, the Plaza de Santo Domingo (officially called Plaza 23 de Mayo) is steeped in history. The Dominicans built a convent here – the first in New Spain – in 1527, of which all that remains today is a restored chapel, the Capilla de la Expiación. Most of the other buildings that flank the square date from the 18th century. The church of Santo Domingo, with its sober facade partly covered in red volcanic *tezontle* stone, was erected completed in 1737. Its tower is capped by a pyramidal pinnacle covered with Talavera tiles *(p131)*. The interior of the church contains statues of saints thought to date from the 16th century, as well as oil paintings by Juan Correa and Alonso López de Herrera. The side altars, antique organ, and the cedarwood choir stalls with carved images of the saints are among the treasures.

The subsidence that led to the demolition of previous churches on this site is widely evident in the square. From the door of the church, the

←

The Torre Latinoamericana skyscraper and *(inset)* its observation deck, with views over the city

↑ The tranquil courtyard of the Museo Franz Mayer, a former hospital turned art museum

INSIDER TIP
On Your Bike

On Plaza de Santo Domingo you'll spot one of the city's 452 stations for Ecobici, the capital's hugely popular public bike-sharing scheme. It's a great way to explore the city. *(www. ecobici.cdmx.gob.mx).*

undulation of the Tuscan-style *portales* (arcade) which runs down the west side of the square, is noticeable. Under the arcade sit scribes, who, for a small fee, will fill out official documents using old manual typewriters; the remaining few of a centuries-old tradition.

    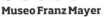

Museo Franz Mayer

📍H3 🏛Avenida Hidalgo 45
Ⓜ Hidalgo, Bellas Artes
🕐10am-5pm Tue-Sun
🌐franzmayer.org.mx

This is the richest collection of applied art in Mexico City. Assembled by German financier and art collector Franz Mayer (1882–1975), it is housed in a 16th-century former hospital. The museum has possibly the most beautiful courtyard in the Historic Center, featuring a delightful fountain.

The collection contains more than 10,000 pieces from Europe, the Far East and colonial-era Mexico. Exhibits include tapestries, furniture, carvings of religious scenes, ceramics, 20,000 antique tiles, and over 1,000 pieces of silverwork. Among the most exquisite objects are a number of inlaid wooden chests. There are also some impressive wooden screens, one of which has a rendering of the conquest of Mexico City on one side and a partial view of the city in the colonial period on the reverse.

Palacio de la Escuela de Medicina

📍K2 🏛Brasil 33, corner of Venezuela Ⓜ Zócalo, Allende 🕐9am-6pm daily
🌐pem.facmed.unam.mx

Now home to the Museum of Mexican Medicine, the Palace of the School of Medicine stands on the site of the building in which the Holy Inquisition carried out its fearsome interrogations from the late 16th to early 19th centuries.

The current building dates from the 18th century, and underwent restoration in the 1970s. The architecture is notable for its Baroque facade – unusually set on the corner of the building – and graceful main courtyard. There are "hanging" arches in each corner of the courtyard, with the supporting pillars set into the wall behind.

A typical 19th-century apothecary's store, transferred in its entirety from Oaxaca *(p234)*, is one of the museum's more unusual features. It has displays on the history of Mexican medicine from pre-Hispanic times, including sacred and medicinal plants.

> **The Palacio de la Escuela de Medecina features a typical 19th-century apothecary's store, transferred in its entirety from Oaxaca.**

A SHORT WALK
THE ALAMEDA CENTRAL

Distance 1 mile (2 km) **Time** 20 minutes
Nearest metro Bellas Artes

This peaceful oasis amidst the surrounding bustle offers shady paths lined with jacaranda trees, decorative fountains and statues, and elegant architecture – a great introduction to the best of the Historic Center. The Alameda takes its name from the *álamos* (poplar trees)

planted here in the late 16th century. Its many statues date mainly from the 1900s, although the central Baroque fountain has been there since the mid-18th century. The most imposing monument is the *Hemiciclo a Juárez*, a marble monument with Doric pillars.

Museo Franz Mayer
(p91) *houses what is probably the finest collection of applied and decorative arts in Mexico. Exhibits date from the 16th to the 19th century.*

The **Museo Nacional de la Estampa** *(National Museum of Graphic Arts; p90) focuses on Mexican graphic design, past and present.*

Iglesia de San Juan de Dios *is an 18th-century church with an unusual concave facade.*

Palacio Postal (p82), *the main post office, has an elegant interior of wrought iron and marble, and houses a postal museum.*

AVENIDA MIGUEL HIDALGO

LÁZARO CÁRDENAS

The **Hemiciclo a Juárez** *monument was inaugurated in 1910 to celebrate the centenary of Mexico's fight for independence.*

Alameda Central

AVENIDA JUÁREZ

The *Art Nouveau facade of the* **Palacio de Bellas Artes** (p78) *is equalled only by its impressive Art Deco interior, with murals by some of the greatest Mexican artists of the 20th century.*

An equestrian statue of Carlos IV guards the entrance to **Museo Nacional de Arte** (p89), *a gallery dedicated to modern Mexican art. The building was constructed between 1904 and 1911.*

Statue of Charles IV

Café Tacuba (p89)

Locator Map
For more detail see p74

The **Museo del Ejército y Fuerza Aérea Mexicanos** *(Museum of the Mexican Army and Air Force) has a collection of weaponry and military memorabilia dating from the Spanish conquest to the 21st century.*

Palacio de Minería *is one of the city's finest 19th-century Neo-Classical buildings.*

La Ópera Bar (p87) *is an old-fashioned restaurant on 5 de Mayo. A bullet hole in the ceiling is said to have been made by famous revolutionary Pancho Villa (p184).*

START

FINISH

TACUBA

FILOMENO MATA

FRANCISCO I MADERO

GANTE

Palacio de Iturbide, *named after the Emperor Agustín de Iturbide (ruled 1821–3), is a superb example of Spanish Colonial architecture.*

0 meters   100   N
0 yards   100

Talavera tiles cover the outside of **Casa de los Azulejos** (p88), *an 18th-century mansion. Inside is a mural by José Clemente Orozco.*

One of Mexico City's first skyscrapers, **Torre Latinoamericana** (p91) was built in the 1950s and has survived many earthquakes.

→ The blue-tiled facade of the Casa de los Azulejos

A SHORT WALK
ZÓCALO

Distance 1.5 miles (2 km) **Time** 25 minutes
Nearest metro Zócalo

The Plaza de la Constitución, invariably known as the Zócalo, is one of the biggest public squares in the world. Walking through this vast open space, visitors can relive history, with the remains of Aztec temples revealed beneath the Spanish Colonial architecture. A giant national flag flies in the middle of this vast paved space, which is dominated by two buildings, the cathedral and the Palacio Nacional. On the square stand other public buildings, restaurants, shops, and hotels.

A caricature of singer David Bowie is among the works of cartoon art in the **Museo de la Caricatura** *(p89).*

A dazzling gold altarpiece is the main feature of the **Templo de la Enseñanzam**, *a late 18th-century Baroque church, which was originally designed as a convent chapel.*

Nacional Monte de Piedad, *a government-run pawn shop, occupies a historic building dating from the 16th century.*

Although damaged by the subsidence affecting the center of Mexico City, the **Catedral Metropolitana** *(p76) is still one of the greatest religious buildings in Latin America.*

Sagrario Metropolitano

FINISH

START

← A Christmas market at the grand Zócalo plaza

Great murals, stained glass, and other decorative details can be seen in the **Antiguo Colegio de San Ildefonso**, *a former seminary.*

Pathways lead through the excavated remains of the Aztec **Templo Mayor** *(p80), unearthed in the 1970s.*

The former archbishop's palace

The first printing press in the Americas was set up in this house in 1536.

Did You Know?

The Aztecs believed their original main square was the center of the universe.

Museo Nacional de las Culturas *has displays on major civilizations of the world.*

The Renaissance **Palacio Nacional** *(p82) houses the offices of the President of Mexico. Inside is a collection of murals by Diego Rivera.*

SEMINARIO

ZÓCALO (PLAZA DE LA CONSTITUCIÓN)

PINO SUAREZ

20 DE NOVIEMBRE

Supreme Court

Mexico's main square is used as a venue for state ceremonial occasions and military parades.

Former city hall

↑ A fountain in the inner courtyard of the Palacio Nacional

AROUND PASEO DE LA REFORMA

Commissioned in the 1860s, by Emperor Maximilian, the Paseo de la Reforma is a grand boulevard linking the Historic Center and the Bosque de Chapultepec (Chapultepec Park). Though it is flanked by tall, modern office buildings today, monumental statues and fountains still adorn the avenue, including the golden Angel of Independence, the symbol of Mexico City.

Until the 1980s this was the city's high-end shopping district, but the fancy boutiques have since migrated to the chic neighborhood of Polanco on the northern edge of Bosque de Chapultepec. The park itself, once the residence of the Aztec emperors, has been a public space since 1530. The castle on the top of the hill at its northeastern end was also Maximilian's home.

AROUND PASEO DE LA REFORMA

Must See

❶ Museo Nacional de Antropología

Experience More

❷ Monumento and Museo de la Revolución
❸ MUCHO Museo del Chocolate
❹ Museo Nacional de San Carlos
❺ Sala de Arte Público Siqueiros
❻ Museo de Arte Moderno
❼ Museo Rufino Tamayo
❽ Castillo de Chapultepec

Eat

① Sala Gastronomica
② Lur
③ Raiz
④ Almara

Drink

⑤ Xaman
⑥ Bukowski's
⑦ El Almacén

Stay

⑧ Camino Real Polanco
⑨ W Mexico City

Did You Know?

The huge, basalt heads for which the Olmecs are best known, may be portraits of high-ranking people.

The museum's entrance hall, providing an insight into the fascinating galleries beyond

MUSEO NACIONAL DE ANTROPOLOGÍA

📍 B4 🏛 Corner of Gandhi and Paseo de la Reforma Ⓜ Auditorio, Chapultepec 🕐 9am-7pm Tue-Sun 🌐 mna.inah.gob.mx

Mexico's ancient civilizations are brought to life through this collection, one of the greatest archaeological museums in the Americas. Entering beneath its huge, hovering canopy, visitors are met by the array of priceless treasures, from the huge Aztec Piedra del Sol to Moctezuma's feather headdress.

Inaugurated in 1964, National Museum of Anthropology was created by Pedro Ramírez Vázquez. The vast and airy space creates a just setting for a world-renowned collection of finds from Mexico's pre-Hispanic cultures. The museum's large, central patio is almost entirely covered by a 275-ft (84-m) long canopy, balanced on a 36-ft (11-m) pillar decorated with bas-reliefs. This canopy is considered to be the largest concrete structure in the world supported by a single pillar. In the entrance hall is a space that is dedicated to temporary exhibitions, which have previously covered themes such as Maya art techniques and desert cultures. There is also an audio-visual display here giving useful background context about Mexico's ancient Mesoamerican eras, civilizations, and cultures (p144).

↑ The main entrance to the Museo Nacional de Antropolgía

📷 PICTURE PERFECT
The Symbol of Mexico

In front of the museum's entrance is a sculpture of the national symbol: an eagle locked in combat with a serpent. The hot pink bird and lime green reptile are a perfect pop of color for Instagram lovers.

Upper Floor

▽ The interconnected galleries on the upper floor of the museum contain the ethnology collection. Grouped roughly in regions, exhibits showcase the traditional lifestyle of the major indigenous groups of Mexico.

Museum Guide

Ground Floor

▲ Laid out around a central patio, the twelve galleries on the ground floor are dedicated to archaeological finds from ancient Mexico. Each room deals with a particular civilization or region of the country.

Outside

▲ Doors lead out to structures built within the grounds of the museum, including reconstructions of Maya temples, a Monte Albán tomb, and a Trascan house. A giant statue of a rain deity, either Chalchiuhtlicue or Tlaloc, stands near the museum's entrance.

ARCHAEOLOGY COLLECTION

Preclassic Era

Beginning with the earliest agricultural settlements in the central plateau around 1700 BC, the Preclassic gallery illustrates the rise of more complex cultures, shown in particular detail through the development of the ceramic arts. Outstanding among the collection are a number of figures influenced by the Olmecs (p272) from the Gulf of Mexico, including the "jaguar-boy" found at Tlapacoya in Mexico state.

Teotihuacán

Centered on the mysterious, ancient city that the Aztecs dubbed "the place where humans became gods," the culture of Teotihuacán (p140) was among the most important of the Classic era in Mesoamerica. The gallery is dominated by the huge stone statue of the water-goddess, Chalchiuhtlicue. Along one wall a reconstruction of the facade of the Temple of Quetzalcoatl reproduces the original blues and reds with which it was painted. Colorful murals of Teotihuacán life adorn the gallery's side walls. Some of the finest pieces are less monumental. They include a variety of pottery vessels for domestic use, such as grain and water storage urns, figurines, and funerary masks showing a talent for lapidary, and obsidian carvings.

Toltecs

As Teotihuacán declined, other cities of the central plateau, Tula in particular, rose to prominence. The founders of Tula (p154) were the Chichimecas from the north, who adopted the name Toltecs, meaning "artists." They soon acquired a reputation as specialists in the military arts. The most noticeable exhibit is a gigantic stone warrior figure known as an Atlante, with which the Toltecs are most commonly associated. These figures were used as pillars in their temples. The Toltec gallery also includes items from other cities of the Postclassic period, including Xochicalco in Morelos. Notable among these exhibits are stone carvings dedicated to the god Quetzalcoatl, and the stylized head of a macaw, which was perhaps used as a ballcourt marker. Xochicalco's most famous monument, the serpent frieze around the base of the temple of Quetzalcoatl, is beautifully illustrated with a photographic mural.

Oaxaca

Following on from the Aztec Hall (p102), this is the first gallery dedicated to the regions of Mexico. It presents the artifacts of the two great peoples of Oaxaca: the Zapotecs (also known as Ben Zaa), builders of the hilltop city of Monte Albán, and their neighbors and successors the Mixtecs, who created Mitla, with its stone friezes. On display are polychrome ceramic pieces from both cultures.

> ### Did You Know?
>
> The inhabitants of Teotihuacán were experts in fashioning obsidian knives.

A sculpture of the Aztec water-goddess Chalchiuhtlicue

↑ A family looking at vivid Cacaxtla frescoes, displayed in the museum

Gulf of Mexico

Among the most spectacular, of all the museum's exhibits are the extraordinary colossal stone heads from the Pre-classic Olmec culture, which flourished from 1200 to 600 BC. The Olmecs also produced smaller, equally remarkable, sculptures of heads and figures in a variety of stone, most of them with the characteristic Olmec features of broad, flat-nosed faces and thick lips, curled downward. The Olmecs share this gallery with the Totonacs from central Veracruz and the Huastecs from the northern shores of the Gulf.

The Maya

There is no doubting the special hold of the Maya on the imagination of visitors to Mexico, whether because of the intricate beauty of their great stone cities in the jungle, such as Palenque in Chiapas (*p244*), or the continuing mystery of their sudden collapse, before the arrival of the Spanish conquistadors. Among the highlights of the Maya gallery are carved stelae, such as the one from Yaxchilán, lintels from the Classic period, and a particularly outstanding

carved head of a young man, found at Palenque. A small, underground gallery contains a reconstruction of the royal tomb of Pakal found beneath Palenque's Temple of the Inscriptions. It also displays artifacts from the site, such as high-quality stucco heads.

Northern and Western Mexico

The sparsely inhabited north-ern deserts never produced the great civilizations traits of central and southern Mexico. Nonetheless, the ceramic art from Paquimé (*p178*) – the most notable of the so-called Oasis cultures – has a distinc-tive elegance, with its geome-tric patterns, smooth-polished surfaces and adornments such as copper or turquoise. The

gallery also contains examples of metalwork, and models of the unique multi-story adobe houses of Casas Grandes. At the height of the Aztec (Mexica) empire, the Tarascans (Purépechas), the dominant culture of the Pacific coast, retained their independence, and with it a distinctive artistic tradition. This gallery provides evidence of their skill in metalworking (they were among the first in the region to use gold, silver, and copper for jewelry and uten-sils), and in pottery. Other items of particular note include the polished earthenware from Classic-era Colima, and the ceramics of the cloisonné technique using different colored clays, which is thought to have originated there.

EXPLORING THE MUSEUM

The galleries on the ground floor are all accessible from the central patio, so your tour of the museum can begin anywhere. The first seven galleries are in chronological order, covering the history of the central plateau. The next five galleries visit the various regions of Mexico, including one dedicated to the great civilization of the Maya. The upper floor is devoted to costumes, houses, and artifacts of the 56 surviving indigenous cultures in Mexico, and explores their religions, social organization, and festivals.

↑ The intricately carved Sun Stone, a highlight of the Aztec Hall

THE AZTEC HALL

The Aztecs

The largest gallery in the museum displays the treasures of the Mexica culture – better known as the Aztecs. When Hernán Cortés and his conquistadors arrived in 1519 (p56), the Aztecs ruled most of what is now Mexico, either directly or indirectly. This gallery gives the visitor a strong sense of the everyday culture of the Aztec people, the power and wealth of their theocratic rulers, and their enormous appetite for blood, sacrifice, war, and conquest.

Large Sculptures

The entrance landing and central section of the gallery are devoted to large stone sculptures. Near the entrance is the Ocelotl-Cuauhxicalli, a 3-ft- (94-cm-) high stone vessel in the form of a jaguar-eagle. It was used as a receptacle to hold the hearts of human sacrificial victims. A statue of Coatlicue, the mother of Coyolxauhqui and later of Huitzilopochtli, is one of the few representations of the goddess in Aztec art. This statue shows her with eagle's claws, a dress made of snakes, and a necklace of hearts and hands. She has been decapitated, and two serpents emanate from her neck to symbolize blood. Other large sculptures are of the goddesses Coyolxauhqui and Cihuateteoa, small-scale representation of a teocalli or temple, and a *tzompantli*, an altar of skulls from the Templo Mayor. On the wall opposite the door, dominating the gallery, is the Sun Stone.

The Aztec People and their History

The section to the right of the entrance describes the Aztec people, their physical appearance and their history. The most conspicuous piece here is a carved round stone, known as the Stone of Tizoc, which records the victories of Tizoc, the seventh ruler of the Aztecs (1481–6). This trachyte stone was found in the Zócalo. Another object of interest is a stone head with inset teeth and eyes to add to its realism. It is thought to represent the common man. Other sculptures represent everyday Aztec people, including a statue of a Mexica noble dressed in robes appropriate to his rank. This part of the museum includes a model of the temple complex that stood at the center of Tenochtitlán. Surrounded by

 PICTURE PERFECT
The Umbrella

Among all the photos of old artifacts, make sure to snap a shot of the central courtyard, dominated by *El Paraguas* (The Umbrella), an inverted fountain. Its massive canopy is balanced on a beautifully carved 36-ft (11-m) bronze pillar.

→ Giant sculpture of the goddess Coyolxauhqui

a wall, it focused upon the Templo Mayor topped by its twin shrines. The rounded temple in front of the Templo Mayor was dedicated to the god Quetzalcoatl.

Sacred Objects

The display cases to the left of the entrance show items used for religious purposes by the Aztecs. One of the most notable is a vase in the form of a pregnant monkey, carved out of obsidian, a hard black, volcanic stone akin to glass. This vase symbolizes the wind loaded with black rain clouds, which will engender growth and fertility. Also on display here is the stone altar on which human sacrificial victims were stretched in order to remove their hearts.

Other Exhibits

Aspects of Aztec daily life are described in other parts of the hall. Notable collections include decorative ceramics, Aztec jewelry made out of bone, gold, wood, crystal, and shells, and clothing that includes animal skins and feathers. The musicality of the Aztecs is shown with a range of instruments, such as flutes and whistles. Along the back wall are documents and drawings explaining the system of tribute that sustained the Aztec economy.

EAT

Sala Gastronomica

This modern restaurant has a menu inspired by the regions of Mexico. Try Veracruz-style eggs for breakfast or classic Oaxacan *mole negro* (dark mole) for lunch.

🅦 salagastronomica.mx
🅒 Mon

 Ⓢ Ⓢ Ⓢ

ETHNOLOGY COLLECTION

Contemporary Cultures

The eleven galleries on the top floor of the museum are devoted to all aspects of Mexico's various indigenous cultures, and include displays dedicated to housing, costumes, religious artifacts, social structures, and festivals. The exhibits focus on the period after the colonial era (*p58*), showcasing how the dozens of different indigenous cultures in Mexico have both preserved and developed their traditions over the centuries.

Starting with an introduction in Gallery 12, the rooms are divided loosely by region, beginning with Gran Nayar in Gallery 13. This covers the cultures of the Náayerite (also known as the Cora), Huichol (Wixáritari), Tepehuan, Nahua, and Mestizos (those of mixed indigenous and European descent) from Nayarit, Jalisco, and Zacatecas, states.

Other highlights include the Oaxaca exhibit (Gallery 17), displaying Mixtec and Zapotec handicrafts from wicker-work and ceramics to jewelry and textiles. In Gallery 21 (The Northwest: Sierras, Deserts and Valleys), the agricultural rituals, basketry, and the Deer Dance of groups such as the Comcaac (Seri), Cochimí, Yaqui (Yoeme), Rarámuri (Tarahumara), and Tepehua are showcased.

63

The number of indigenous languages spoken in Mexico.

↑ An exhibit of festival costumes, found among the ethnology collection

EXPERIENCE MORE

Monumento and Museo de la Revolución

📍G3 🏛Plaza de la República Ⓜ️Revolución 🕐Noon–8pm Mon–Sat (to 10pm Fri & Sat), 10am–8pm Sun 🌐mrm.mx

The striking dome-topped cube that is the Monument to the Revolution was designed as part of a parliament building under the dictator Porfirio Díaz (p61). Due to unanticipated problems with the marshy ground, it was never completed.

Then, in 1932, as an alternative to demolishing it, the architect Carlos Obregón Santacilia proposed that it be converted into a monument celebrating the 1910 revolution that put an end to the *Porfiriato*. Stone cladding and sculptures were added, and the remains of revolutionary heroes such as Francisco Villa were interred at the base of the columns. The austerity of the monument's functional and Art Deco styling is relieved by details in bronze. The statues, sculpted by Oliverio Martínez de Hoyos, represent independence, the 19th-century liberal reform, and the post-revolutionary agrarian and labor laws.

At the base of the monument is a museum dedicated to the 50-year period from the expulsion of the French in 1867 to the 1917 revolutionary constitution. The exhibits on display include photographs, documents, reproductions of period newspapers, carriages, and contemporary clothing.

MUCHO Museo del Chocolate

📍G4 🏛Calle Milan 45 Ⓜ️Cuauhtémoc 🕐11am–5pm daily 🌐mucho.org.mx

Housed in a restored early-20th-century residence, the tooth-tingling Chocolate Museum is dedicated to chocolate, which the Aztecs considered to be a gift from the gods. Its permanent collection contains artifacts from Europe, Asia, and the Americas, and the production process is explained from the cultivation of cacao to the making of chocolate. (Note that the exhibits are in Spanish only.)

Temporary exhibitions cover an eclectic range of topics, from cacao-loving insects to chocolate's aphrodisiac qualities.

PLUSH POLANCO

Just north of the Paseo de la Reforma is one of the city's most chic neighborhoods, Polanco. Its streets are lined with boutiques, cocktail bars, night-clubs, and upscale hotels and restaurants. Much of Polanco's appeal lies with it being less hectic than downtown, and many people buzz around on EcoBici bicycles (p91), which are available to hire from charging stations on the main streets.

Workshops and courses are also available, and you can satisfy your chocolate cravings in the shop with tasting samples.

Museo Nacional de San Carlos

📍 G2 🏛 Puente de Alvarado 50 Ⓜ Hidalgo, Revolución 🕐 10am–6pm Tue–Sun 🌐 mnsancarlos.inba.gob.mx

Occupying an imposing Neo-Classical building, this museum has the oldest and most important collection of European art in Latin America. The bulk of the collection consists of paintings spanning the 14th to the early 20th century, including notable examples of the Flemish, French, Italian, and Spanish schools. Among the highlights are engravings by Goya and sculptures by Rodin.

Galleries on the upper floor house the permanent collection. Pride of place at the entrance is given to *La Encarnación*, a stunning gilded altarpiece dating from 1465, by the Aragonian painter Pere Espallargues.

At one time the building was home to a "museum of strange objects," but this was later moved to the nearby **Museo Universitario del Chopo** (Chopo University Museum). This fabulous twin-towered Art Nouveau structure, nicknamed "the Crystal Palace," focuses on contemporary art and performing arts.

Museo Universitario del Chopo

⊛ 🏛 Calle Dr. Enrique Gonzalez Martinez 10 🕐 11:30am–7pm Tue–Sun 🌐 chopo.unam.mx

←

Fountains in front of the Monumento a la Revolución on Plaza de la República

↑ Exploring the artwork on display at the Museo Nacional de San Carlos

Sala de Arte Público Siqueiros

📍 B4 🏛 Tres Picos 29 Ⓜ Auditorio, Polanco 🕐 10am–6pm Tue–Sun 🌐 saps-latallera.org

This was the home and studio of the celebrated Mexican muralist David Alfaro Siqueiros (1896–1974). The painter's life and work are represented here by a collection that includes finished pieces, as well as drawings, plans, models, and photo-montages of his many murals. There is also a selection of photographs and documents charting Siqueiros' life, which was singularly eventful. It included two prison terms, one of which was for his part in a plot to kill Leon Trotsky (*p121*). In spite of this, his painting was popular, and in the 1940s and 1950s the state commissioned him to produce several works.

The ground-floor gallery is the site of the mural *Maternity*, which was originally designed for a school. The upper floor-galleries contain paintings by Siqueiros. The second-floor gallery is devoted to the work of other artists, both contemporary Mexican and international.

DRINK

Xaman

This cozy cocktail bar makes an ideal spot for a quiet drink, with an unusual shaman-themed decor.

📍 F4 🏛 Copenhague 6 🚫 Mon 🌐 xaman.bar

Bukowski's

Named after the notoriously booze-fueled American writer, this bohemian bar is appropriately sited above a bookshop. Live jazz nights are regularly held here.

📍 E4 🏛 Hamburgo 126 🌐 pendulo.com/especial/bukowski-bar

El Almacén

One of the city's oldest LGBT+-friendly bars, this unpretentious club is famous for its good-humored drag shows.

📍 E5 🏛 Florencia 37-B 📞 (55) 37 19 19 25 🚫 Mon

↑ A visitor photographing Frida Kahlo's *Las Dos Fridas* at the Museo de Arte Moderno

Museo de Arte Moderno

📍 C5 **🏛 Corner of Paseo de la Reforma and Gandhi** **Ⓜ Chapultepec** **🕐 10:15am–5:30pm Tue-Sun** **🌐 mam.inba.gob.mx**

A wide range of 20th- and 21st-century Mexican painting and sculpture is housed in the Museum of Modern Art. The collection includes works by all the well-known figures – Rufino Tamayo, Diego Rivera, David Alfaro Siqueiros, and Frida Kahlo – as well as artists who do not belong to the mainstream established by the muralists and others since the revolution. International artists who have worked in Mexico are also represented.

The museum has a fine array of oils by Tamayo and several works by Francisco Toledo, his fellow Oaxacan. Among the other highlights are Frida Kahlo's *The Two Fridas*, Diego Rivera's portrait of Lupe Marín, and José Clemente Orozco's *Las Soldaderas*. Contemporary artists displayed include Alberto Castro Leñero, Irma Palacios, and Emilio Ortiz.

Sculptures are exhibited in the gardens, and the adjacent circular gallery has temporary exhibitions of modern Mexican and international art.

 HIDDEN GEM
Casa Estudio Luis Barragán

On the southwest corner of Bosque de Chapultepec *(p110)* is the home of Pritzker-Prize-winning Luis Barragán (1902–88). Visit by booking a guided tour *(www.casaluisbarragan.org)*.

Museo Rufino Tamayo

📍 C5 **🏛 Corner of Paseo de la Reforma and Gandhi** **Ⓜ Chapultepec** **🕐 10am–6pm Tue-Sun** **🌐 museotamayo.org**

This outstanding collection of modern painting and sculpture was assembled by one of Mexico's foremost 20th-century artists, Rufino Tamayo, and his wife Olga. It occupies a stunning, futuristic, concrete-and-glass building which is set among the trees of Bosque de Chapultepec *(p110)*. The building was designed by renowned Mexican architects Teodoro González de León and Abraham Zabludovsky, and was awarded the National Prize for Arts and Sciences in 1982.

Housed within this light and airy gallery are some 800 paintings in all, as well as drawings, sculptures, and graphic art. There are a number of paintings by Rufino Tamayo himself, and many modern artists, including international names such as Andy Warhol, Salvador Dalí, and René Magritte.

8

Castillo de Chapultepec

📍 C5 🏛 Bosque de Chapultepec Ⓜ Chapultepec

The hill that forms the highest point of Bosque de Chapultepec once stood on the lakeshore across the water from Tenochtitlán, the Aztec's capital city. On its summit is the 18th-century Chapultepec Castle, begun in the late 1800s and completed in 1864.

A crucial battle was fought here in 1847, when young army cadets died trying to defend the fortress against invading US troops. In the 1860s, the castle became the palace of Emperor Maximilian. Subsequently it was an official residence for the president.

Today the castle houses the **Museo Nacional de Historia** (National History Museum), which covers Mexican history from the Conquest to the revolution. Exhibits include items relating to historical figures, such as the glasses worn by former president Benito Juárez (*p61*). The walls of the museum are decorated with large murals showing historical events.

In the castle's grounds is the Galería de Historia, known as the Museo del Caracol (Snail Museum) because of its shape. Here visitors are guided through a series of dioramas that illustrate scenes from the struggle for independence up to the 1917 Constitution.

Museo Nacional de Historia

 🏛 Bosque de Chapultepec 🕐 9am–5pm Tue–Sun 🌐 mnh.inah. gob.mx

Stained glass by Dr. Atl in the Castillo de Chapultepec; *(inset)* the castle's grand facade ↓

EAT

Lur
This stylish restaurant specializes in Basque cuisine, mixing old and new influences.

📍 B4 🏛 Presidente Masaryk 86 🌐 restaurantelur.com

$$$

Raiz
One of the city's leading gourmet restaurants, Raiz bases its contemporary Mexican cuisine on local ingredients.

📍 B4 🏛 Schiller 331 🌐 restauranteraiz.com

$$$

Almara
This restaurant fuses Mediterranean and modern Mexican cuisines, plus an extensive wine list.

📍 E4 🏛 Corner of Varsovia and Hamburgo 🌐 almara.rest

$$$

STAY

Camino Real Polanco
A chic, colorful hotel opposite the Bosque de Chapultepec.

📍 C4 🏛 Calz General Mariano Escobedo 🌐 caminoreal.com

$$$

W Mexico City
An ultramodern, luxury hotel with a cool and quirky style.

📍 A4 🏛 Camino Real Polanco 🌐 marriott.com

$$$

A LONG WALK
BOSQUE DE CHAPULTEPEC

Distance 5.5 miles (9 km) **Time** 2 hours **Terrain** An easy walk on well-kept footpaths **Nearest metro** Chapultepec

The city's biggest park provides plenty of footpaths and shady lawns where you can escape the noise of traffic and city bustle. A favorite weekend recreational spot for residents of Mexico City, Chapultepec has been a public park since the 16th century. Its attractions include a zoo, a boating lake, a number of museums and galleries, and occasionally live, open-air entertainment. It is well worth making the climb up to the castle terrace, which offers stunning views across the city.

↑ Diego Rivera's Fuente de Tláloc fountain in the eastern half of the park

Mexico's national concert hall, **Auditorio Nacional,** *is considered one of the best in the world.*

The **Fuente de Tláloc** *fountain was designed by artist Diego Rivera. Tlaloc was the central Mexican rain deity (p287), and one of the most important gods in the pantheon.*

The **"Papalote" Museo del Niño** *children's museum has over 400 interactive exhibits, organized into five themes: the human body, expression, the world, "Conscience," and communication. A giant video screen shows educational movies.*

Auditorio Nacional

Zoológico de Chapultepec

Lago Mayor de Chapultepec

La Feria de Chapultepec

Residencia Presidencial Los Pinos

Fuente de Tláloc

MUTEC

Museo del Niño

Constituyentes
FINISH

JOSÉ CEBALLOS

0 meters 600

0 yards 600

N ↑

The house of muralist David Alfaro Siqueiros is now a museum, **Sala de Arte Público Siqueiros**, displaying his paintings and documents relating to his life (p107).

One of the city's highlights, the **Museo Nacional de Antropología** (p100) has a world-famous collection of ancient relics.

Works by Tamayo himself and other painters are on show in **Museo Rufino Tamayo** (p109).

Opened in 1964, the **Museo de Arte Moderno** (p109) has a collection of works by modern Mexican artists.

The **Monumento a los Niños Héroes** (Monument to the Boy Heroes) honors the army cadets who died defending Chapultepec castle from the US in 1847.

Once the residence of Mexican rulers, **Castillo de Chapultepec** (p109) offers views of the park and of the Paseo de la Reforma.

AROUND PASEO DE LA REFORMA

Bosque de Chapultepec

Locator Map
For more details see p98

AV. PRESIDENTE MASARIK

Sala de Arte Público Siqueiros

DARIO

RUBÉN

CALZADA MAHATMA GANDHI

DARWIN

LEIBNITZ LEIBNITZ

VICTOR HUGO

PLAZA MELCHOR OCAMPO

CIRCUITO INTERIOR

Museo Rufino Tamayo

CALZADA GEN. M. ESCOBEDO

RÍO LERMA

DE

Museo Nacional de Antropologia

LA REFORMA

PASEO DE LA REFORMA

SEVILLA

Lago de Chapultepec

Museo de Arte Moderno

Torrre Mayor

HAMBURGO

Sevilla Ⓜ

SALAMANCA

COLEGIO MILITAR

CALZADA MAHATMA GANDHI

CALZADA DEL CERRO

START ▶ Ⓜ Chapultepec

TAMPICO

PUEBLA

SONORA

Castillo de Chapultepec

Monumento a los Niños Héroes

VERACRUZ

DURANGO

Bosque de Chapultepec

Museo de Caracol

MELGAR

GRAN AVENIDA

JUAN ESCUTIA

AVENIDA DE LOS CONSTITUYENTES

GEN. RAFAEL REBOLLAR

→ Visitors to Bosque de Chapultepec enjoying the deckchairs and boats

SAN ÁNGEL AND COYOACÁN

At the time of the Spanish conquest, Coyoacán was a small town on the shore of Lake Texcoco. Hernán Cortés set up his headquarters here in 1521 while the former Aztec capital of Tenochtitlán nearby was rebuilt. Nearby San Ángel was then a village called Tenanitla – it became known as San Ángel in the 17th century, after the foundation of the convent-school of San Angelo Mártir.

Until the 20th century both San Ángel and Coyoacán were rural communities outside Mexico city. The growth of the metropolis has since swallowed them up, but both retain most of their Spanish Colonial architecture. Much favored as a place of residence by artists and writers, the area has been the home of several famous people, including Diego Rivera, Frida Kahlo, and Russian revolutionary Leon Trotsky.

SAN ÁNGEL AND COYOACÁN

Must See
❶ Museo Frida Kahlo

Experience More
❷ Plaza San Jacinto
❸ Museo de El Carmen
❹ Museo de Arte Carrillo Gil
❺ Museo Estudio Diego Rivera
❻ Avenida Francisco Sosa
❼ Museo Nacional de la Acuarela
❽ Museo Nacional de las Intervenciones
❾ Museo Casa de León Trotsky

Eat
① San Angel Inn
② Ruta de la Seda
③ Churreria General de la Republica

MUSEO FRIDA KAHLO

📍 S3 🏠 Londres 247 Ⓜ Coyoacán 🕐 10am–5:45pm Tue & Thu–Sun, 11am–5:45 Wed Ⓦ museofridakahlo.org.mx

The home of arguably Mexico's most famous artist is a popular visitor attraction. A tour of the museum offers an intimate insight into Kahlo's complex life, with many of her personal belongings on display.

Better known as Casa Azul (Blue House), this is where painter Frida Kahlo was born and died. She painted some famous works here, many inspired by the pain she suffered as a result of her multiple crippling injuries. This house is a treasure trove of paintings and artifacts associated with her life and that of her lover Diego Rivera, with whom she shared the house. On display are letters and diaries as well as ceramics and other everyday items. Frida's wheelchair and one of the corsets she had to wear because of her disability are also on display. Book in advance as there are long lines to purchase tickets on the day.

TOP 3 UNMISSABLE ARTWORKS

Portrait of My Father (1952)
Kahlo painted this with hints of brown to recall the sepia-toned images her father, a photographer, used to take.

My Family (1949)
One of several unfinished pieces in the house, this shows Kahlo's family tree.

Viva la Vida (1954)
Kahlo's last finished piece, painted just days before her death, is full of life and joy in the shapes, colors, and words in the watermelon.

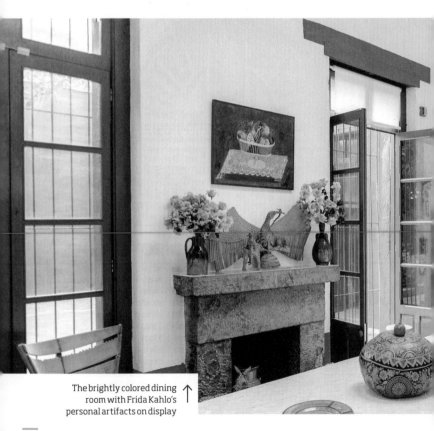

The brightly colored dining room with Frida Kahlo's personal artifacts on display ↑

↑ The iconic blue exterior of the museum, from which the building takes its name

↑ An exhibition dedicated to the artist's wardrobe on display at Casa Azul

6 Jul, 1907

▷ Frida is born Magdalena Carmen Frieda Calderon in the Casa Azul. She often told people she was born in 1910, to coincide with the revolution.

17 Sep, 1925

Frida's back is broken in a streetcar accident. During her convalescence she begins to paint seriously.

21 Aug, 1929

▷ Frida marries artist Diego Rivera. It is Rivera's third marriage; he is 20 years older than his bride.

1929–1930

Kahlo begins wearing traditional clothing, especially that of matriarchal indigenous cultures, to express her anti-colonial and feminist beliefs.

1930–33

Frida and Rivera live in the United States while Rivera works on several commissions.

Nov, 1938

◁ Frida's first solo exhibition is held in New York City. She becomes a sensation for her unique look as much as her art.

Nov, 1939

Frida and Rivera divorce, both having had affairs over the years. The couple remarry the following year.

1940s

▷ Frida's lifelong health problems worsen, but she still paints, teaches, is politically active, and attends exhibitions at home and abroad.

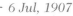

Apr, 1953

Frida's first solo exhibition in Mexico. Her health is so bad that she arrives in an ambulance and is carried to a bed where she remains throughout the event.

13 Jul, 1954

Frida dies in Casa Azul. The same day, her body is taken to lie in state at the Palacio de Bellas Artes.

↑ Handicraft and art market at the Plaza San Jacinto

EXPERIENCE MORE

 2

Plaza San Jacinto

N4 ⌂ San Ángel
Ⓜ Miguel Ángel de Quevedo

On Saturdays this square, which forms the center of San Ángel, is an excellent place to shop for Mexican handicrafts, either at the outdoor stalls or in El Bazaar Sábado, which is located in a 17th-century house in the northwest corner.

The 16th-century Iglesia de San Jacinto, just off the square, was originally annexed to a Dominican monastery of the same name. The church has a fine dome. Inside, the carved wooden screen and the onyx font are both worth seeing.

The most impressive building on the north side of the square is the Casa del Risco (also known as the Casa del Mirador), a well-preserved, 18th-century house built for the Marqués de San Miguel de Aguayo and donated to the nation in 1963. Built around an inner courtyard with an grand fountain, the house features a wealth of colonial-era furniture and decor.

 PICTURE PERFECT
San Ángel in Bloom

Just north of Plaza San Jacinto is the Mercado de Flores de San Ángel (flower market). The stalls are lit up in the evening, making it a great time to take photos of the beautiful flowers on display.

 3

Museo de El Carmen

N4 ⌂ Avenida Revolución 9 Ⓜ Miguel Ángel de Quevedo ⏱10am–5pm Tue–Sun Ⓦ elcarmen.inah.gob.mx

The Carmelite monastery-school of San Angelo Mártir, built in 1615, gave its name to the San Ángel district. The three beautiful domes that rise above it, elaborately decorated with colorful tiles, are still a symbol of the area. Later the monastery and its church became known as El Carmen. Since 1929 it has served as a museum of furniture, paintings, and other artistic and historical objects from the colonial period.

Much of the original interior is preserved, including the monks' cells. In crypt 11, mummified bodies, which were disinterred by troops during the revolution, are displayed in glass-topped coffins. The chapel on the first floor contains an 18th-century gold-painted altarpiece inset with oil paintings of saints.

4

Museo de Arte Carrillo Gil

🔲N3 ⌂ Avenida Revolución 1608 Ⓜ Miguel Ángel de Quevedo ⏱10am–6pm Tue–Sun Ⓦ museodearte carrillogil.com

This light and airy gallery on three floors has temporary exhibitions and sometimes shows the collection of art that embraces some of the finest 20th-century Mexican artists. The collection was assembled by Dr. Alvar Carrillo Gil and his wife, Carmen. It includes works by Diego Rivera, José Clemente Orozco, and David Alfaro Siqueiros. Among the Rivera canvases are a number of works from the artist's Cubist period. Less well-known, but equally interesting, are paintings by Austrian Wolfgang Paalen (1905–59) and Gunther Gerzso (1915–2000).

Dr. Carrillo, who studied medicine in Paris, was himself a painter of some note, and a close friend of Orozco.

Museo Estudio Diego Rivera

📍 M3 🏛 Corner of Calle Diego Rivera and Altavista Ⓜ Viveros, Barranca del Muerto 🕐 10am–6pm Tue–Sun 🌐 estudiodiegorivera. bellasartes.gob.mx

One of the most outstanding 20th-century architects of Mexico, Juan O'Gorman, built these twin houses in 1931–2 for two of the country's most distinguished painters, Diego Rivera and Frida Kahlo. Surrounded by a cactus hedge, the houses are connected by a rooftop bridge, over which Frida used to take Diego his meals. *The Two Fridas* and several other of her renowned

Inside the Museo Estudio Diego Rivera and *(inset)* the museum's colorful exterior

works were painted here. Behind her house is a building her father used as a photographic studio.

The large living room/studio in Rivera's house contains an assortment of his personal belongings, from paintbrushes to huge, papier-mâché skeletons and pre-Hispanic pottery. Other rooms are devoted to temporary exhibitions.

EAT

San Ángel Inn
Housed in a 17th-century hacienda, this elegant restaurant is renowned for its Mexican cuisine and live music, and has been attracting famous patrons since the mid-20th-century.

📍 M4 🏛 Calle Diego Rivera 50 🌐 san angelinn.com

$$$

Ruta de la Seda
A café-patisserie with beautifully presented homemade cakes make it a local favorite. It has a focus on organic and fair-trade produce.

📍 R4 🏛 Aurora 1 🌐 caferutadelaseda. com

$$$

Churreria General de la Republica
This bustling café offers dozens of varieties of churros, stuffed with all sorts of sweet treats, or dusted with spices, all freshly made to order.

📍 S3 🏛 Allende 38 🌐 chgr.com.mx

$$$

⑥
Avenida Francisco Sosa

📍Q3 🏛Between San Ángel and Coyoacán Ⓜ Miguel Ángel de Quevedo

Coyoacán's most attractive street is also one of the oldest colonial-era streets in Latin America, dating back around 500 years. Running roughly a mile (1.5 km) between Avenida Universidad and the Jardín Centenario in Coyoacán *(p122)*, it is lined with handsome residences.

At the beginning of it stands the quaint, 17th-century chapel of San Antonio Panzacola. Continuing down the street there are a number of very attractive residences, such as the Casa de la Campana (No 303) and No 319, which has a replica of one of the Atlante towering statues from the Toltec site of Tula *(p154)*. No 383 is another interesting colonial-era house, thought to have been constructed in the 18th century by Pedro de Alvarado, the Spanish conqueror of Mexico and Guatemala. The house next door belonged to his son. About halfway along the avenue is the pleasant Plaza Santa Catarina. On this square stand a church and

the Casa de la Cultura Jesús Reyes Heroles, a pleasant colonial-era building with patios and well-tended gardens. It houses a cultural center for art and literary events. A short way farther along the avenida, at No 77, is the Italian Cultural Institute.

---

⑦
Museo Nacional de la Acuarela

📍Q4 🏛Salvador Novo 88 Ⓜ Miguel Ángel de Quevedo 🕐10am–6pm daily 🌐acuarela.org.mx

Dedicated primarily to some of the finest works by Mexican watercolor artists from the 19th century to the present day, this museum is located in a small, two-story house set in a pretty garden.

The larger part of the collection consists of works by contemporary artists, including many winners of the Salón Nacional de la Acuarela annual prize for watercolors. Embracing a wide range of styles and subject matter, it may surprise those who think of watercolors primarily in terms of delicate landscapes.

Two outstanding canvases are *La Carrera del Fuego* and *Jazz*, both by Ángel Mauro

The inner courtyard of Museo Casa de León Trotsky ↑

Rodríguez, on display on the ground floor.

There is an international room containing a selection of paintings by artists from all over the Americas, as well as Spain and Italy, including Australian artists Robert Wade and Janet Walsh.

A separate gallery in the garden outside houses temporary exhibitions.

---

⑧
Museo Nacional de las Intervenciones

📍S3 🏛Corner of General Anaya & Calle 20 de Agosto Ⓜ General Anaya 🕐9am–6pm Tue–Sun 🌐intervenciones.inah.gob.mx

This former convent still bears the bullet holes from a battle that took place here between US and Mexican forces in 1847. Today it is a museum dedicated to the foreign invasions of Mexico since its

←

The Casa de la Cultura Jesús Reyes Heroles on Avenida Francisco Sosa independence in 1821. The collection consists of weapons, flags, and other artifacts, including a throne and saber belonging to Emperor Agustín (ruled 1821–3) and a death mask of the Emperor Maximilian (*p61*), as well as paintings, maps, and models.

Adjoining the museum is the former convent church, which houses religious paintings dating from the 16th to the 18th centuries. These include *La Asunción* by the 16th-century painter Luis Juárez and the 17th-century work *La Virgen y San Ildefonso* by Manuel de Echave.

To frustrate would-be assassins, Trotsky fitted the windows and doors with armor-plating, raised the height of the surrounding wall, and blocked off most of the windows that overlooked the street, among other things. All this foiled one attempt on his life: about 80 bullet holes can still be seen in the outer walls.

However, these precautions did not stop Ramón Mercader, a regular visitor to the house,

who had won his victim's confidence. The room where the murder took place is just as it was at the time, complete with the chair and table where Trotsky was sitting when he died. Trotsky's typewriter, books, and other possessions can be seen where he left them. One of the photographs on display shows him on his arrival in Mexico in 1937, standing on the quay in Tampico with his wife Natalia and Frida Kahlo.

9

Museo Casa de León Trotsky

🗺 S2 🏛 Avenida Río Churubusco 410 Ⓜ Coyoacán 🕙 10am–5pm Tue–Sun 🌐 museotrotsky.com

Leon Trotsky, the Russian revolutionary, lived in this house from 1939 until his assassination in 1940. Before moving here he lived with the artists Diego Rivera and Frida Kahlo (*p116*).

THE ASSASSINATION OF TROTSKY

The intellectual Leon Trotsky was born Lev Davidovich Bronstein, in Russia, in 1879. He played a leading role in the Bolshevik seizure of power in 1917 and in forming the Red Army to fight the Russian Civil War of 1918-20. But Lenin's death in 1924 led to a power struggle within the ranks of the victorious revolutionaries, and in 1927 Trotsky was forced into exile by his rival, Joseph Stalin. He was granted asylum in Mexico in 1937 but even across the Atlantic he was not safe from Stalin's purge of all his opponents. On August 20, 1940, he was fatally wounded by Ramón Mercader, who pierced his skull with an ice-pick.

A SHORT WALK
COYOACÁN

Distance 1.5 miles (2 km) **Time** 25 minutes
Nearest metro Coyoacán

The lovely suburb of Coyoacán has been a favorite area for many famous Mexicans, from Hernán Cortés to Frida Kahlo. The area is an ideal place for a stroll, packed with cafés, restaurants, and *cantinas*. Calle Felipe Carrillo Puerto, heading south out of the plaza, is a good place to shop for souvenirs. Coyoacán is also known in Mexico City for its delicious ice-cream. The weekend is a particularly great time to explore the area, as a lively craft fair operates in its two main squares, Jardín Centenario and Plaza Hidalgo.

The north side of **Plaza Hidalgo** *is taken up by the distinctive 15th-century Casa de Cortés, which is now used for government offices.*

The **Casa de Cortés** *faces the church of San Juan Bautista across the spacious Plaza Hidalgo square, which centers on a bandstand.*

Indoor craft bazaar (open at weekends)

Gateway of a former monastery

The narrow, pretty street of **Avenida Francisco Sosa** *(p120) leads to the neighborhood of San Ángel. It is lined with handsome mansions, which were built by wealthy families in colonial times.*

Cantina La Coyoacana

CABALLOCALCO

FELIPE CARRILLO PUERTO

ORTEGA

START

FINISH

Jardín Centenario *was once the atrium of the monastery of San Juan Bautista, of which only the church remains.*

Casa de Diego de Ordaz *is named after a Spanish conquistador. At one corner is an ornate niche with a statue of the Virgin Mary.*

Once part of a convent, the **Iglesia de San Juan Bautista** *was originally built in the 16th century. Though much altered, it still has a number of interesting relief sculptures on its facade.*

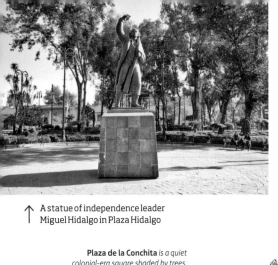

↑ A statue of independence leader Miguel Hidalgo in Plaza Hidalgo

Locator Map
For more detail see p114

The tiny **Iglesia de la Conchita** church has an intricately carved, Mudéjar-style facade.

Plaza de la Conchita *is a quiet colonial-era square shaded by trees, and features a stone cross in the middle. It's considered one of the prettiest spots in Coyoacán.*

FERNANDEZ LEAL

VALLARTA

HIGUERA

SAN FRANCISCO

CARRANZA

VENUSTIANO

Meditation
(1980), a statue by Rocío Peredo

Casa del Teatro

| 0 meters | | 100 | N |
| 0 yards | | 100 | |

↖

The 16th-century **Casa de la Malinche** *is the former home of Hernán Cortés's translator and mistress "La Malinche." It is now a preschool.*

→
The elaborate interior of the San Juan Bautista church

A LONG WALK
SAN ÁNGEL
TO COYOACÁN

Distance 2.5 miles (4 km) **Time** 50 minutes
Terrain An easy walk on well-kept footpaths
Nearest metro Chapultepec

Few parts of Mexico City can boast a domestic architecture of the colonial and pre-revolutionary eras as
well-preserved as that of Coyoacán and San Ángel. This
walk connects the two squares at the heart of these
districts, both of which are well-known in the city for
their weekend craft fairs. The walk often follows tree-
lined, cobbled streets. Along the way are churches,
museums, art galleries, and monuments, as well as
some picturesque places to stop for a meal.

*Nex to San Antonio
Panzacola is an old stone
bridge over a tributary of
the Río Magdalena. Cross
this and you come to one
of the prettiest streets
in the city, **Avenida
Francisco Sosa** (p120).*

*Cross Avenida Insurgentes and you will
come to the **Parque de la Bombilla**, the
small, wooded park that surrounds the
monument to General Álvaro Obregón,
assassinated nearby in July 1928.*

*Leave Plaza San
Jacinto (p118)
via Calle Madero.
At the end of this
road you will pass
the **Centro
Cultural San
Ángel** on the right.*

*At Avenida Revolución, cross over
to the **Museo de El Carmen**, which
contains some fine religious paintings
and colonial-era furniture. Afterwards,
head to the cobbled street of Avenida
La Paz where there are some good
restaurants to stop for a break.*

*Continue on through the
tranquil, green oases of
Plaza Frederico Gamba
and **Parque Tagle**.*

Did You Know?

General Obregón's arm,
lost in battle, used
to be kept in the
monument in Parque
de la Bombilla.

0 meters — 600
0 yards — 600
N ↑

Locator Map
For more detail see p114

Cafés and shops
lining the borders
of the Plaza del
Centenario

*Halfway along Francisco Sosa you
come to the enchanting **Plaza
Santa Catarina** where story-tellers
gather on Sunday lunchtimes.*

*Turn down Calle Salvador Novo for a short
detour to visit a gallery of watercolor paintings, the **Museo Nacional de la Acuarela**.*

*At the end of Francisco
Sosa you arrive at the
twin arches of what was
once the gateway into
the convent of **San
Juan Bautista**. This
then leads into the
pleasant square of
Jardín Centenario
at the heart of
Coyoacán (p122).*

The charming Iglesia de
Santa Catarina on the
square of the same name

Must See

1 Xochimilco

Experience More

2 Avenida Insurgentes Sur
3 Basílica de Santa María de Guadalupe
4 Tlatelolco and Plaza de las Tres Culturas
5 Mercado de La Merced
6 Universidad Nacional Autónoma de Mexico (UNAM)
7 Museo Anahuacalli
8 Museo Soumaya
9 Pirámide de Cuicuilco
10 Tlalpan

BEYOND THE CENTER

In the 1870s, Porfirio Díaz presided over a massive extension of the city's infrastructure, and its rapid growth continued into the 20th century. While the outer edges of the city comprise shantytowns and workaday suburbs, hidden among them are a number of gems such as the floating gardens of Xochimilco and the magnificent murals around the university campus. It's easy to zip between the neighborhoods by bus and taxi, so don't miss the chance to step outside the bounds of the city center and explore the lesser-known highlights.

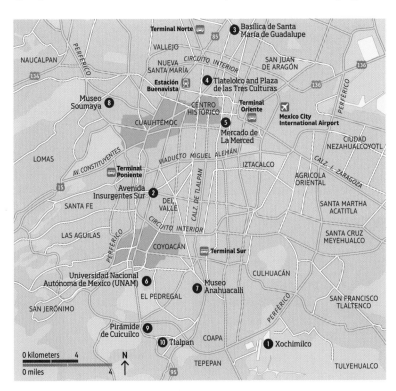

❶

XOCHIMILCO

📍 Avenida Guadalupe I Ramírez s/n, San Juan Ⓜ Xochimilco

This network of canals and vegetable plots that were created by the Aztecs, and are still in use today. Families flock here on Sundays, hiring colorfully decorated boats to explore the waterways, accompanied by mariachis bands that create a uniquely Mexican party atmosphere.

The History of Xochimilco

Known as "the place of the flower fields" in Nahuatl, the language spoken by the Aztecs, Xochimilco was once a lakeside village connected by a causeway to Tenochtitlán, the Aztec city where the Historic Center of Mexico City now stands. Today it is the only part of Mexico City still to have the canals and semi-floating flower and vegetable gardens, or *chinampas*, built by the Aztecs. The *chinampas* were originally created on a base of aquatic roots that were then covered with soil. They remain an important source of flowers and vegetables to Mexico City even today.

Xochimilco Today

A favorite weekend pastime – popular with tourists as well as the city's inhabitants – is to rent one of the many brightly decorated *trajineras* (punts), which have roofs and a table down the middle. A local boatman poles the punt along between banks shaded by willows. Waterborne mariachis will provide entertainment while smaller boats sell typical Mexican snacks and drinks, such as *pulque*, a slightly sour drink made from fermented sap, often served with fruit and nuts.

The northern part of Xochimilco's wetlands has been preserved as the Parque Ecológico de Xochimilco, and serves as an important habitat for birds such as storks, hummingbirds, eagles, and egrets. Since 2019, the park has been undergoing a long-needed rehabilitation, but the Cuemanco Plant Market is still worth a visit (open 8am–6pm daily). It lies on the edge of the park, and its alleys are crammed with flower and plant stalls.

→ Mexican fare being served from a smaller boat to visitors abroad a *trajinera* (punt)

← A mariachi band providing musical entertainment to a waterborne audience

INSIDER TIP
Trajinera Tours

Hire a *trajinera* (punt) from the canal-side piers, to tour the Aztec canals. Prices range from $3 per hour to $40 for six hours. They operate daily with a roof to protect against the elements.

↑ Rows of colorful *trajineras* stacked up on the canals at Xochimilco

EXPERIENCE MORE

② Avenida Insurgentes

 South from Glorieta de Insurgentes Ⓜ San Antonio, Barranca del Muerto

The Avenida Insurgentes runs just over 18 miles (30 km) from the capital's border with Mexico state in the north to the start of the highway to Cuernavaca in the south, and is said to be the longest street in Latin America.

Its southern (Sur) stretch has several sights of interest. Just a few blocks south of its junction with the Viaducto Miguel Alemán stands the World Trade Center, formerly the Hotel de México. This is without doubt one of the most prominent buildings on the Avenida. Its slim, glass tower is surmounted by a huge circular section that has a revolving floor.

The Polyforum Siqueiros, one of Mexico City's most audacious works of modern architecture, is next door

> **The Polyforum Siqueiros on Avenida Insurgentes Sur is one of Mexico City's most audacious works of modern architecture.**

to the World Trade Center. Its upper floor, which is reached by twin, circular staircases, is topped by an octagonal dome. This is decorated by one of the largest murals in the world: *March of Humanity*, by David Alfaro Siqueiros (1896–1974).

At Eje 6 Sur and Insurgentes is the Ciudad de los Deportes, which includes a soccer stadium and the Plaza México arena. Reputedly the world's largest bullring by seating capacity, it holds up to 60,000 people and is surrounded by statues commemorating famous bullfighters, including Manuel Rodríguez ("Manolete"), who was in the arena's inaugural program in 1946.

Just before the junction with Barranca del Muerto is the Teatro de los Insurgentes, built in the early 1950s by architect Alejandro Prieto. The curved facade is adorned with an allegorical mural by artist Diego Rivera. Completed in 1953, the mural centers on a huge pair of hands holding a mask, around which are gathered key revolutionary and independence heroes.

---

③ Basílica de Santa María de Guadalupe

 Plaza de las Americas 1 Ⓜ La Villa Ⓣ 6am–9pm daily Ⓦ virgende guadalupe.org.mx

The richest and most visited Catholic shrine in the Americas is a complex of buildings at the foot of Cerro del Tepeyac hill. Legend says it was here that a dark-skinned Virgin Mary miraculously appeared to a shepherd, Juan Diego, in 1531. She is named after the Virgin of Guadalupe in Extremadura, Spain.

The Antigua Basílica was built in the early 1700s. Twin towers flank its Baroque facade, which features relief carvings of the Virgin. It is overshadowed by the circular, modern church that now stands beside it, which can hold up to 10,000 worshippers. An object of veneration inside it is Diego's tunic on which the image of the Virgin is said to have been imprinted as proof of the miracle.

The Virgin is supposed to have appeared four times in all. The impressive Capilla del Pocito – a chapel regarded as one of the finest achievements of Mexican Baroque architecture – was constructed on the site of her fourth appearance. It is roughly elliptical in shape and its domed roof is faced with dazzling blue and white Talavera tiles, a style brought to Mexico in the 16th century by Dominican monks from Talavera de la Reina, Spain.

Also in the complex is the Capilla de Indios, the house in which Juan Diego is said to have lived after the Virgin's first appearance until his death in 1548.

Tlatelolco and Plaza de las Tres Culturas

🚇 Eje Central & Ricardo Flores Magón Ⓜ Tlatelolco, Garibaldi ⏰ 8am–6pm daily 🌐 tlatelolco.inah.gob.mx

The remains of the ceremonial center of Tlatelolco form a major part of the Plaza de las Tres Culturas. The square gets its name (The Three Cultures) from the mix of modern, colonial, and pre-Hispanic architecture that has developed around it. A powerful earthquake in 2017 caused some damage, but even so this centuries-old site is still standing.

Tlatelolco, the "twin city" of the Aztec capital, Tenochtitlán *(p78)*, was the most important commercial center of its day. The site here has a *templo mayor* (main temple) similar to that of Tenochtitlán. There are also smaller temples including the "calendar temple," which owes its name to the glyphs adorning three of its sides, representing dates in the Aztecs' ritual calendar. In the northwest corner of the complex are the remains of the carved "wall of serpents," which marked the boundary of the ceremonial center.

The Spanish erected their own temples and shrines on the site, including the Templo de Santiago – a Catholic church in an almost militaristic style. In front of the Templo de Santiago is a plaque that reads: "On 13 August 1521, heroically defended by Cuauhtémoc, Tlatelolco fell into the hands of Cortés. It was neither triumph nor defeat, but the painful birth of the *mestizo* nation that is Mexico today."

The modern era is represented by several buildings, particularly the concrete-and-glass foreign ministry tower. Scattered around the plaza are sculptures by artist Federico Silva. Between the monastery and the nearby residential tower block is a 1944 mural by David Alfaro Siqueiros. Entitled *Cuauhtémoc Against the Myth*, it combines sculpture with alfresco painting, and represents Cuauhtémoc, the last Aztec emperor, who was killed by the Spanish.

The modern church of the Basílica de Santa María de Guadalupe

Jardín Botánico
⊗ 🅐 Cto. Zona Deportiva s/n
🕐 9am-5pm daily (to 3pm Sat
& Sun) 🌐 ib.unam.mx

7   🍴 🛍️

Museo Anahuacalli

🅐 Museo 150 🕐 11am-
5:30pm Tue-Sun 🌐 museo
anahuacalli.org.mx

This museum was conceived
and created by muralist Diego
Rivera to house his collection
of pre-Hispanic art, and was
completed after his death by
multiple artists, including
Rivera's daughter. Built of
black volcanic stone, it takes
the form of a pyramid. The
collection consists of around
2,000 pieces that represent
most of the indigenous
civilizations of Mexico. There
are funerary urns, masks, and
sculptures from the ancient
culture of Teotihuacán (p140).

The studio, although never
actually used by Rivera, has
been set up as if it were, with
his materials and half-finished
works on display. A smaller
gallery next to the pyramid
contains an exhibition of
papier-mâché sculpture
relating to the Day of
the Dead, celebrated
October 31 to
November 2 (p221).

5

Mercado de La Merced

🅐 Anillo de Circunvalación
& Calle Callejón de
Carretones 🅜 Merced
🕐 6am-7pm daily

Said to be one of the biggest
markets in the Americas, La
Merced has over 5,000 stalls.
It occupies the spot on which
an Aztec market stood prior
to the conquest by the
Spanish (p57).

La Merced is divided into
seven sections, six of which
specialize in different types of
merchandise, while the last is
a traditional market.

The Mercado area is well
known for prostitution, and
can be dangerous at night.

6

Universidad Nacional Autónoma de México (UNAM)

🅐 Ciudad Universitaria
🅜 Universidad, Ciudad
Universitaria 🕐 7am-
9:30pm daily 🌐 unam.mx

The largest university in Latin
America is also a UNESCO
World Heritage site. It occupies
a vast campus in the south
of the city. Many of the most
interesting buildings are
decorated with incredible
murals. Over the entrance of
the striking stadium – the

 The colorful food
market of the Mercado
de La Merced

symbol of the 1968 Mexico
Olympics – is a high-relief
mural by Diego Rivera, while
the rectory tower is adorned
with dramatic designs by David
Alfaro Siqueiros. Nearby is the
Biblioteca Central (Central
Library), whose tower is
covered with mosaics of
colored tiles, made by Juan
O'Gorman from 1950 to 1956.
Each wall illustrates a period
of Mexican history and its
scientific achievements.

A separate complex of
buildings farther south
includes one of the city's
major performing arts centers:
the Sala Nezahualcóyotl (www.
musica.unam.mx). The **Museo
Universitario de Arte
Contemporáneo (MUAC)**,
housed in an angular, modern
building flooded with light,
exhibits the largest collection
of contemporary art in Mexico.
Close to the Olympic stadium
is the **Jardín Botánico**. The
garden has a cactus collection,
an arboretum, and a section
devoted to jungle plants.

**Museo Universitario de
Arte Contemporáneo
(MUAC)**

🅐 Insurgentes 3000
🕐 10am-6pm Wed-Sun
(to 8pm Thu & Sat) 🌐 muac.
unam.mx

Museo Soumaya

🏛 **Blvd Miguel de Cervantes Saavedra & Presa Falcón**
🕐 **10:30am-6:30pm daily**
🌐 **soumaya.com.mx**

This curvaceous modern building, designed by Mexican architect Fernando Romero, houses one of the country's most outstanding collections of European, Mexican, and pre-Colombian art. The stunning gallery has more than 65,000 pieces spanning three millennia, including European masterpieces by da Vinci, Rodin, and Rubens.

The Mexican collection includes murals by Rivera, Orozco, Tamayo, and Siqueiros, as well as pre-Hispanic artifacts and religious icons.

Pirámide de Cuicuilco

🏛 **Avenida Insurgentes Sur & Periférico** 📞 **(55) 56 06 97 58** 🕐 **9am-5pm daily**

This pyramid belongs to the earliest known urban civilization in the Valley of Mexico, founded around 700 BC. It is all that is left of the ceremonial center of a settlement thought to have comprised as many as 20,000 inhabitants at its peak.

The surviving structure is a truncated, layered cone, just 82 ft (25 m) high but 328 ft (100 m) across. The eruption of a nearby volcano, Xitle, forced the inhabitants of the area to flee around AD 100. The solidified lava, which can be as much as 26 ft (8 m) deep, makes excavation of the area difficult. However, a museum on the site exhibits the pottery, tools, and spearheads that have been found.

Tlalpan

🏛 **Mex 95, 15 miles (25 km) S of city center**

In the age of the Spanish viceroys, Tlalpan was a favorite country retreat for both ordinary Mexicans and the nobility. As a result, a large number of elegant mansions and haciendas were built here from the early 18th century onward.

Visitors to the old town, now the seat of Mexico City's largest *delegación* (suburban area), can stroll along narrow streets and admire the beautiful architecture, which dates from the 17th to the 20th centuries. The 18th-century Casa Chata, the Casa del Marqués de Vivanco, and the Casa del Conde de Regla are among some of the outstanding buildings here.

In the central Plaza de la Constitución, with its *Porfiriato*-era bandstand and busts of national heroes scattered around, is the Capilla del Rosario, a 17th-century chapel with a Baroque facade. In the same square stands the tree from which 11 patriots, who rebelled against the French occupation under Emperor Maximilian I, were hanged in 1866.

The former country house of General Antonio López de Santa Anna, the victor of the Battle of the Alamo *(p60)*, stands at the corner of San Fernando and Madero. He was named president of Mexico 11 times.

INSIDER TIP
Gooooal!

For a truly Mexican experience, catch a soccer match at Estadio Azteca *(www.estadio azteca.com.mx)*. The season's highlight is the Súper Clásico between Chivas de Guadalajara and Club América.

← The striking architecture of the Museo Soumaya, and *(inset)* visitors studying the art on display

EXPERIENCE
MEXICO

A boat trip on the river in the Sumidero Canyon

AROUND MEXICO CITY

Snowcapped volcanoes tower over the country's central plateau – a series of vast plains and broad valleys. Great civilizations flourished here and built extensive cities and awesome ceremonial sites such as Tula and Teotihuacán. After the arrival of the Spanish in the early 16th century, missionaries fanned out from these sites to explore and conquer the vast territories later consolidated as New Spain. As they spread out, they dotted the region with fortress-like convents and opulent churches. Meanwhile, the discovery of precious metals sparked the development of mining towns, and the rich volcanic soil led to endless fields of crops that belonged to huge estates, run from imposing haciendas.

Today busy highways radiate from Mexico City to burgeoning cities in the neighboring states. So far, however, the incursions of modern Mexico into the region have not significantly disturbed the area's natural beauty, protected in part by a series of national parks.

AROUND MEXICO CITY

Must Sees

1 Teotihuacán
2 Museo Nacional del Virreinato
3 Puebla

Experience More

4 Pachuca
5 San Agustín Acolman
6 Huasca
7 Mineral del Monte
8 Tula
9 Cholula
10 Valle de Bravo

11 Xochicalco
12 Cuernavaca
13 Malinalco
14 Tepoztlán
15 Popocatépetl and Iztaccíhuatl
16 Cacaxtla and Xochitécatl
17 Tlaxcala
18 Toluca
19 Cantona
20 Convento de San Nicolas de Tolentino de Actopan
21 Taxco

Chapulhuacan

Jacala

HIDALGO

Ixmiquilpan

Querétaro   QUERÉTARO
Huichapán
CONVENTO DE SAN NICOLÁS DE TOLENTINO DE ACTOPAN **20**

Celaya
San Juan del Río

Salvatierra

Mixquiahuala

Tlaxcoapan

BAJÍO AND THE CENTRAL COAST *p190*

TULA **8**
Tula de Allende

Acámbaro

Acambay
Tepeji del Río
Tizayucan

El Oro

Morelia

Atlacomulco

MUSEO NACIONAL DEL VIRREINATO **2**

Tzitzio

MEXICO
Cuautlán
Mexico City International Airport

Ixtahuaca de Rayon
Jiquipilco
Tlanepantla

Zitácuaro

Toluca International Airport

Mexico City

El Devanador

MICHOACÁN

TOLUCA **18**

15

Ajusco
12,894 ft (3,930 m)

Las Anonas

VALLE DE BRAVO **10**

Tenango

MALINALCO
13

Nocupétaro

Nevado de Toluca 15,387 ft (4,690 m)

TEPOZTLÁN **14**

Tenancingo

Tiquicheo

134

Tejupilco

CUERNAVACA **12**

Ixtapan de la Sal

XOCHICALCO **11**

Churumuco de Morelos

Huetamo

Bejucos

Zacatepec

Amatepec

TAXCO **21**

Ciudad Altamirano

Huitzuco

Arcelia
Teloloapán
Iguala

GUERRERO

Los Fogones

Apipilulco

Rio Balsas

0 kilometers   50

0 miles   50

N ↑

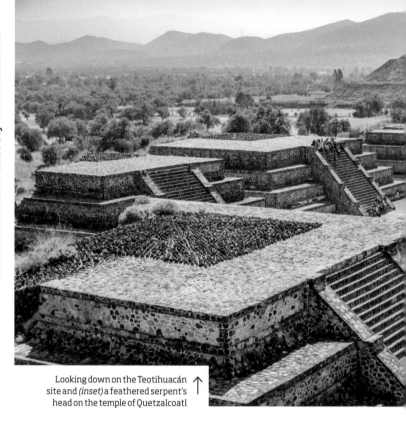

Looking down on the Teotihuacán site and *(inset)* a feathered serpent's head on the temple of Quetzalcoatl

TEOTIHUACÁN

🅰B6 **🚗** Mex 132D, 29 miles (47 km) NE of Mexico City, Mexico State **🕐** 9am–5pm daily; Museum: 8am–5pm daily **🌐** teotihuacan.inah.gob.mx

Walking down Teotihuacán's Avenue of the Dead, with one vast pyramid in front and another behind, is one of the most awe-inspiring experiences in the Americas. The magnificent monuments of this ancient site bear witness to a mysterious culture that dominated the region for five centuries.

Teotihuacán is one of the most impressive cities of the ancient world. Founded before the Christian era, this colossal urban center once housed up to 125,000 people and covered over 8 sq miles (20 sq km). It dominated life in the region for 500 years before being destroyed (possibly by its own people) and abandoned, around AD 650. Later, the site was held sacred by the Aztecs, who believed it had been built by giants. The ceremonial center, with its temples, palaces, and pyramids, bears witness to the city's splendor. However, the first inhabitants' origin, way of life, and even demise remain a mystery. Teotihuacán is an active archaeological site, with new discoveries made regularly. Today, it's still not known who built Teotihuacán.

Exploring the remarkable ruins, with the Pyramid of the Sun rising behind

PICTURE PERFECT
Time it Right

Teotihuacán is a very popular day trip from Mexico City. Its best to arrive early if you want the opportunity to take some photos of the empty enigmatic ruins before the midday crowds start to arrive.

The Superimposed Buildings (Edificios Superpuestos)

Quetzalpapalotl Palace Complex (p142)

Plaza of the Moon

Entrance 3

Pyramid of the Moon

Entrance 2

Entrance 4

Avenue of the Dead, running the length of the site

Palaces of Tetitla, Atetelco, Zacuala, and Yayahuala (p142)

Mexico City

Palace of Tepantitla (p142)

Mural fragment depicting a colossal jaguar

Entrance 1

Pyramid of the Sun, ranking among the biggest in the world

Restaurant

Museum (p142)

The Citadel

Entrance 5

Temple of Quetzalcoatl, decorated by masks of the plumed serpent Quetzalcoatl

Living quarters for the ruling classes

↑ Layout of the of the Teotihuacán archaeological site

EXPLORING TEOTIHUACÁN

To fully explore this colossal and awesome site, visitors should be prepared for long walks over uneven ground and stiff climbs up steep stairways – all at an altitude of 7,550 ft (2,300 m) and often under a hot tropical sun. Comfortable shoes, a hat, and sunblock are a must, plus rain gear in summer.

The Museum

The on-site museum is just south of the Pyramid of the Sun. It displays artifacts that were found at Teotihuacán, explanatory maps and diagrams, and, beneath the glass floor of its main hall, a scale model of the city.

The shady gardens outside are a good place to rest during a tour of the site. They are planted with botanical species native to the area and decorated with an original, partially restored, mural depicting feathered Teotihuacán sculptures.

Outlying Palaces

Several impressive ancient dwelling complexes are situated beyond the fence and road that ring the site.

Just east of the Pyramid of the Sun lies the Palace of Tepantitla, which contains the most important and colorful murals discovered so far at Teotihuacán. These include representations of elaborately dressed priests, the rain god Tlaloc, and his carefree paradise, known as Tlalocan, where miniature human figures frolic in an Eden-like setting. West of the site, and best reached by car, are four other palaces – Tetitla, Atetelco, Zacuala, and Yayahuala – which have great examples of frescoes, murals, and wall paintings.

Quetzalpapalotl Palace Complex

This maze of residential and temple structures grew slowly over several centuries. The last part to be built was probably the elegant Palace of Quetzalpapalotl, uncovered in 1962 and reconstructed with mostly original materials. It sits atop the now buried Temple of the Feathered Conches (2nd–3rd century AD). The Jaguar Palace, just to the west, has a large courtyard faced by a portico and a stepped temple base.

THE UNEARTHING OF TEOTIHUACÁN

For over a 1,000 years after its decline, the crumbled ruins of Teotihuacán remained hidden below a layer of earth and vegetation. Despite being venerated by the Aztecs, the site was never noticed by Cortés and his men when they passed by during their retreat from Tenochtitlán in 1520. The structures visible today, a mere tenth of the city, were excavated at digs that began in 1864.

Murals in the Jaguar Palace show plumed jaguars playing instruments

Entrance to lower level

Exit from lower level

Did You Know?

The Pyramid of the Sun is half the height of the Great Pyramid of Egypt, but has a similar sized base.

An illustration of the Quetzalpapalotl Palace complex ↑

Palacio de Quetzalpapalotl and *(inset)* a mural found at the nearby Jaguar Palace ↑

Palace of Quetzalpapalotl, named for the mythological creatures carved into its courtyard pillars

Decorative merlons symbolizing the calendar crown the courtyard

A huge stone serpent's head juts out from the top of a staircase and guards the porticoed entrance to the Palace of Quetzalpapalotl.

Temple of the Feathered Conches, an older structure found beneath the Palace of Quetzalpapalotl

Entrance to Palace of Quetzalpapalotl

Plaza of the Moon

MESOAMERICA

Mexico is strewn with many incredible reminders of the Mesoamerican civilizations that once lived here. The term Mesoamerica refers to a geographical region whose people shared a broadly similar culture before the arrival of the Spanish. It covers what is now central and southern Mexico, and other parts of Central America.

ANCIENT CIVILIZATIONS

The civilizations of Mesoamerica are normally divided into "highland" (especially the Valley of Mexico) and "lowland," such as the Maya in the Yucatán Peninsula. Despite the distances between them, the various cultures had many things in common, including gods, a calendar, and building practices, but they had different languages and customs.

Some cultures existed concurrently, but often - as in the case of the Mixtecs and the Zapotecs - one group would take over the territories of its predecessors. In some cases, the rise and fall of cultures - like the one based at Teotihuacán (p140) - is still a mystery to this day.

↑ A clay doll made by an Olmec artisan

PRECLASSIC AND CLASSIC PERIODS

The first era of Mesoamerica, known as the Preclassic period, lasted from around 1500 BC to AD 0. Its most notable culture is that of the Olmecs (1400-600 BC), who are often called the *cultura madre* (mother culture) because of their influence on later civilizations. Their main sites, at San Lorenzo and La Venta, wielded political, economic, and religious authority over big regions and a large population - but even so, the civilzation eventually faded into obscurity.

The Maya (p298) were the longest surviving Mesoamerican civilization (c 1000 BC-AD 1500),

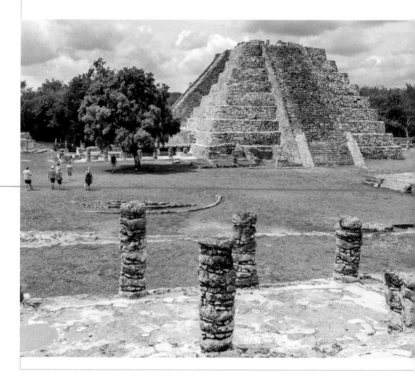

and their descendents (p238) still live in Mexico. The powerful Maya Empire spread from southern Mexico into Central America, building extensive ceremonial centers.

The Zapotecs were another long-lasting Mesoamerican culture, rising to prominence around 500 BC. They produced some of the earliest forms of writing in ancient Mexico. The Zapotec civilization ended around AD 900, coinciding with the end of the Classic period, but, as with the Maya, their culture carries on in present-day Mexico.

THE POSTCLASSIC ERA

This period (AD 900-1500) gave rise to multiple cultures that existed at the same time across Mexico. The militarized and artistic Toltecs (900-1200) were based in Tula (p154). Successors of the nearby Zapotecs, the Miztecs (1100-1450) built the ceremonial center Mitla (p252), and produced detailed codices, picture histories. The Tarascans (1350-1529) formed a formidable empire in central Mexico, rivalling the Aztecs (1200-1520), whose vast empire was overthrown by the Spanish. Beginning in the 1520s, Spain rapidly conquered Mexico and systemically destroyed its remaining civilizations, and by the 17th century only ruins remained.

↑ The ruins of a pyramid at Mayapán, a Maya site in the Yucatan Peninsula

MESOAMERICAN RELICS

Chacmool

These carved figures can be seen at many archaeological sites. The stone dishes placed on their stomachs are thought to have held sacrificial offerings.

Pyramids

Stepped and then crowned with a temple, Mesoamerican pyramids had different uses in different cultures, from human sacrifice to funerary rites.

Food

Many foods that are now eaten all over the world originated in Mesoamerica. They include tomatoes, chilies, and corn (maize).

The Wheel

Although the wheel was known, it was used only for nonfunctional objects such as toys. Most burdens were carried by porters or by canoe.

Jade

This green stone was more highly prized than gold in Mesoamerica. It was used for art and jewelry as well as being a key material for religious items.

Obsidian

A hard, glassy stone, obsidian was used instead of metals, which were not used until the 6th century, and never for functional objects.

2

MUSEO NACIONAL DEL VIRREINATO

⌂A6 ⬛Plaza Hidalgo 99, Tepotzotlán, 27 miles (44 km) N of Mexico City, Mexico State ⏲9am–4:45pm Tue–Sun ⬜virreinato.inah.gob.mx

Within the Iglesia de San Francisco Javier and its cloisters, school rooms, and gardens, splendid art, furniture, and reliquaries recreate the daily life of the former Jesuit college.

Mexico's most complete collection of colonial-era art and artifacts, one of its finest Baroque churches, and a splendid former Jesuit college built in the 17th and 18th centuries together make up this stunning museum covering Mexico's viceregal era. The church and college buildings, a vast complex with courtyards and gardens in the village of Tepotzotlán, were nearly complete when the Jesuits were expelled from New Spain in 1767. Restored and opened as a museum in 1964, exhibits include treasures preserved in situ as well as pieces from collections around the country.

Iglesia de San Francisco Javier

Built in the late 1600s, this majestic Baroque church is famous for its elegant 18th-century additions: the richly decorated Churrigueresque facade and tower, the exuberant gold altars, a trio of unusual chapels on one side, and the Miguel Cabrera murals in the chancel and cross vaults. The facade and interior are both prime examples of Mexican High Baroque. Together they form a harmonious whole equaled only by Santa Prisca in Taxco *(p161)* and San Cayetano near Guanajuato *(p199)*.

The main altar is dedicated to St. Francis Xavier, patron saint of the Jesuit college.

Entrance from museum

The altar to the Virgin of Guadalupe centers on a Miguel Cabrera painting of the patron saint of Mexico.

↑ The Capilla de los Novicios, once used by college residents, now part of the museum

Camarín de la Virgen, a profusely decorated octagonal chamber, once served as a dressing room for the Virgin of Loreto – the statue's vestments and jewels were changed regularly.

GALLERY GUIDE

Most of the collection is displayed on the entrance level of the former college building. The upper floor contains exhibits on artisan guilds, convent workshops, and female religious orders, while the lower level houses the old kitchen, rare stone sculptures, temporary exhibits, and the museum store.

The altar to St. Stanislaus Kostka honors a Polish Jesuit who served as a model to the students of the institution.

The dome rising above the intersection of the Latin Cross nave is best seen from a viewpoint in the museum.

The altar to St. Ignatius Loyola shows the founder of the Jesuits with a book displaying the order's motto.

The bell tower has 13 bells hanging on three levels under a tiled dome topped by a filigreed iron cross.

Pulpit

The Altar to the Virgen de la Luz is adorned with a multitude of cherubs and angels, which surround the central image of the Virgin and Child.

The imagery and style of the frontispiece echoes that of the altars inside, while the abundance of finely carved limestone hints at the brilliant interior.

So-called estípite pilasters form the verticals of the altars. Inspired by the proportions of the human figure, estípites taper off at the base, thus appearing to be upside down.

Corridor

The Casa de Loreto is said to be a replica of the Virgin Mary's Nazareth home, which angels moved to Loreto in Italy when the Muslims invaded the Holy Land.

Relicario de an José was built to house relics revered by the Jesuits – resembling the inside of a treasure chest.

↑ Illustration of Iglesia de San Francisco Javier, part of the Museo Nacional del Virreinato

147

3

PUEBLA

 C7 Puebla ✈🚍 𝑖 Avenida Palafox y Mendoza; www.turismopuebla.gob.mx

Founded in 1531, Puebla combines exquisite Spanish Colonial architecture with the vibrant buzz of a cosmopolitan city. Its rich Spanish heritage is still evident today in the finely preserved old center, with sumptuous palaces, churches, and museums.

①

Estrella de Puebla

🏠 Osa Mayor 2520 🕐 3:30–10pm Mon-Fri, 11am-10pm Sat & Sun 🌐 viajapor puebla.mx

Puebla's Big-Wheel stands tall in the Angelópolis district and is one of the city's most popular modern attractions.

From the top, which is more than 260 ft (80 m) above the ground, passengers are rewarded with breathtaking views over the charming city of Puebla and, on a clear day, may even be able to glimpse the volcanoes of Popocatépetl and Iztaccíhuatl (p158) west of the city.

②

Catedral de Puebla

🏠 16 de Septiembre s/n 🌐 arquidiocesisde puebla.mx

The second largest cathedral in Mexico, after the one in the capital, Catedral de Puebla was built in a mix of Renaissance and Baroque styles. The pillars around the large atrium – the plaza in front of the building – are surmounted by statues of angels, symbols of the town whose full name is Puebla de los Angeles ("People of the Angels").

Inside there are five naves and 14 side chapels. The main altar, known as the ciprés, was

designed by Manuel Tolsá in 1797. Standing on an octagonal base, it has two superimposed "temples" supported by Corinthian columns, crowned by a tiled dome in imitation of that of St. Peter's in Rome. Behind the ciprés is the Altar de los Reyes whose dome was painted by Cristóbal de Villalpando in 1688.

③

Teleferico de Puebla

🏠 Calzada Ignacio Zaragoza 🕐 2pm-10pm Mon, 10am-10pm Tue-Sun 🌐 visit-puebla.mx

Puebla's cable car quickly become one of the city's top

🔍 HIDDEN GEM
Alley of the Frogs

Near the Zócalo (main square), Callejón de los Sapos is in the Artists' Quarter, which hosts an arts and crafts market on Sunday mornings. Its name comes from floods that drew many frogs.

←

The impressive City Hall standing on Puebla's main square (Zócalo)

attractions after opening in 2016. The four-minute journey zips across the Xanenetla leisure park and offers a chance to admire the largest urban mural in the world, as well as stunning views over the city and volcanoes beyond.

④ Secret Tunnels of Puebla

🏠 Bulevar 5 de Mayo 208, Barrio de Xanenetla
🕐 10am–4pm Tue–Sun
🌐 viajaporpuebla.mx

Discovered in 2015, a 6-mile (10-km) network of tunnels runs beneath the center of Puebla, thought to have been constructed up to 500 years ago. Some of the tunnels are still in a state of disrepair and not easy to find. The best part to explore is the Pasaje Histórico 5 de Mayo, which is well-lit and has historical artifacts on display.

⑤ Museo de los Hermanos

🏠 6 Oriente No. 206
📞 (222) 242 10 76
🕐 10am–6pm Tue–Sun

This museum of revolutionary memorabilia is housed in the same building where the event said to have sparked the Mexican Revolution (*p60*) took place. On November 19, 1910, Aquiles Serdán – a shoemaker and political activist – resisted arrest for his revolutionary activities, and he and around a dozen others, including his family, were killed by the police.

⑥ Taller Uriarte Talavera

🏠 4 Poniente No 911
🕐 10am–3pm Mon–Fri
🌐 uriartetalavera.com.mx

Guided tours of this Talavera pottery workshop show the production process from the early purifying of the clay, to the painting, glazing, and final firing of the piece.

TOP 4 ART MUSEUMS

Museo Internacional del Barroco
🏠 Atlixcáyotl 2501
🌐 mib.puebla.gob.mx
Imaginative displays around Puebla's Baroque heritage.

Museo Amparo
🏠 2 Sur No 708
🌐 museoamparo.com
A collection of Mesoamerican- and colonial-era art.

Centro Cultural Ex-Convento de Santa Rosa
🏠 14 Poniente No 305
📞 (222) 232 77 92
A former convent, displaying crafts produced in Puebla.

Museo de Arte Religioso de Santa Mónica
🏠 18 Poniente No 103
📞 (222) 232 01 78
Ecclesiastical artifacts, art, and sculpture.

A SHORT WALK
PUEBLA

Distance 1.5 miles (2.5 km) **Time** 30 minutes
Nearest bus stop 8 Poniente - 2 Norte

Puebla is best known for the beautiful Talavera tiles that adorn its walls, domes, and interiors; for *mole poblano*, the thick sauce enriched with chocolate that originated here; and for being the site of an important battle against the French on May 5, 1862. The streets of the compact city center are lined with churches, mansions, and handsome old buildings, and are a delight to stroll around.

Teatro Principal

6 ORIENTE

4 ORIENTE

*Built in the 17th century as part of an orphanage, the **Templo de San Cristóbal** is noted for its collection of sculptures.*

Calle 6 Oriente *is known for its shops selling handmade candies, crystallized fruits, and rompope (eggnog).*

4 NORTE

6 ORIENTE

*The Revolution of 1910 supposedly began in this house, which is now a museum: the **Museo de los Hermanos** (p149).*

START

FINISH

Iglesia de Santa Clara

*The 18th-century **Casa del Alfeñique** is so named because its delicate white ornamental plasterwork resembles* alfeñique, *a sugar and almond paste. It now houses the state museum.*

2 NORTE

2 ORIENTE

VIPS *restaurant occupies this metal-framed building dating from the early 1900s.*

Diners at the arcade
↓ opposite the leafy
Plaza Principal

*The facade of **Casa de los Muñecos** – now a restaurant – is covered with decorative red tiles.*

AVENIDA MAXIMO

City Hall

Plaza Principal
(Zócalo)

Diners at the arcade opposite the leafy Plaza Principal

Barrio del Artista *(Artist's Quarter) is an attractive corner of the city.*

PUEBLA

Locator Map
For more detail see p149

↑ Colorful artwork underfoot in the Barrio del Artista, Puebla's Artists' Quarter

El Parián

Did You Know?

Crafts from the Artists' Quarter are sold in a small market, El Parián.

8 NORTE

6 NORTE

Casa de las Bóvedas

2 ORIENTE

Iglesia de la Compañía

C[I]ÓN DE SAPOS

3 ORIENTE

Hotel Colonial

A. CAMACHO

4 SUR

Plazuela de los Sapos
is the scene of a Sunday morning flea market.

3 ORIENTE

5 ORIENTE

2 SUR

At the heart of the city's 17th-century **cathedral** *(p148) is an octagonal altar by Manuel Tolsá. One of the two 226-ft (69-m) bell towers can be climbed for a view of the city and the nearby volcanoes (p158).*

The 50,000 volumes in the historic **Biblioteca Palafoxiana** *library, housed in the former bishop's palace, include a rare 16th-century Bible and atlas.*

Tourist information

| 0 meters | 100 |
| 0 yards | 100 |

N

EXPERIENCE MORE

4

Pachuca

 C4 ⊙ Hidalgo ⊞ ⓘ Camino Real de La Plata 340; (771) 718 44 89

Pachuca, capital of Hidalgo state, lies in the heart of a rich mining area. The center of town, with its steep, narrow lanes and small squares, retains some buildings from the two mining booms of the 16th and 18th centuries.

The tower in Plaza de la Independencia, the 130-ft (40-m) Neo-Classical Reloj Monumental (Monumental Clock), has an eight-bell carillon made by the creators of the Big Ben bell in London.

Undoubtedly, the most significant colonial-era complex is the late-16th-century Ex-Convento de San Francisco and its adjoining church. The church contains the remains of the 3rd-century martyr St. Columba, whose mummified body was brought here in the 18th century. Part of the massive former monastery building

houses the **Fototeca Nacional and Museo de Fotografía**. The latter has exhibits on the history of photography and shows selections from the one million photos on file at the former (the National Photographic Archive). One section is dedicated to the Casasola Archive, an outstanding chronicle of the Mexican Revolution and post-revolutionary daily life. It is also worth seeing the photographs and mining equipment at the **Archivo Histórico y Museo de Minería**.

On the southern outskirts of Pachuca is the Parque David Ben Gurion, featuring a huge, stunning mosaic made from around seven million tiles by Hidalgo-born artist Byron Gálvez Avilés. The park was founded in 2005 by the city's Jewish community as a tribute to David Ben Gurion, Israel's first prime minister.

On the other side of town, the Santa Apolonia hill provides amazing views.

Fototeca Nacional and Museo de Fotografía

⊙ ⓐ Casasola ⓒ (771) 714 36 53 ⓞ 10am–6pm Tue–Sun

🔍 HIDDEN GEM
Pachuca Football Club

The soccer-obsessed town of Pachuca is home to Mexico's oldest club, as well as the Centro Interactivo Mundo Fútbol, a fun interactive soccer museum (www.mundofutbol.com).

Archivo Histórico y Museo de Minería

⊛⊛⊛ ⓐ Mina 110 ⓒ (771) 715 09 76 ⓞ 10am–6pm Tue–Sun

5

San Agustín Acolman

 B6 ⓐ Calzada De Los Agustinos, Acolman, Mexico State ⓞ 10am–5pm daily 🔳 inah.gob.mx/paseos/exacolman

One of Mexico's oldest monasteries, San Agustín Acolman was founded in 1536 by Augustinian monks who came here to convert the local indigenous people. It is notable for its atrium, a Christian version of the pre-Hispanic ceremonial plaza, where crowds of indigenous disciples would gather to hear the new religion preached from a

The imposing Reloj Monumental, in Plaza de la Independencia, and (inset) brightly colored houses on Pachuca's hillside

→
A bridge over the canyon of Prismas Basálticos, near Huasca

chapel balcony above. The fortress-like building now houses colonial-era artwork.

The forbidding aspect of the monastery is softened, however, by the adjoining church's beautiful Plateresque facade, which is characterized by classic Italian Renaissance columns, richly decorated door arches, and a choir window replicating the portal below. The sparse interior of the nave is notable for its Gothic fan vaulting adorned with rich frescoes.

Huasca

C4 **Hidalgo** **Plaza Principal; (771) 792 07 47**

The picturesque village of Huasca is best known for its *haciendas de beneficio*, where mineral ores were refined. San Miguel Regla 2 miles (3 km) northeast of town, is a particularly popular spot with visitors, and is now a hotel. More impressive is **Hacienda Santa María Regla**, which has vaulted cellars, and patios with stone drag mills and melting ovens. From here visitors can access the spectacular 9-mile (15-km) canyon Prismas Basálticos, whose walls are made up of red and ocher basalt hexagons.

Hacienda Santa María Regla

 4.5 miles (7 km) NE of Huasca **Daily** **haciendaderegla.com.mx**

Mineral del Monte

C4 **Hidalgo** **Rubén Licona Ruiz 1; (771) 797 05 10**

Also known as Real del Monte, this mining town used to be the richest in the area. Gold and silver were discovered here before the Conquest (*p57*), and the Spanish started mining in the mid-1500s.

The town's steep streets, stairways, and small squares are lined with low buildings. The houses with high sloping roofs and chimneys indicate a Cornish influence, the legacy left by the 350 Cornishmen employed by the English company that ran the mines between 1824 and 1848. They are also responsible for *pastes*, a local specialty based on the Cornish pasty, as well as for introducing soccer to Mexico.

The town has several museums dedicated to its British industrial heritage, such as the Museo Casa Grande, the Museo de Sitio Mina de Acosta, and the **Museo del Paste**, dedicated to the Cornish pasty.

Museo del Paste

Av Juaréz 114 Barrio el Portezuelo **10am-6pm Wed-Mon** **museodelpaste.com**

EAT

The British miners who worked in Mineral del Monte are responsible for the area's popular pastes. Pachuca is home to some of the best places to try them.

Pastes Kikos
C4 **Guanajuato & Blvd del Minero, Pachuca** **(771) 273 05 47**

$$⑤$⑤

Pastes El Billar
C4 **Avenida Revolución 504-A, Pachuca** **(771) 713 37 38**

$⑤$⑤

Restaurant La Blanca
C4 **Calle Mariano Matamoros 201, Pachuca** **(771) 715 18 96**

$⑤$⑤

↑ The giant Atlantes warrior statues at the Toltec site of Tula

Tula

🗺️ C4 🚗 Off Mex 57, 53 miles (85 km) N of Mexico City, Hidalgo 📞 (773) 100 36 54 🕐 9am–5pm daily

The most important Toltec site in Mexico, Tula flourished as a great urban center from AD 900 to 1200, after the decline of Teotihuacán (*p140*) and prior to the rise of Tenochtitlán (*p78*). At its peak, the city covered up to 6 sq miles (16 sq km) and had an estimated population of 40,000. Then inner strife, invasions, and fire destroyed the Toltec empire and this, its capital. Only remnants of the main palaces, temples, and ballcourts survive on a wind-swept hill overlooking the small town of Tula de Allende.

The site is most famous for its giant stone sculptures, the Atlantes, some of which are reproductions. At a height of 15 ft (4.6 m), these four figures in battle gear crown the Pyramid of Tlahuiz-calpantecuhtli, or the Morning Star. Together with a massive serpent and other pillars, they probably once supported an ornately carved roof.

Certain stylistic elements at Tula – such as the column-filled Palacio Quemado (Burnt Palace), the *chacmool* sculptures, and the huge size of Ballcourt No 2 – underline the site's similarity to the Maya city of Chichén Itzá (*p294*). It was once thought that Toltec king Topiltzín was driven out of Tula and fled to the Yucatán Peninsula (*p276*) where he ushered in a cultural renaissance. However, recent theories suggest that the similarities are a result of Maya influence on Tula, and not vice versa.

Cholula

🗺️ C7 🚗 Puebla 🚌 ℹ️ Portal Guerrero 3, 4 Norte; (222) 261 23 93

In pre-Hispanic times, Cholula was a sacred city and a large and important commercial center. Before subjecting it to one of the bloodiest massacres of the Spanish Conquest, Cortés described

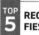

TOP 5 REGIONAL FIESTAS

Chalma Pilgrimages
Pilgrims make their way to the El Señor de Chalma shrine at Easter.

Fiesta de los Tiznados
A festival held on January 21 in Tepoztlán, in remembrance of the ancient Tepoztec king.

El Día de la Batalla de Puebla
Commemroating the Battle of Puebla, military parades take palce on May 5.

Fiesta de la Virgen de la Caridad
An image of the Virgin is carried for 3 miles (5 km) through Huamantla in mid-August.

Reto al Tepozteco
Villagers race up Tepozteco Hill in early September.

it as "the most beautiful city outside Spain."

The arcade on the west side of Cholula's large *zócalo* (main square) shelters restaurants and cafés. Opposite is the fortified, Franciscan **Convento de San Gabriel**. Founded in 1529 on the site of a temple to Quetzalcoatl, the main church has a single nave with rib vaulting and Gothic tracery. On the left of the atrium is the Capilla Real, which was built for indigenous converts. It acquired its 49 mosque-like domes in the early part of the 18th century.

To the east is the **Zona Arqueológica**, a site which is dominated by the remains of the largest pyramid ever built in Mesoamerica, at 213 ft

→ The beautiful tile-covered church of San Francisco Acatepec

(65 m) high. Since the 1930s, archaelogists have dug 5 miles (8 km) of tunnels through this Great Pyramid, identifying at least four stages of construction between 200 BC and AD 800.

Opposite the entrance to the tunnel is a museum with a large cutaway model of the pyramid, as well as artifacts from the site. On top of the pyramid sits the 1874 church of Nuestra Señora de los Remedios. The wonderful view from the atrium takes in Puebla *(p148)*, the volcanoes, and Cholula's many other churches.

The extraordinary folk-Baroque church of Santa María Tonantzintla, 3 miles (5 km) south of Cholula, has an interior that is bursting with colorful saints, fruit, angels, and cherubs. Begun in the 16th century, it took its craftsmen 200 years to complete. A farther 1 mile (1.5 km) south, the church of San Francisco Acatepec has a facade entirely covered in colorful Talavera tiles *(p131)*.

Convento de San Gabriel
🏠 Corner of Calle 2 Sur and Avenida Morelos ⏰ 9am-5pm daily

Zona Arqueológica
♿ 🏠 Avenida Morelos 📞 (222) 247 90 81 ⏰ 9am-6pm daily

↑ View over Valle de Bravo and its lake, a popular spot for hang gliding

 10

Valle de Bravo

🅰 C5 🏠 Mexico State 🚌 ℹ Rincón de San Vicente; www.turismovalledebravo.gob.mx

Set among pine-covered volcanic mountains, this pretty colonial-era town achieved popularity in the 1950s after the construction of an artificial lake. Easy access from Mexico City makes the town a favorite weekend destination for the capital's elite, but during the week peace returns to the cobbled streets.

Local attractions such as the waterfalls of Cascadas Velo de Novia, the **Santuario de Piedra Herrada** butterfly reserve, and the peaceful **Carmel Maranathá** temple all make the most of the beautiful natural scenery. The area is also a popular place to enjoy activities, with lots of opportunities for hang gliding, hiking, horseback riding, and waterskiing.

Santuario de Piedra Herrada
♿ 🏠 San Mateo Almomoloa 📞 (722) 511 11 27 ⏰ 9am-4pm daily

Carmel Maranathá
🏠 Carretera México Valle de Bravo ⏰ 10am-2pm & 4-7pm Mon-Fri 🌐 carmel maranatha.wixsite.com/ocd-en-valle

The pyramidal ruins at Xochicalco and *(inset)* a bas-relief carving on the Pyramid of the Feathered Serpent

Xochicalco

🅰A7 🅾Off Mex 95, 25 miles (40 km) SW of Cuernavaca
🕘9am–6pm daily (Museum: to 5pm) 🌐inah.gob.mx

The extensive ruins of Xochicalco Archaeological Zone are all that remains of an important city-state that rose to prominence after the decline of Teotihuacán (*p140*). The city flourished from AD 700 to 900, before being eclipsed by the rise of the Toltecs (*p144*).

About 30 percent of the site has been unearthed, including three ballcourts and the remains of several pyramidal structures. An on-site museum displays artifacts found during archaeological work. As well as being a fascinating place to explore, the site's location on a plateau offers incredible views of the surrounding area.

The Pyramid of the Plumed Serpent, excavated between 1777 and 1994, is considered one of the nation's most beautiful monuments. It features remarkably well-preserved bas-reliefs of serpents, glyphs, and Maya-style figures.

Cuernavaca

🅰A7 🅾Morelos 🚌
ℹAvenida Motolinía 2; www.cuernavaca.gob mx

Inhabited since 1200 BC, Cuernavaca is one of the oldest cities in Mexico. Today it is a popular weekend destination from Mexico City, and full of history and culture for visitors to discover.

The **Palacio de Cortés** was built by the Spanish on the site of Aztec pyramids they had destroyed. It served as Cortés's residence until his return to Spain in 1540. Known for a series of Diego Rivera murals depicting Mexico's history, it also contains the Museo Regional Cuauhnáhuac, which has a fine collection of historical artifacts.

The fortress-like Catedral de la Asunción, dating from the 1520s, has murals thought to have been painted by artists brought over from China or the Philippines. The **Museo Robert Brady**, situated in a former cloister, holds the art and craft collection of this American artist.

> Xochicalco's Pyramid of the Plumed Serpent, excavated between 1777 and 1994, is considered one of the nation's most beautiful monuments.

La Tallera is the former studio of the great muralist David Alfaro Siqueiros (1896–1974). Revolutionary politics shaped his life and work, and inspired the aesthetic behind his ambitious projects.

A few blocks from the main *zócalo* (square) is the **Museo de Arte Indígena Contemporáneo**, which focuses on works by contemporary indigenous artists.

Palacio de Cortés
🎨🕐🏛 🏠Avenida Leyva 100 📞(777) 312 69 96 ⏰Tue–Sun

Museo Robert Brady
🎨💬 🏠Netzahualcóyotl 4 ⏰10am–6pm Tue–Sun 🌐museorobertbrady.com

La Tallera
🎨🕐 🏠Venus 52, Jardín de Cuernavaca ⏰10am–6pm Tue–Sun 🌐saps-latallera.org

Museo de Arte Indígena Contemporáneo
🎨💬 🏠Avenida Morelos 275 📞(777) 310 57 00 ⏰10am–5pm Tue–Sun

 13

Malinalco

🅰A7 🏠Mexico State 💬 ℹRincón de San Vicente; www.malinalco.gob.mx

This charming town is nestled in a valley, surrounded by steep volcanic hills. An Aztec ceremonial center sits on a narrow ledge 20 minutes' climb above town.

Its main structure, the House of the Eagle (Cuauhcalli), is carved entirely out of the rock. The building is thought to have been used for initiation ceremonies of high-ranking Aztec knights. Behind it stand the remains of the Temple of the Sun and the Tzinacalli Edifice, where the bodies of knights killed in combat were deified.

A reproduction of the temple facade and the inner chamber can be seen in the **Museo Universitario Dr. Luis Mario Scheider**.

Museo Universitario Dr. Luis Mario Scheider
🎨 🏠Calle Amajac 📞(714) 147 12 88 ⏰10am–5:30pm Tue–Sun

 14

Tepoztlán

🅰A7 🏠Morelos 💬 ℹ22 Avenida Revolución de 1910; www.infotepoz.com

Lying in a lush green valley, Tepoztlán is surrounded by spectacular volcanic rock formations. The town's main landmark is the massive, fortified Ex-Convento Dominico de la Natividad, although the building is in a state of disrepair. The market on Plaza Santo Domingo, meanwhile, is a great place to browse. You'll find everything from fresh fruit to Mexican handicrafts.

A tiring but worthwhile climb above the town stands the Santuario del Cerro Tepozteco, a shrine dedicated to Tepoztecatl, the ancient god of pulque – an alcoholic beverage made from the agave plant.

For lovers of pre-Hispanic art, the **Museo Carlos Pellicer** holds a small but interesting collection, the legacy of the Tabascan poet and anthropologist Carlos Pellicer, who lived in Tepoztlán.

Museo Carlos Pellicer
🎨🕐 🏠González 📞(739) 395 10 98 ⏰10am–6pm Tue–Sun

 # EAT

Tepoznieves
This is the original branch of a local chain that offers more than 100 delicious flavors of ice cream and sorbet.

🅰A7 🏠Avenida 5 de Mayo No 21, Tepoztlán 🌐nieves-tepoznieves.com

💲💲💲

STAY

Hostería Las Quintas
Spacious rooms in a hotel surrounded by botanical gardens.

🅲C5 🏠Blvd Gustavo Díaz Ordaz No 9, Cuernavaca 🌐hosteria lasquintas.com.mx

💲💲💲

↑ Visitors exploring the Aztec ruins above the town of Malinalco

15

Popocatépetl and Iztaccíhuatl

B7 Mexico State
iztapopo.conanp.gob.mx

The snow-capped volcanoes of Popocatépetl, or Popo, ("Smoking Mountain") and Iztaccíhuatl ("Sleeping Lady") are the second and third highest peaks in Mexico. On a clear day, they are two of Mexico's most awesome sights.

According to legend, the warrior Popocatépetl fell in love with Iztaccíhuatl, an Aztec princess. To win her hand, he defeated a great rival in battle. Wrongly believing him to be dead, the princess herself then died of a broken heart. In his grief, Popocatépetl turned himself and his princess into these two adjacent mountains. The outline of Iztaccíhuatl bears a resemblance to that of a sleeping woman.

The Paso de Cortés, a saddle between the two peaks accessible by car, is an ideal base for walks on Iztaccíhuatl, but ascents of the peak itself should be left to experienced climbers and those who have hired a guide. Such services are offered by the park.

Access to the area around Popocatépetl volcano is restricted because of seismic activity. If you plan to hike, check posted warnings and contact your embassy or SECTUR (Secretaría de Turismo) for the latest information.

16

Cacaxtla and Xochitécatl

C7 Off Mex 119, 19 miles (30 km) NW of Puebla, Tlaxcala (246) 416 00 00
9am–5:30pm daily

Cacaxtla was the capital of the Olmeca-Xicalanca, a Gulf Coast group who dominated this area from the 7th to 10th centuries AD. Some of Mexico's best-preserved murals, probably painted by Maya artists, were discovered here in 1974.

The 72-ft- (22-m-) high *Mural de la Batalla* depicts a violent battle between jaguar and eagle warriors, with no fewer than 48 human figures in vibrant colors.

Two other extraordinary murals are in Edificio A. The *Hombre-jaguar* represents a lord dressed in a jaguar skin, surrounded by a border of sea creatures. The *Hombre-ave* is a "bird-man" painted in black with an eagle headdress. He holds a blue serpent staff and stands on a plumed snake. Heads of corn around the edge have small human faces.

Perched on a neighboring peak just 1.5 miles (2 km) away is another Olmeca-Xicalanca site, Xochitécatl. Situated atop an extinct volcano overlooking the surrounding valley, Xochitécatl is thought to have been used as a ritual ceremonial center in conjunction with Cacaxtla. Dating from about 800 BC, its pyramids and other main buildings flank two plazas.

→
The lavish exterior of the Basílica de Ocotlán, situated above Tlaxcala

⑰ Tlaxcala

AC6 **A**Tlaxcala 🚌
ℹ Corner of Avenida Juárez and Lardizábal; www.turismotlaxcala.com

Often seen as a provincial backwater, the city of Tlaxcala is, in fact, one of the country's colonial-era treasures. Its seclusion is partly due to the historical independence of the local people, the Tlaxcaltecas. During the Conquest they took up arms against their old enemy, the Aztecs, joining Cortés to conquer Tenochtitlán.

The so-called Ciudad Roja (Red City) is dominated by earthy tones of terracotta and ocher. In the center is the spacious tree-filled *zócalo* (main plaza). The colorful and richly decorated brick, tile, and stucco facade of the Parroquia de San José dominates the northwest corner of the square. At the entrance to this church two fonts have pedestals depicting Camaxtli, the ancient

Tlaxcalan god of war and hunting, and the Spanish imperial coat of arms.

Across Plaza Xicoténcatl to the south, a path leads uphill to the cathedral, which has a stunning Moorish-style coffered ceiling and contains the font used to baptize the four local chiefs who allied with Cortés. The **Museo Regional**, in the cloisters next door, has a collection of pre-Hispanic pieces, including a large stone figure of Camaxtli, the god of war. The two rooms upstairs are dedicated to colonial-era art.

The **Museo Vivo de Artes y Tradiciones Populares de Tlaxcala** is a fascinating living museum where artisans demonstrate their techniques.

Housed in a 19th-century former hospital, the impressive **Museo de Arte de Tlaxcala** contains some of artist Frida Kahlo's early works. Around the corner is the fascinating **Museo de la Memoria de Tlaxcala**, focused on the town's history.

On a hill above the city, the twin-towered Basílica de Ocotlán is one of the most lavish Churrigueresque churches in Mexico. The

 HIDDEN GEM
Puppet Story

The town of Huamantla, east of Tlaxcala, is famous for its puppetry, as the Rosete Aranda puppet company was founded here in 1850. Learn more at the National Puppet Museum (*Parque Juárez 50*).

18th-century facade combines hexagonal brick and white stucco decoration, and the interior is an explosion of Baroque giltwork.

Museo Regional
⊘ **A** Ex-Convento de San Francisco, off Plaza Xicoténcatl **(** (246) 462 02 62 **O** 10am–6pm Tue–Sun

Museo Vivo de Artes y Tradiciones Populares de Tlaxcala
⊘⊘ **A** Blvd Emilio Sánchez Piedras 1 **(** (246) 462 57 04 **O** 9am–6pm Tue–Sun

Museo de Arte de Tlaxcala
⊘ **A** Plaza de la Constitución 21 **(** (246) 466 03 52 **O** 10am–6pm Tue–Sun

Museo de la Memoria de Tlaxcala
⊘⊘⊘ **A** Avenida Independencia 3 **(** (246) 466 07 91 **O** 10am–5pm daily

 ←
A hiker climbs to the snowy peak of Popocatépetl volcano

↑ Striking stained glass by Leopoldo Flores, at Toluca's Cosmovitral Jardín Botánico

⑱ Toluca

🅰 A7 🄰 Mexico State ✈🚌
ℹ Plaza Fray Andrés de Castro; www.toluca.gob.mx

At 8,790 ft (2,680 m) above sea level, Toluca is the highest state capital in the country.

Founded by the Spaniards in the late 17th century, Toluca is full of fine buildings. The Neo-Classical cathedral, a massive late-19th-century pile, dominates the main square, Plaza de los Mártires. Nearby are the 18th-century Templo de la Santa Veracruz and the 19th-century Portales, a series of arched walkways lined with cafés and shops. To the north is the **Museo de Bellas Artes**, which exhibits Mexican art from the last four centuries. Nearby, the **Cosmovitral Jardín Botánico** shows botanical specimens in the beautiful old market, its walls and ceiling ablaze with colorful stained glass. The Central de Abastos is the city's main food market, with around 2,000 stalls – making it one of the largest in Mexico.

To the southeast, the suburb of Metepec is famous for its brightly colored, ceramic *árboles de la vida* (trees of life), loosely based on the story of Adam and Eve.

There's also plenty more to see in the surrounding area, making Toluca a great base for exploring the region. To the west is the **Centro Cultural Mexiquense**, a large complex of museums devoted to modern art, local history, and regional crafts. A short drive southwest is the extinct, snow-capped Nevado de Toluca volcano. A dirt road leads almost to the top, and hikers can descend into the crater. The hilltop ceremonial center of Teotenango is south of Toluca. Dating from AD 900, the extensive site features restored pyramids, plazas, a ballcourt, and a museum.

 PICTURE PERFECT
Rare Pyramid

A photo of the rounded pyramid of Calixtlahuaca, 25 minutes north of Toluca, makes a great contrast to Mexico's other ruins. It was built in the 7th century BC as a site of pilgrimage for the Otomi.

125,000

The number of pieces of stained glass in Toluca's Cosmovitral Jardín Botánico

Museo de Bellas Artes
♿ 🄰 Santos Degollado 102, Poniente 📞 (722) 215 53 29 🕐 10am–6pm Tue–Sun

Cosmovitral Jardín Botánico
♿♿ 🄰 Juárez & Lerdo s/n 📞 (722) 214 67 85 🕐 10am–6pm Tue–Sun (to 3pm Sun)

Central de Abastos
🄰 Jose Lopez Portillo Km 4 📞 (722) 210 01 12 🕐 7am–8:30pm daily

Centro Cultural Mexiquense
🄰 Blvd Jesús Reyes Heroles 302 📞 (722) 274 12 00 🕐 10am–6pm Tue–Sun (to 3pm Sun)

19

Cantona

D5 **19 miles (30 km) NE of Oriental, Puebla** **9am–6pm daily** **inah. gob.mx**

The remains of a once major city occupy a vast area of low hills beside a lava field. Little is known about the history of Cantona but it was probably inhabited from about AD 700 to 950. One of the most built-up of all Mesoamerican cities, it may have supported a population of 80,000.

A full visit will take at least two hours. A signposted route from the parking lot sets off on one of the *calzadas*, or cobbled streets, which connect the various parts of Cantona. This leads past the ruins of houses and patios before climbing to the Acrópolis, the cluster of public buildings at the heart of the city. Soon the route reaches the first of 24 ballcourts excavated here – more than at any other site in Mexico. Of these, 12 are unusual in that they form parts of complexes with a pyramid at one end and the playing area at the other.

 20

Convento de San Nicolás de Tolentino de Actopan

C4 **Lerdo de Tejada, Actopan, Hidalgo** **(772) 728 35 80** **9am–5pm Tue–Sun**

Built in the 1550s, the imposing Convent of San Nicolás de Tolentino de Actopan is one of Mexico's most remarkable and best-preserved 16th-century fortress-monasteries. Even more spectacular than its Plateresque facade, square Moorish tower, and vaulted open chapel are its frescoes, which are considered the most beautiful and extensive from this era in Mexico.

 21

Taxco

C5 **Guerrero** **Avenida de los Plateros 126; (762) 622 07 98**

Set against a spectacular rugged mountainside, Taxco is one of the least spoiled colonial-era towns in Mexico. Its history is inextricably tied to the local silver boom, and today many of its attractions focus on the industry. Housed in the main handicrafts center, the Museo de la Platería offers an immersive experience of the silver production process. The Mina Prehispánica de Taxco runs tours exploring historic mine shafts. Taxco's silver market, Mercado de Plata, is a great place to buy silver at reasonable prices.

The success of those who grew rich from the silver mines have also left their mark on the town, such as with the grand Iglesia De Santa Prisca. It is a fantastic exmple of the Churriguer-esque style of Mexican architecture.

Museo de la Platería

Patio de las Artesanias, Plaza Borda 1 **(762) 622 06 58** **9am–6pm Tue–Sun**

Mina Prehispánica de Taxco

Cerro de la Mision 32 **(762) 622 82 86** **9am–6pm daily**

Mercado de Plata

Calle de Fundiciones y de Mora **(762) 625 86 70** **10:30am–6pm Sat**

Iglesia De Santa Prisca

José de La Borda 1 **(762) 622 01 83** **9am–7pm Mon–Sat, 10am–8:15pm Sun**

↑ The colonial-era town of Taxco, famous for its silver mining

A SHORT WALK
TAXCO

Distance 0.5 miles (1 km) **Time** 15 minutes **Nearest bus stop** Central de Autobuses Estrella Blanca

Exploring Taxco on foot takes you along steep cobble-stoned streets and narrow alleys lined with laid-back cafés and restaurants. In the historic center is the magnificent, Baroque Iglesia de Santa Prisca, a testament to the wealth brought into this silver boom town during the colonial era. The town's fortunes were revived with the arrival of silver designer William Spratling in 1932, who established Taxco as a center for silversmiths.

PLAZUELA DE BERNAL

FINISH

START

Overlooking the main square, **Casa Borda** *was built by the Borda family in 1759 for the parish priest. Today, it holds exhibitions by local artists.*

An intimate and lively square, **Plaza Borda** *is lined with charming old buildings. There are numerous restaurants and bars nearby. In addition, the area abounds with silver shops, filled with the high-quality pieces for which Taxco's many silversmiths are famous.*

Casa Figueroa *was built for the Count of Cadena. It has a dark and interesting history involving subterfuge and murder.*

PLAZA BORDA

OJEDA

CUAUHTEMOC

← The cathedral towers rising above the old buildings of Taxco's old town

Casa Humboldt is named after Baron von Humboldt, the German naturalist, who spent a night here in 1803. It is a beautifully maintained building containing a museum of religious art, the Museo de Arte Virreinal.

Museo Guillermo Spratling contains William Spratling's collection of pre-Hispanic artifacts and works of art from around the world.

Santa Prisca has an octagonal dome covered with colorful tiles. Rising behind the church's twin towers, it is an unmistakable landmark that can be seen from all over the city.

CALLE JUAN RUIZ DE ALARCÓN

DELGADO

CALLE DE LA VERACRUZ

EL ARCO

0 meters 25
0 yards 25
N

The magnificent **Iglesia de Santa Prisca** (p161), with its Churrigueresque facade and ornate sculptures, dominates the Plaza Borda. It was paid for by José de la Borda, who made his fortune by discovering important deposits of silver. No expense was spared in construction, which took seven years (1751–58).

Bar Berta claims to be where the Margarita cocktail was invented.

Did You Know?

Silver ingots were found in the icehouse of Taxco's Casa Figueroa.

BAJA CALIFORNIA

Indigenous peoples such as the Cochimí, Kiliwa, Kumeyaay, and Guaycura have inhabited the Baja peninsula for over 10,000 years. Baja was virtually ignored by European explorers until 1697, when Jesuit missionaries began establishing isolated churches across the peninsula. The Europeans brought diseases to the area, which turned into epidemics that decimated the region's population – by the early 1800s the indigenous population was virtually extinct, and Baja remained a desolate place well into the 20th century. The border city of Tijuana began to flourish after US Prohibition in the 1920s turned it into a party town for citizens of neighboring California, a reputation it retains today. In 1930 the peninsula was divided in two: Baja California in the north, and Baja California Sur in the south. Though it became popular with US fishermen and adventurers such as John Steinbeck, growth in the rest of Baja was sluggish until the completion of the Transpeninsular Highway (Hwy 1) in 1973.

Today Baja California is a major holiday destination, particularly the southern resort towns such as Cabo San Lucas. Even the parts of the peninsula that remain swathed in isolated desert or crisscrossed by arid mountain chains exude a charm for more adventurous travelers looking for an epic road trip.

0 kilometers 150
0 miles 150
N ↑

San Diego

Salton
Sea

Mexicali
International
Airport

TIJUANA ④ ✈ Tijuana
International
Airport

Mexicali ✈

Rosarito

VALLE DE GUADALUPE ①

ENSENADA ②

Santo Tomás

El Chinero

Colonet

San Felipe

Camalú

Parque Natural
San Pedro Mártir

BAJA CALIFORNIA
NORTE

El Rosarito

San Fernando

Cataviña

Parque Natural
del Desierto Central

Isla
Cedros

Bahía
Sebastian
Vizcaíno

Isla Natividad

Bahía Tortugas

Pacific
Ocean

BAJA CALIFORNIA

Experience

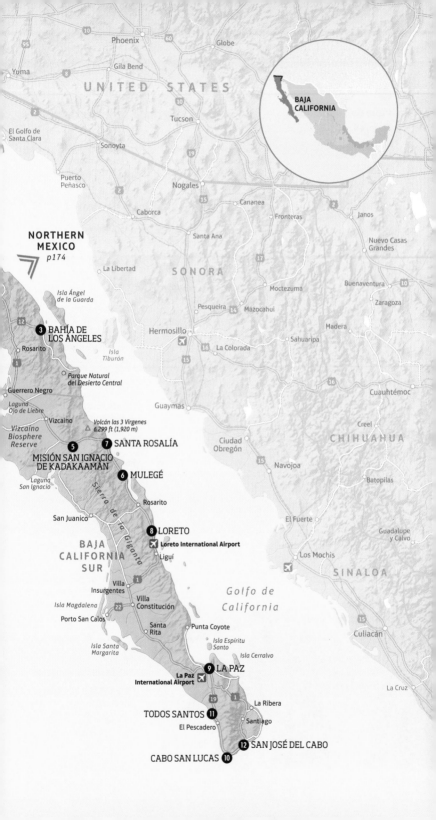

EXPERIENCE

❶ Valle de Guadalupe

 D1 ☐ Baja California
ℹ Paseo de los Héroes
10289, Tijuana; www.
bajanorte.com

The vineyards of Guadalupe Valley have received international acclaim since the 1990s. The villages of Francisco Zarco in the north and San Antonio de las Minas in the south anchor the valley's 60 vineyards. The **Museo de la Vid y el Vino** provides an introduction to the region, and most wineries offer tours and tastings.

Museo de la Vid y el Vino

⊘ ☐ Carretera Federal Tecate-Ensenada Km. 81.33 ⏲ 9am–5pm Tue–Sun 🌐 matra.temp.domains/~museodelvinobc/index.php

❷ Ensenada

 D1 ☐ Baja California
✖ ✉ ℹ Blvd Lázaro Cárdenas 609; www.
bajanorte.com/ensenada

This busy port and cruise-ship destination is popular with sportfishing fans, surfers, and divers, as well as foodies who come here for the town's famous fish tacos.

The city's landmarks include the twin-towered church of Nuestra Señora de Guadalupe and the giant sculpted heads of three national heroes – Juárez, Hidalgo, and Carranza – on the Plaza Cívica.

Several old buildings have been repurposed and are now dedicated to preserving local history. Just inland, the **Museo Histórico Regional de Ensenada** was built in 1886 as a military barracks; today its cells are galleries chronicling the history of the town. The **Riviera de Ensenada**, near the waterfront, was a hotel in the 1930s but now houses exhibitions and a history museum. In the lobby is a remarkable 3D mural showing the 18th-century Jesuit missions of the Californias.

The huge complex opposite the Riviera is the Caracol (Museo de Ciencas), an interactive science museum showcasing Baja California's geology and environments.

Bodegas de Santo Tomás makes some of Baja's finest wine from grapes grown in vineyards near town; it offers daily tours and wine tasting. Ensenada's small but lively "party district" clusters around the old-fashioned Hussong's Cantina on Avenida Ruíz, founded in the 19th century by the German Hussong family, still a powerful force in the city.

Museo Histórico Regional de Ensenada

☐ Gastélum 56 ☎ (646) 178 36 92 ⏲ 9am–5pm Tue–Sun

Riviera de Ensenada

☐ Blvd Lázaro Cárdenas 1421 ☎ (646) 176 43 10 ⏲ 8am–8pm daily

Bodegas de Santo Tomás

⊘ 🕐 🕐 🕐 ☐ Av Miramar 666 ⏲ Daily 🌐 santo-tomas.com

TOP 3 REGIONAL FIESTAS

Carnival
One of Mexico's best Pre-Lent Carnivals is held in La Paz.

Vendimia Wine Festival
In August, growers and producers show off their wares in Ensenada.

Baja 1000
A grueling off-road race Ensenada to La Paz (or vice versa every other year) in November.

❸ Bahía de los Angeles

 E2 ☐ Baja California
🌐 bajanorte.com

Located on the beautiful bay of the same name, the town of Bahía de los Angeles is a tranquil spot, even by Baja standards. Popular with

↑ Visitor photographing a vineyard in the Valle de Guadalupe

The Millennial Arch on the busy Avenida Revolución in Tijuana ↑

sportfishing enthusiasts, it also offers opportunities for diving and kayaking around the numerous islands in the bay. Other attractions include trips across a spectacular desert landscape to see pre-historic rock paintings (p170), and the well-preserved San Borja mission.

Boats are available to visit various offshore islands, but visiting or camping on the islands requires a permit. You can obtain one from the reserve office in town.

4

Tijuana

🅐 D1 🏠 Baja California 🛫🚌 ℹ️ HSBC Centro, Av Revolución 791; www.tijuana.gob.mx

A well-known party town, Tijuana is one of the world's busiest border cities, just 20 miles (32 km) from the US city of San Diego, California.

Towering skyscrapers and massive shopping malls are a measure of its modernity, but Tijuana's focus is the cluster of bars, clubs, and souvenir stalls on Avenida Revolución. Even in this busy leisure district, however, you'll find

Did You Know?

Caesar salad was invented in Tijuana by Caesar Cardini at Hotel Caesar (Av Revolución 1079).

history close by – two blocks west of Revolución, the elegant Catedral de Nuestra Señora de Guadalupe, built in 1909 was designated a cathedral in 1964.

Tijuana also has a few cultural attractions, the main one being the **Centro Cultural Tijuana** where concerts and art exhibitions are held. At the same location is the illuminating **Museo de las Californias**, which chronicles the history of Baja California.

Centro Cultural Tijuana
♿😐🕐 🏠 Paseo de los Héroes 9350 🕐 10am-7pm daily 🌐 cecut.gob.mx

Museo de las Californias
♿ 🏠 Paseo de los Héroes 9350 📞 (664) 687 96 35 🕐 10am-7pm Tue-Sun

---

THE MEXICO-US BORDER

The US and Mexico are separated by a heavily guarded land border that runs for 1,950 miles (3,140 km). Around 50 million people cross every year at Tijuana alone. When crossing from the US into Mexico there are no customs checks, and only casual checks for pedestrians. Stop at the *migración* office for a Mexican entry form, or "FMT" (these are not handed out automatically).

Always allow more time heading into the US, and be prepared for a line - crossing the border at Tijuana can take up to three hours. For Tijuana Airport, use the CBX skybridge, which connects to the San Diego side (www.crossborderxpress.com).

5

Misión San Ignacio de Kadakaamán

⚠E2 ⌂Hidalgo 1916, Juan Batista, San Ignacio, Baja California Sur

Standing among thousands of date palms, this church is one of the best-preserved and prettiest missions in Baja California. Although originally founded by Jesuits in 1728, the church seen today was actually built in 1786 by Dominicans. Its whitewashed Baroque facade, with masonry details in reddish lava stone,

holds four polygonal windows and four niches containing carvings of saints. The interior has original furniture and altarpieces, as well as a beautiful main altar.

In the canyons near the town of San Ignacio are some ancient cave paintings. To visit the caves, you must be accompanied by an approved guide, who must be booked in advance from a group such as Baja Unbound (www.baja-unbound.com) or INAH (615 122 73 89). The **Museo de las Pinturas Rupestres de San Ignacio** also has exhibits on the cave paintings.

↑ The Jesuit Misión San Ignacio de Kadakaamán in San Ignacio

Museo de las Pinturas Rupestres de San Ignacio
⌂ Prof Gilberto Valdivia Péna █ (615) 154 02 22 🕐 8am-5pm Mon-Sat

---

6

Mulegé

⚠E2 ⌂Baja California Sur

This pretty town has a lovely church, founded by Jesuit missionaries in 1705. Set on a bluff, it delights visitors with its superb views of the Santa Rosalía river below. Not far away is the **Museo Mulegé**, which has displays on the town's history. It is housed in a former prison, a whitewashed building complete with tiny, crenellated towers.

Mulegé is popular with scuba divers, but for some of the best beaches in Mexico take the road south out of Mulegé, past the Bahía Concepción. The water here

→

The Santa Rosalía river near the town of Santa Rosalía

BAJA'S ANCIENT CAVE PAINTINGS

The exact age of Baja's cave paintings is unknown, but some may date from 1200 BC. The best-preserved are found in the Cueva de las Flechas (Cave of the Arrows) and the Cueva Pintada (Painted Cave). A visit to these sites, in the San Pablo canyon, involves a two- or three-day camping trip with mules; organize tours at least 48 hours in advance at the INAH office in San Ignacio.

> **Santa Rosalía's Iglesia de Santa Bárbara is a prefabricated church by Gustave Eiffel, designer of the Eiffel Tower.**

changes dramatically from deep blue to an intense green.

Museo Mulegé
 Cananea **(** (613) 132 73 04 ⏰ 8am–3pm Mon–Fri

---

❼
Santa Rosalía

🅐 E2 📍 Baja California Sur 🚌🚐 ℹ️ Carretera Transpeninsular, Km. 220; (615) 152 23 11

This small town was founded by a French copper-mining company in the 1880s. The company moved on in the 1950s, but left engines from their railroad and some of the mine installations, which can still be seen today. Mining restarted here in 2015 after a US$1.6 billion investment. Overlooking the town is a mining museum, the **Museo de Historia de la Minería de Santa Rosalía**.

Among the town's pretty sights are the many two-story timber buildings with verandas, which give it a Caribbean look. Another is the Iglesia de Santa Bárbara, a prefabricated church by Gustave Eiffel, designer of the Eiffel Tower.

Museo de Historia de la Minería de Santa Rosalía
 🏠 Jean-Michel Cousteau 1 **(** (615) 152 29 99 ⏰ 8am–3pm Mon–Sat

---

❽
Loreto

🅐 E2 📍 Baja California Sur 🚐 ℹ️ Corner of Francisco Madero and Salvatierra; (613) 13 50 411

Loreto is best known as a magnet for sportfishing. There is also good diving, kayaking, and snorkeling to be found here around the offshore islands of Isla del Carmen and Coronado.

The heart of the town is the area around Plaza Cívica and the superbly restored Misión Nuestra Señora de Loreto. This mission was the first in the Californias, where Jesuit missionaries embarked on a campaign to evangelize (and hence subdue) the indigenous population. The **Museo de las Misiones** inside explains how this was accomplished and displays period artifacts.

Some 22 miles (36km) southwest of Loreto, the **Misión San Francisco Javier de Viggé-Biaundó**, completed in 1758, is one of the most isolated churches in Baja.

Museo de las Misiones
 🏠 Salvatierra 16 **(** (613) 135 04 41 ⏰ 9am–12:45pm & 1:45–6pm Tue–Sun

Misión San Francisco Javier de Viggé-Biaundó
🏠 23893 San Javier ⏰ 8am–5pm daily

BEACHES OF BAJA

Playa El Requesón
A dazzling sandbar in the Bahía Concepción near Mulegé.

Bahía Chileno
Best of the beaches between Cabo and San José (p173).

Playa Los Cerritos
This gorgeous bone-white beach lies south of Todos Santos (p173).

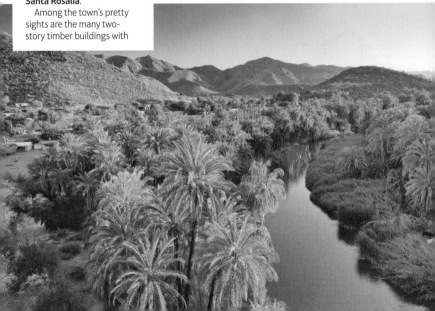

EAT

Taquería Hermanos González

La Paz is famous for its taco stands, and this one is a local legend. Also known as "Super Tacos de Baja California," it serves up tasty fried-fish and shrimp tacos with homemade salsa.

🅰E3 🏠Santos Degollado 110, La Paz 📞(612) 186 87 92

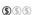

Rancho Viejo

One of the best taco joints in La Paz. Signature dishes include *arrachera* (steak) tacos and roast potatoes stuffed with cheese, mushrooms, and marinated pork.

🅰E3 🏠Márquez de León 228, La Paz 📞(612) 128 46 47

La Paz

🅰E3 🏠Baja California Sur ✈️🚌⛴ ℹ️Carretera Transpeninsular, Km. 5.5; www.lapaz.gob.mx

The capital of Baja California Sur, La Paz sits beside the largest bay on the Sea of Cortés, at the foot of a peninsula endowed with some excellent, and often half-deserted, beaches. Its curving, 3-mile (5-km) *malecón* (waterfront promenade) is lined with palm trees, hotels, and restaurants and is a lovely place for a stroll.

La Paz owes its foundation to the abundance of pearls in nearby waters, and its fortunes have often risen and fallen with those of the pearl industry. Nowadays its economy increasingly relies on tourism and its status as a premier sportfishing spot.

La Paz's **Museo Regional de Antropología e Historia** has interesting displays on pre-Hispanic rock paintings and other aspects of Baja's indigenous heritage, as well as on its struggle for independence.

The **Centro Cultural La Paz**, housed in the restored 1910 Palacio Municipal, has Baja-themed exhibitions.

Fine beaches lie between La Paz and the port of Pichilingue. The most pristine is Playa de Balandra, while Playa de Tecolote attracts locals at the weekend.

The nearby islands are popular with divers for their reefs, caves, and shipwrecks, and many also have fine beaches. Isla Espíritu Santo offers fantastic sailing opportunities and the chance to swim with wild sea lions. Fin whales and whale sharks are common from November to March; Baja Outdoor Activities in La Paz is a dependable operator (*www.kayactivities.com*).

Museo Regional de Antropología e Historia

 🏠Corner of 5 de Mayo and Altamirano 📞(612) 122 01 62 🕐9am–6pm daily

Centro Cultural La Paz

🏠16 de Septiembre 120 📞(612) 122 00 65 🕐8am–8pm Mon–Fri, 10am–6pm Sat

---

Cabo San Lucas

🅰F3 🏠Baja California Sur 🚌 ℹ️visitaloscabos.travel

In Cabo San Lucas it often seems that the official language is English due to the large numbers of foreign tourists. The town is famous for its romantic "Lovers' Beach." Accessible by boat, it is set among the jagged rocks known as Los Frailes (The Friars), which seem to form the tip of the peninsula. The beach is framed by a rock archway considered to link the waters of the Pacific with those of the Sea of Cortés.

One of the world's best game-fishing locations, the town has a sizable marina and a waterfront strip crowded with bars, clubs, and restaurants. Farther inland, much of Cabo San Lucas's old town remains intact.

Beach activities are concentrated on the long Playa El Médano, where the swimming is safest and jet-skis can be rented. The diving is excellent around Los Frailes, where there is an immense underwater canyon.

Between Cabo San Lucas and San José del Cabo are a number of top-class golf courses and some absolutely stunning beaches.

 11

Todos Santos

 E3 ⬆ Baja California Sur ℹ Plaza San José, San José del Cabo; www.todos santos.com

The wonderfully preserved old town of Todos Santos is packed with cafés and art galleries. On the main road, Juárez, is Hotel California. This 1950s gem features Mexican and Mudéjar decor – though claims that this is the hotel from the Eagles' famous 1970s song have been denied.

Plaza Todos Santos marks the heart of town, and is home to the attractive colonial-era Misión de Nuestra Señora del Pilar de la Paz. Although the church was mostly rebuilt in the 1960s, the revered image of Mary inside is thought to date back to the 1730s.

On nearby beaches, it's possible for visitors to watch the release of turtles by Tortugueros Las Playitas (www.todostortugueros.org), which runs a successful sea turtle recovery program. Make sure that you watch from a distance and do not interfere with the turtle release, as this is harmful to the animals.

 12

San José del Cabo

 F3 ⬆ Baja California Sur ✈🚌 ℹ Plaza San José; www.loscabos.gob.mx

The town of San José del Cabo is centered around the shady Plaza Mijares, where there is an arts and crafts market on weekends. To the south, the streets slope downward to the beachfront boulevard with its modern tourist hotels, condos, and resort complexes. On the east side of the town is a palm-fringed estuary, home to over 200 different species of birds. To the east is the village of Pueblo la Playa, which has beautiful white-sand beaches, often deserted.

A weekly Art Walk is held at 5pm on Thursdays from November to June (www. artcabo.com), offering a great introduction to the town's art scene. Local galleries stay open late, including the lauded Frank Arnold Gallery (Comonfort 1137).

WHALE-WATCHING

Two dozen species of cetaceans are found off the Baja coasts, from the small vaquita to the world's largest animal, the blue whale. These magnificent mammals can be spotted with binoculars from several vantage points along the shore at Guerrero Negro, or in the whale sanctuaries of the Vizcaíno Biosphere Reserve. You can also join an organized whale-watching trip, but be sure to choose a reputable company that will not approach the creatures too closely (p39).

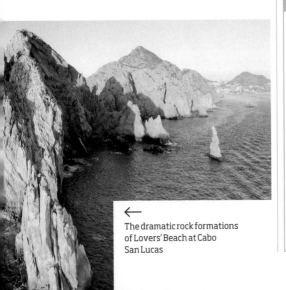

← The dramatic rock formations of Lovers' Beach at Cabo San Lucas

NORTHERN MEXICO

With its stark mountains and arid plains, giant cacti, and men on horseback, the north is the Mexico of popular imagination. Two mountain ranges – the eastern and western Sierra Madre – cross this great territory, and between them lies the Chihuahuan Desert, the largest in North America. The region is delimited to the north by the 1,950-mile (3,140-km) border with the United States. Receiving influences from the cultures on either side of it, the border region – almost a third of the country – is defined by its unique blend of languages, music, and food.

Though no great pre-Hispanic civilization ever developed in this region, contemporary indigenous communities, such as the Rarámuri, hold on to a traditional way of life quite apart from modern Mexican society. And while the land is sparsely-populated and often austere, the mountains pf northern Mexico conceal beautiful places where cool pine forests, placid lakes, and thunderous waterfalls can be found. The incredible Copper Canyon is traversed by one of the world's most spectacular railroads, known as "El Chepe."

NORTHERN MEXICO

Must Sees
1 Paquimé
2 Copper Canyon

Experience More
3 Chihuahua
4 Hermosillo
5 Mazatlán
6 Monterrey
7 Álamos
8 Durango
9 Saltillo
10 Hidalgo del Parral

① ✏️

PAQUIMÉ

Ⓐ F1 **Ⓐ** 5 miles (8 km) SW of Casas Grandes, Chihuahua **Ⓒ** (55) 55 12 25 93
Ⓞ 9am–5pm Tue–Sun

**The enigmatic ruins of Paquimé are the most significant remains of
a sophisticated civilization in northern Mexico. Isolated and hard to
reach, the site is often deserted; its simple adobe houses, ballcourts,
and plazas, surrounded by arid hills, create a haunting experience.**

This extraordinary complex of adobe buildings, set on a plateau overlooking the Casas Grandes River, is quite unlike other central and southern Mexican sites. The site flourished between the 10th and 14th centuries and probably housed over 3,000 people. Its partial destruction by fire in about 1340 and the disappearance of its inhabitants before the arrival of the Spanish have yet to be fully explained.

At the entrance is the Museo de las Culturas del Norte, which has been designed to mimic the ruins of the defence towers that once stood here. It contains original ceramics as well as a model of the city as it would have looked in its heyday. Beyond here you can tour the ruins via a self-guided trail. The signage is in English and Spanish.

Walls of packed earth, up to 5 ft (1.5 m) thick, a mazelike construction, and "apartment buildings" as much as five floors high with internal staircases are among the site's characteristic features. The houses also contain stoves for heating and beds in the form of alcoves. Low doorways in the shape of a thick "T" may have been partly for defence purposes. An impressive network of channels brought spring water from 5 miles (8 km) away for filtration and storage in deep wells. From here it was channeled to domestic and agricultural users, while another system of conduits drained away the waste. The inhabitants of Paquimé raised macaws for ceremonial purposes. The low, adobe pens with circular entrances, in which the birds were kept, remain intact.

←

A Paquimé
pot, found
at the site

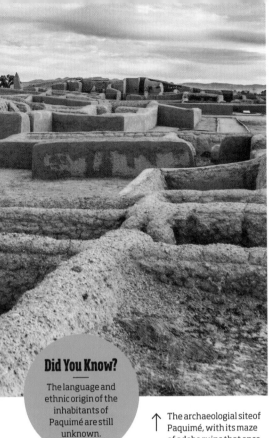

A PIECE OF PAQUIMÉ

Unique to Paquimé is a particularly fine type of pottery, which is distinguished by a high polish and geometric or anthropomorphic designs. The most typical colors are black and reddish brown on a buff background. Many examples of this pottery have been discovered at the archaeological site and are on display in the museum. Today, the style has been revived by local potters, some of whom request high prices for a single piece. More modestly priced pieces can be bought in the nearby town of Casas Grandes Viejo. The pots are made by hand using the pinching method, whereby a ball of clay is pinched into a round flat shape, then pressed into a bowl shape.

Did You Know?

The language and ethnic origin of the inhabitants of Paquimé are still unknown.

↑ The archaeologial site of Paquimé, with its maze of adobe ruins that once housed thousands

① Visitors are often able to explore the ancient adobe buildings at Paquimé completely undisturbed.

② The sheer size of the ancient adobe walls can only be fully appreciated when standing next to them.

③ The Cultural Museum features exhibitions that offer a fascinating insite into this sophisticated civilization.

2

COPPER CANYON

 F2 🏠 Chihuahua 🚆🚌 🌐 visitmexico.com

The rugged mountains of the Sierra Tarahumara contain a system of mesmerizing canyons. Collectively known as the Copper Canyon, the main gorges have depths of more than 6,561 ft (2,000 m). Riding the Copper Canyon railway, you'll be transported from sweat-soaked plains to cool pine-smothered mountains. Hidden within the valleys are bubbling cascades, historic missions, and villages that haven't changed in decades.

① Creel

🏠 Chihuahua **ℹ** Artesanías Misión, Av Tarahumara, Centro; (635) 429 33 20

Redolent of wood smoke and fresh mountain air, the small logging town of Creel is the main road and rail gateway to the largely unspoiled Sierra Tarahumara and the Copper Canyon. While small (it has only 4,000 inhabitants), Creel is an excellent place to join the spectacular El Chepe railroad (p182), or to disembark and spend a few days exploring the pine-clad mountains. However, adventurous travelers looking for outdoor activities should note that winters can be extremely cold in Creel, as this town stands at an altitude of over 7,550 ft (2,300 m).

Near the railroad station are the town plaza and Creel's main street, Calle López Mateos. Two churches stand on the square along with the Artesanías Misión shop, which gives informal advice to visitors as well as selling crafts made by the local indigenous community, the Rarámuri (also known as the Tarahumara).

On the other side of the railroad tracks is the **Casa de las Artesanías**, an interesting government-run museum and craft shop housed in a former railway station. Displays cover a variety of crafts from the region ranging, the story of railway tycoon Enrique Creel (after whom the town is named), the numerous Jesuit missions in the area, and the culture of the Rarámuri. Most notable is the glass case that contains mummified bodies found in the nearby hills.

The perfect spot around the town for a relaxing stroll or a picnic is at Lago Arareco, which is just 3 miles (5 km) to the south. The U-shaped lake is totally surrounded by unusual rock formations and a fragrant pine forest. A few miles farther along the same road is the beginning

Cascada de ⑥ Basaseachi
16
25
227
Río Candameño
San Juanito
Bocoyna
Creel ①
Lago Arareco
Recohuata
Cascada Cusárare
El Divisadero ④
Cusárare
Bahuichivo
77
San Rafael
28
Chínipas
Río Urique
Río Chínipos
Cerocahui
③ El Chepe Railroad
Urique
209
⑤ Batopilas
25
El Descanso
Río El Fuerte
Río Urique
San Javier
Choix
Río San Miguel
② El Fuerte

0 kilometers   40
0 miles   40
N ↑

↑ The rugged mountain peaks of the spectacular Copper Canyon

 Must See

TOP 3 WAYS TO EXPLORE

Horseback
⌂ Hotel Paraiso del Oso, Cerocahui, Chihuahua
ⓦ mexicohorse.com
Experience the canyons on horseback, a truly traditional way to travel in this old cowboy country.

Mountain Bike
⌂ 46 Avenida Lopez Mateos, Creel, Chihuahua
ⓦ amigos3.com
Lake Arareco, the San Ignacio Mission, and surrounding attractions make easy day-trips by bike from Creel.

Train
El Chepe operates scenic train journeys through the canyons (p182).

of a 2.5-mile (4-km) trail that winds through a scenic canyon to Cascada Cusárare, a 100-ft (30-m) waterfall.

Other attractions within easy reach of Creel include the hot springs at Recohuata, some 12 miles (20 km) south, the Valle de los Hongos ("Valley of the Mushrooms"), which takes its name from the mushroom-shaped rock formations found here, and El Divisadero (p182), the viewpoint that looks out over the breathtaking Copper Canyon. Tours to various sights, including helicopter trips over the canyons, are available in town.

Casa de las Artesanías
⊗ ⓗ ⌂ Avenida Ferrocarril 178 ☎ (635) 456 00 80
🕓 9am–6pm daily (to 1pm Sun)

② **El Fuerte**

⌂ Sinaloa 🛈 Plaza de Armas; (698) 893 0349

Founded in the 16th century, El Fuerte is an enchanting colonial-era town with a river running through it. The town makes a far more appealing starting point to the Copper Canyon train ride than Los Mochis. The center, packed full of brightly painted houses, is small and easy to navigate on foot. The town focuses on the elegant Plaza de Armas, which features the grand Palacio Municipal, a modest 18th-century church, Iglesia Sagrado de Corazón, and the 17th-century fort (fuerte) itself. Though a replica of the original Spanish outpost, the Museo Fuerte Mirador contains historical artifacts, old photos, and local Yoreme arts and crafts. There are splendid views of the town from here.

Among several stories associated with El Fuerte, is the legend of the masked bandit El Zorro, which became popular thanks to the movies. It is believed that Don Diego de la Vega (El Zorro) was born in the town, and lived there for some years.

THE RARÁMURI

The Rarámuri (also called the Tarahumara) moved up into the mountains of the Sierra Madre Occidental about 400 years ago to avoid the Spanish missionaries. Since then, they have kept themselves very much apart from the rest of Mexico, preferring to live in small self-sufficient farming communities. The name Rarámuri means "runners", and the culture is known for its traditional sport of rarajipari, which involves teams of runners kicking a wooden ball for huge distances across rugged mountain slopes. Participants wear sandals on their feet, and matches can last for several days.

↑ A train making its way through the Copper Canyon with (inset) passengers enjoying the ride

③

El Chepe Railroad

🚉 Multiple stations 🕐 Wed
🌐 chepe.com.mx

One of the world's great railroads, the Chihuahua al Pacífico ("El Chepe" for short) took almost a century to complete. With 86 tunnels and 37 bridges, this engineering marvel was conceived in the days before the Panama Canal was a fast route across the continent. It takes around 13 hours to travel the 415 miles (670 km) from Chihuahua to Los Mochis on the Pacific coast. The most spectacular scenery is between Creel and El Fuerte, a stretch that drops more than 6,550 ft (2,000 m).

Most people see the Copper Canyon area by train, and there are two to choose from. The Chepe Express is a luxury tourist service between Los Mochis and Creel (with stops at El Fuerte and Divisadero only). The Chepe Regional, much cheaper but still comfortable, runs the full route between Los Mochis and Chihuahua. Note that each train only runs in each direction three days a week (see website for details).

④

El Divisadero

🚉 Chihuahua, 80 miles
(131 km) S of Creel 🚉

El Chepe trains stop for 15 minutes to allow passengers to admire the jaw-dropping "one-hundred-mile" vista into the precipitous depths canyons at El Divisadero, a tiny station high in the mountains. It is true that Divisadero is basically just a train stop but there are some little food and souvenir stalls and next to the viewpoint, with its own great views and a restaurant, is a hotel for those who wish to spend longer contemplating the magnificent panorama. Minibus tours can also be arranged to the viewpoint.

🔍 HIDDEN GEM
The Lost Mission

An easy hike along the canyon from Batopilas, the 18th-century Misión de San Miguel de Satevó stands in a desolate landscape of cactuses and scrub. A testament to the zeal of the Jesuit missionaries who came here in the 1600s, it was abandoned for decades before being restored in the 1990s.

⑤
Batopilas

 Chihuahua

Barely more than a single street wide, and clinging to the riverbank at the bottom of a mile (1.5-km) deep canyon, Batopilas is one of Mexico's hidden treasures. And it was treasure, in the form of silver, that brought the Spanish, and later the noted US politician Alexander Shepherd, to this remote spot. Although once a wealthy silver mining town, today Batopilas is popular as a base for hiking excursions in the canyons.

Not the least remarkable fact about this place is that it was built when the only way in and out was by mule train over the mountains. Today, it can still take three hours to traverse the 37 miles (60 km) of dirt road that link Batopilas with the Creel-to-Guachochi highway. As it descends, the road drops over 7,000 ft (2,100 m) down the canyon wall via a hair-raising sequence of bends.

Batopilas was the birthplace of Manuel Gómez Morín, who formed PAN (Partido de Acción Nacional), the main opposition party to the long-running PRI. There is little more than a plaque and a bust to mark the fact, but monuments to another former resident, Alexander Shepherd, abound. Shepherd, the last governor of Washington DC, created the Batopilas Mining Company in the 1890s. The ruins of his home, Hacienda San Miguel, now overgrown with wild fig and bougainvillea, lie just across the river from the town entrance. Much of the aqueduct he built is still intact, and his hydroelectric plant, which made Batopilas the second electrified town in Mexico, is working again. The Hacienda Rio Batopilas, which is now an upscale hotel, is another noteworthy edifice with fanciful colonnades and arches.

---

⑥
Cascada de Basaseachi

Chihuahua, 124 miles (200 km) N of Creel

🕐 5am–10pm daily

A three-hour drive northwest of Creel is the dramatic Basaseáchic Falls. At almost 1,000 ft (300 m) high, this is the third highest waterfall in North America. The towering falls are surrounded by a vast national park, with excellent walking trails and campgrounds, as well as other waterfalls. Visit in the rainy season (mid-June to August), when the falls are fullest (May is the driest month).

→ The beautiful Cascade de Basaseachi, tumbling down the rock face to a pool below

EXPERIENCE MORE

❸
Chihuahua

F2 ⬛ Chihuahua ✈🚗🚌
ℹ Palacio de Gobierno;
www.chihuahua.gob.mx

The ghosts of two Mexican heroes, Pancho Villa and Father Miguel Hidalgo (p59), seem to haunt the streets of Chihuahua. Set among rugged hills in a semi-desert landscape, it owes its foundation to the rich veins of silver discovered nearby in the colonial period. The city's aqueduct, referred to by locals as "los arquitos" (the arches), dates from that era. Its best-preserved section is at the intersection of Calle 56 and Calle Allende.

The Plaza de Armas, the main square of Chihuahua, is dominated by the cathedral. This impressive, twin-towered building in rose-colored stone dates from the 18th century. Its 1920s altar of Italian marble is particularly fine. A side chapel contains a museum of religious art, open on weekdays.

The Palacio de Gobierno on Plaza Hidalgo (to the northeast of the main square) is a late-19th-century building. Its courtyard features striking murals by Aarón Piña Mora that illustrate episodes from Chihuahuan history. There is also an eternal

flame commemorating independence hero Father Hidalgo – it marks the spot where he was executed in 1811 after leading a rebellion against the Spanish crown. Two blocks away, on Avenida Juárez, the Palacio Federal preserves within its walls the remains of the church tower that served as Hidalgo's cell. It contains a few poignant reminders of the priest's incarceration and fate, including a tiny lantern with which he illuminated the last few nights of his life.

Undoubtedly the best-known Chihuahuan resident was Francisco "Pancho" Villa,

the hero of the 1910–20 revolutionary war. The **Museo Histórico de la Revolución** features the bullet-riddled Dodge at whose wheel he met his end in 1923. The museum is situated in his former house, and much of his furniture and other household goods are still here. The galleries recount the story of the revolution.

Perhaps the finest house in the city is the Quinta Gameros, to the southeast of the Plaza de Armas, which houses the **Centro Cultural Universitario Quinta Gameros**. It is worth paying the admission price for this exquisite Art Nouveau mansion just to see the dining room with its fantastic wood carvings. The rooms upstairs house permanent exhibitions, including paintings and sculptures by Mexican artist Luis Aragón.

Exhibits in the **Museo Casa de Juárez** primarily focus on Benito Juárez and the three difficult years he spent here during the French Intervention.

Museo Histórico de la Revolución
♿ 📷 ⬛ Calle 10a 3010
📞 (614) 416 29 58 ⏰ 9am–1pm & 3–7pm Tue–Sat, 9am–5pm Sun

PANCHO VILLA (C 1878–1923)

A member of a bandit group as a young man, Francisco "Pancho" Villa became an influential leader of the revolution after joining the campaign to depose Porfirio Díaz in 1910. His excellent military strategies and charismatic leadership inspired great loyalty in his División del Norte army and made him a folk hero, particularly around Chihuahua where he had his headquarters. In 1920 Álvaro Obregón took power and encouraged Villa to retire to a hacienda in Canutillo (Durango). Three years later, on a trip into Hidalgo del Parral, he was assassinated.

← People relaxing in front of the attractive rose-colored cathedral of Chihuahua

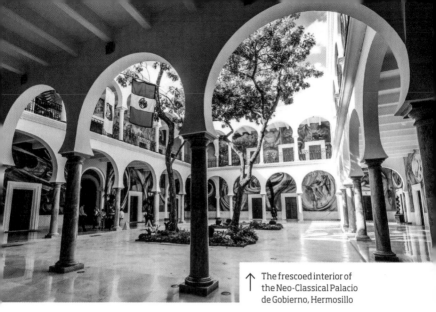

↑ The frescoed interior of the Neo-Classical Palacio de Gobierno, Hermosillo

Centro Cultural Universitario Quinta Gameros

🎨 ⓢ 🏠 Paseo Bolívar 401 📞 (614) 238 20 05 🕐 11am-7pm Tue-Sun

Museo Casa de Juárez

🎨 🏠 Juárez 321 📞 (614) 410 42 58 🕐 9am-6pm Tue-Sun

---

❹

Hermosillo

🅰 E2 🏠 Sonora 🚆🚌 ℹ Calle Comonfort; www.isc.gob.mx

Sonora's busy, thriving capital city – where cattle ranchers rub shoulders with car workers – has a quieter, prettier side too. Centered on the Plaza Zaragoza, with its lacy white bandstand, its outstanding

Did You Know?

The Chihuahua dog breed hails from Mexico. They likely descend from dogs bred by the Toltecs.

feature is the 19th-century cathedral with its twin towers and pale yellow dome, each surmounted by a cross. The cathedral's dazzling white facade is a blend of architectural styles, with Neo-Classical predominating. It is remarkably harmonious, considering it took over a century to build.

Opposite the cathedral, on the east side of the plaza, is the Neo-Classical **Palacio de Gobierno**. Equally stunning with its pure white facade, the palace contains frescoes that were painted in the 1980s by three artists whose inspiration ranged from indigenous creation myths to the Mexican Revolution.

Another half a mile (1 km) to the east, the **Museo de Sonora** resides in a beautifully restored building that was once the state penitentiary. Galleries cover the geology and ecology of the state and its development from pre-historic times to the present.

Dominating the city center is the Cerro de la Campana (Bell Hill). It is crowned by radio masts and illuminated at night. You can hike or take a taxi up to enjoy panoramic views over the city.

Palacio de Gobierno

🎨 🏠 Calle Comonfort 📞 (662) 213 11 70 🕐 Mon-Sat

Museo de Sonora

🎨 🏛 🏠 Jesús García Final 📞 (662) 217 27 14 🕐 10am-6pm Tue-Sat, 9am-4pm Sun

---

TOP 4 REGIONAL FIESTAS

Easter
The Rarámuri Easter ceremony in Cusarare and Norogachi is a re-enactment of the Crucifixion story.

Fiesta de las Flores
Floats display flowers and battle motifs at this spring festival in Nogales.

Día de la Marina
Guaymas hosts mock naval battles on June 1 to honor the Mexican navy.

Nuestra Señora del Refugio
In Durango, men in long animal-skin tunics perform the Matachines dance on July 4.

↑ Sunbathers on the sandy shorefront of Mazatlán

⑤

Mazatlán

 F3 Sinaloa 🚗🚌
ℹ Av del Mar 882, Tellería;
www.gomazatlan.com

Mazatlán is one of Mexico's most northerly major resorts. An agreeable climate and almost 12 miles (20 km) of beaches make it extremely popular. Another attraction is the Mazatlán Pre-Lent Carnival, claimed to be the third largest in the world, after those of Rio and New Orleans.

A waterfront boulevard connects the narrow streets and 19th-century architecture

of the old town with the expensive beach hotels of the touristic Zona Dorada (Golden Zone). Of the offshore islands, Venados, Lobos, and Pájaros all offer an enticing combination of wildlife and uncrowded, sandy beaches, and are easily and cheaply reached by small boats. The misleadingly named Isla de la Piedra, however, is not actually an island but a peninsula across the estuary. Famous for its sandy beaches fringed with coconut palms, it is the site of one of Mexico's largest tourist developments, the Estrella de Mar.

Historic Mazatlán is worth visiting for its beautifully restored, Italianate Teatro Ángela Peralta named after a famous Mazatlán-born opera singer, and its intriguing cathedral – Neo-Gothic on the outside, exuberantly Baroque on the inside. Both buildings date from the 19th century. However, Mazatlán's oldest church is the Iglesia de San José, built in 1842 on the slopes of the Cerro de la Nevería (Icebox Hill). The hill,

> **Mazatlán's waterfront boulevard connects the narrow streets of the old town with the expensive beach hotels of the Zona Dorada (Golden Zone).**

which offers a spectacular view of the city by day or night, acquired its name from the 19th-century practice of storing imported ice in a tunnel carved into the hillside.

For sensational views over Mazatlán, it's worth hiking to the top of the Cerro de Crestón, the dramatic peak at the southern edge of the city, which is topped by a lighthouse (El Faro).

Note that as of 2020, the US government's travel advisory for the state of Sinaloa is Level 4, meaning "Do Not Travel"; this is due to high crime levels in the region. When visiting Mazatlán, it's advisable to keep your explorations to the Zona Dorada and historic town center.

 GREAT VIEW
Sky Room

Have an evening drink in the panoramic bar of the Hotel Posada Freeman (Olas Altas 79) for awe-inspiring views over Mazatlán's old town, with lights twinkling along the *malecón* (esplanade).

Monterrey

🅰C2 🅰Nuevo León ✈🚌
ℹ Washington 2000
Oriente; www.nl.gob.mx

Mexico's third largest city, Monterrey is a thriving commercial center ringed by jagged mountain peaks. It is home to some striking contemporary skyscrapers, including T.Op Torre 1, the nation's tallest building (1,002 ft/305 m).

On the Gran Plaza, MARCO (Museo de Arte Contemporáneo) houses Latin American modern art. Also on the plaza, the Catedral Metropolitana contains vivid murals created by Mexican painter Ángel Zárraga in the 1940s. The Museo del Palacio occupies the Palacio de Gobierno, with exhibits charting the history of the state. It has two sister museums: the Museo de Historia Mexicana focuses on national history, while the Museo del Noreste covers the history of northeast Mexico.

The main attraction of the Parque Fundidora is the Museo del Acero Horno-3, a remarkable museum built out of the remains of a steel mill, tracing the history of Monterrey's steel industry.

East of the Gran Plaza lies Barrio Antiguo, the oldest part of downtown, sprinkled with painted adobe houses, art galleries, bars, and clubs.

The beautifully renovated Obispado, the old bishop's palace, tops the hill to the west of downtown Monterrey. Completed in 1787, it now contains the Museo Regional de Nuevo León.

Monterrey is also home to Cervecería Cuauhtémoc Moctezuma brewery, established in 1890.

MARCO

 🅰Corner Zuazua and Jardón �🕐10am-6pm Tue-Sun (to 8pm Wed)
🆆marco.org.mx

Palacio de Gobierno

🅰5 de Mayo s/n 🕐10am-8pm Tue & Sun, 10am-6pm Wed-Sat 🆆3museos.com

Museo del Acero Horno-3

⊗ 🅰Parque Fundidora 🕐10am-6pm Tue-Thu, 11am-7pm Fri-Sun 🆆horno3.org

Obispado

🅰Calle Rafael J. Vergel 1730 📞(818) 346 04 04

---

⑦ Álamos

🅰F2 🅰Sonora 🚌
ℹ Guadalupe Victoria 5; (647) 428 04 50

A colonial-era jewel, on the western edge of the Sierra Madre Occidental, Álamos owed its fame and fortune to the silver discovered here in the 17th century. However, its restoration is largely due to a community of US immigrants.

It is the restored Sonoran mansions, with their interior patios and large windows with wrought-iron grilles, that give the town its flavor. Tours of some of these homes take place every Saturday.

Other Álamos highlights include the Baroque Parroquia de la Purísima Concepción. Its bell tower has china plates, allegedly donated by local women, embedded in its walls. Sadly, most of the plates were broken in the revolution. The nearby **Museo Costumbrista** charts local history, while the **Museo María Félix** is a small homage to local-born María Félix (1914–2002), a legendary Mexican actress who starred in almost 50 films over a 28-year career.

Museo Costumbrista

 🅰Guadalupe Victoria 1 📞(647) 428 00 53 🕐10am-6pm Wed-Sun

Museo María Félix

⊗ 🅰Francisco I. Madero 310 🕐10am-4pm Wed-Sun

↑ The Baroque Parroquia de la Purísima Concepción in Álamos

⑧ Durango

ⒶG3 **Ⓜ**Durango **✕⊠**
🛈Florida 1106, Barrio
del Calvario; www.
visitdurango.mx

This city's main attraction
is its association with the
movie industry, particularly
1950s' Westerns. Many of its
restaurants and shops have
cowboy themes.

On the north flank of Plaza
de Armas stands the Baroque
cathedral. A few blocks west is
the Palacio de Gobierno, known
for its striking set of 20th-
century murals. The Casa de
Cultural Banamex, a late-18th-
century mansion east of the
plaza, now houses a museum
where the original interior can
still be seen. The exquisite Art
Nouveau Teatro Ricardo
Castro holds what is reputedly
the country's largest hand-
carved relief made from a
single piece of wood.

The 18th-century Palacio de
Zambrano is now the **Museo
General Francisco Villa**,

HOLLYWOOD IN MEXICO

Clear blue skies and
magical, semidesert
landscapes made
Durango a favorite
location for the movie
industry for many
years, especially for
Westerns. The stars
who have filmed here
range from John Wayne
and Kirk Douglas to
Anthony Quinn and Jack
Nicholson. Some of the
best-known movies
shot near Durango
include John Huston's
The Unforgiven and
Sam Peckinpah's *The
Wild Bunch* and *Pat
Garrett and Billy the Kid*.
A few Hollywood
locations can be visited,
including the Villa del
Oeste (officially called
Condado Chávez).

1898

The year Durango
was first used as a
film location.

which chronicles the history
of the region since the
Mexican Revolution. The
**Museo de Arte Guillermo
Ceniceros** preserves the
legacy of the eponymous
muralist, while the **Paseo
Túnel de Minería** celebrates
the city's mining heritage.

There are several Western
movie locations to visit
outside the city, most notably
Villa del Oeste.

Museo General Francisco Villa

⊘ **Ⓐ**5 de Febrero 800
🕙10am–6pm Tue–Fri, 11am–
6pm Sat & Sun **🌐**museo
villa.iced.mx

Museo de Arte Guillermo Ceniceros

⊘ **Ⓐ**Serdán 1225 **🕙**10am–
7pm Tue–Fri, 11am–6pm
Sat & Sun **🌐**guillermo
ceniceros.com

Paseo Túnel de Minería

⊘⊘ **Ⓐ**Calle Lic. Benito
Juárez 313 **☎**(618) 137 53 61
🕙10am–10pm Tue–Sun

Villa del Oeste

 ⒶMex 45, 7 miles (12 km)
N of Durango **☎**(618) 137 43
86 **🕙**Tue–Sun

⑨ Saltillo

ⒶB2 **Ⓜ**Coahuila **✕⊠**
🛈Calle Ignacio Allende 124;
www.saltillo.gob.mx

Dubbed "the city of columns"
because of the number of
buildings characterized by
Neo-Classical colonnades,
Saltillo is also famous for

what is probably the most
beautiful cathedral in
northeast Mexico. Dominating
the old Plaza de Armas, the
Churrigueresque facade of
the 18th century Catedral
de Santiago de Saltillo has
six columns richly embellished
with carved flowers, fruit, and
shells. The silverwork of the
font is so fine that the piece is
often exhibited elsewhere and
replaced in the cathedral by a
photograph.

On the opposite side of the
plaza is the state government
headquarters, the Palacio de
Gobierno, which contains a
mural charting the history of
Coahuila. The other building
of note in the center is the
Templo de San Esteban,
which stands out for its
attractive, tiled cupola, as
well as its history, as it served
as a hospital for injured
Mexican troops during the
US invasion of Mexico (*p60*).

Saltillo is also home to a
number of museums. The
Museo de las Aves de México,
is dedicated to the birds of
Mexico, and contains a
collection of stuffed birds,
covering over 670 different
species. The **Museo del
Desierto** aims to promote a
greater understanding of the

Catedral de Santiago de
Saltillo rising above the
rooftops of Saltillo

biodiversity of desert ecology. The fascinating **Museo de la Revolución Mexicana** chronicles the 1910 revolution, and the **Museo de los Presidentes Coahuilenses** honors the five Mexican presidents to hail from Coahuila.

Museo de las Aves de México

🔄 📷 🏠 Calle Hidalgo 151 ☎ (844) 414 01 67 🕐 10am-6pm Tue-Sat, 11am-6pm Sun

Museo del Desierto

🏠 Carlos Abedrop Dávila 3745 🕐 10am-5pm Tue-Sun 🌐 museodeldesierto.org

Museo de la Revolución Mexicana

🏠 Hidalgo Sur 167 ☎ (844) 410 47 94 🕐 10am-6pm Tue-Sun

Museo de los Presidentes Coahuilenses

🏠 Nicolás Bravo Sur 264 🕐 10am-6pm Tue-Sun 🌐 museopresidentes.org.mx

> Dubbed "the city of columns" because of the number of buildings characterized by Neo-Classical colonnades, Saltillo is also famous for its beautiful cathedra.

⑩
Hidalgo del Parral

🅰 F2 🏠 Chihuahua 🚌 ℹ Mina La Prieta; (627) 525 44 00

Most famous as the site of Pancho Villa's murder, Parral (as it is usually known) was founded in 1631. It owes its existence to the gold and silver mines, and at the end of the 19th century it was one of the most opulent cities in Mexico. Its churches are noted for the chunks of ore that went into their construction.

At the corner of Calle Primo de Verdad and Riva Palacio is the splendid **Casa de Alvarado**, built at the start of the 20th century. Notice the anguished face over the main door, which is said to be that of a local mine worker.

Casa de Alvarado

🏠 Calle Riva Palacio No 2 ☎ (627) 522 02 90 🕐 10am-5pm daily

BAJÍO AND THE CENTRAL COAST

After defeating the Aztec empire in 1521, Spanish soldiers marched across central Mexico to conquer the region's nomadic indigenous tribes. Missionaries also came to spread Christianity, and adventurers to seek their fortune. Soon, opulent, Spanish-style cities were founded in the area, some becoming the principal suppliers of silver and gold to the Spanish royal family. In the early 19th century, general discontent with Spanish rule began to simmer here, and the first armed uprising by rebels earned the region the title "the Cradle of Independence." Ferocious battles were fought in the cities of Guanajuato and Morelia, until Mexico declared its independence from Spain in 1821.

This Mexican heartland – known as Bajío – remains a relatively prosperous region, thanks to its rich agricultural lands, thriving industry, and increasingly popular tourist attractions. Charming, well-preserved towns built during colonial times characterize the states, where sun-drenched coastlines and humid jungles adjoin cactus-strewn mesas and snow-capped volcanoes.

BAJÍO AND THE CENTRAL COAST

Pacific Ocean

0 kilometers 100
0 miles 100

N
↑

GUADALAJARA

A B4 **A** Jalisco ☒ 📧 **ℹ** Morelos 102; (33) 3668 16 00

In the 20th century, an industrial boom transformed Guadalajara from a provincial city into a modern metropolis. A broad industrial belt and sprawling suburbs now ring the center, but downtown around the cathedral, the colonial-era plazas and gardens seem unchanged since the days of the conquistadors.

① Mercado Libertad

A Dionisio Rodríguez 52 **◷** 8am–8pm daily

The largest indoor market in Latin America opened in 1958, a seemingly chaotic warren of stalls. Just about every product imaginable is sold, from tacky souvenirs to dried iguanas – be sure to haggle. The lower levels are dedicated to food and cheap restaurants.

② Cathedral Basílica

A Plaza de Armas

Construction of this enormous cathedral began shortly after Guadalajara was founded in 1542. However, it was not finished until the early 17th century, and then in a medley of styles. Two earthquakes, in 1750 and 1818, destroyed the original facade and towers. They were replaced in the mid-19th century by the present yellow-tiled twin spires.

③ Museo Regional de Guadalajara

A Calle Liceo 60 **☎** (33) 613 27 03 **◷** 9am–5pm Tue–Sun

A lovely former seminary dating from 1699 is now the home of the Regional Museum of Guadalajara. The galleries have displays on palaeontology, archaeology, and prehistory. Exhibits include a complete mammoth skeleton, and a replica of a shaft tomb discovered in Zapopan. Upstairs are displays about indigenous cultures and paintings by Jalisco artists from the colonial era to the present day.

④ Palacio de Gobierno

A Corner of Moreno and Avenida Corona **☎** (33) 366 818 02 **◷** 9am–6pm Mon–Fri

The Baroque Government Palace is the seat of the Jalisco state government. Murals by José Clemente Orozco adorn the main staircase, the dome of the former chapel, and the upstairs congress chambers. They celebrate independence hero Miguel Hidalgo, who proclaimed the abolition of slavery in Mexico here in 1810.

⑤ Instituto Cultural Cabanas

A Cabañas 8 **◷** 10am–6pm Tue–Sun **W** hospicio cabanas.jalisco.gob.mx

Founded in 1805 and now a UNESCO World Heritage site,

← Guadalajara's imposing cathedral, facing onto the Plaza de Armas

this former hospice is the largest Spanish Colonial edifice in the Americas and one of Mexico's finest Neo-Classical buildings. The structure, with its central dome and 22 courtyards, was the work of Manuel Tolsá.

For most of its history, the site was an orphanage, housing up to 3,000 children. In 1979 it was restored and turned into an exhibition center and a school for the performing and fine arts.

Frescoes by José Clemente Orozco, executed in the late 1930s, cover the interior of the former chapel, with the central *Man in Flames* in the dome. These masterworks take as their themes the Conquest, political terror, and the dehu-manization of modern man.

The Plaza Tapatía, fronting the building, marks the end of a pedestrian zone extending from the cathedral. Nearby is Mercado Libertad, which is one of Latin America's largest covered markets.

MARIACHI MUSIC

Modern mariachi music emerged in Jalisco in the 19th century - don't leave Guadalajara without hearing it played live at the Plaza de los Mariachis. Mariachi bands stroll between the no-frills bars of this short pedestrianized street (be prepared to pay for a song). Friday and Saturday nights are the best times to visit.

⑥ Basílica de Zapopan

🏛 **Calle Eva Briseño 152, Zapopan, 4 miles (7 km) NW of center** 📞 **(33) 3633 66 14** 🕑 **7am–9pm for mass daily**

The early 18th-century Basílica de Zapopan is home to one of the most revered religious relics in Mexico, the Virgen de Zapopan. The small corn-paste statue was presen-ted to the local indigenous people by a Franciscan friar in the 16th century and is believed to bring relief from natural catastrophes.

⑦ 🖐 Museo Huichol Wixárika de Zapopan

🏛 **Calle Eva Briseño 152** 📞 **(33) 3636 44 30** 🕑 **10am–2pm & 3–6pm Mon–Sat, 9am–2pm Sun**

This small museum next to the basilica displays Huichol (Wixáritari) traditional clothing and artifacts. It also sells handi-crafts, including shamanic yarn paintings *(cuadros de estambre)*, and beaded prayer bowls *(kuka or chaquira)*. The entrance is in the arcade to the right of the basilica entrance.

❷

GUANAJUATO

🅰B4 🏠Guanajuato ✈🚌 ℹ️ Plaza de la Paz 14; (473) 732 24 64

One of Mexico's most beautiful colonial-era cities climbs out of a rugged ravine and up bald hills that once supplied a quarter of New Spain's silver output. Its illustrious past as a rich and influential mining city is easily visible in the incredible buildings found along the maze of streets and alleys in the historic center.

①

Teatro Juárez

🏠Sopena s/n 📞 (473) 732 25 21 🕙10am-6pm Tue-Sun

Statues of the Muses crown the facade of this Neo-Classical theater. Below them a wide stairway flanked by bronze lions leads up to a stately foyer and Moorish-style auditorium. This is the main venue for the Festival Cervantino held in October. Music, dance, and theater groups from all over the world gather in Guanajuato for this cultural highlight dedicated to the Spanish writer Miguel Cervantes, creator of

Don Quixote. It began in the 1950s with Cervantes inspired plays staged by students here. The city's Spanish Colonial buildings provide settings for performances, which feature period costumes and horses.

---

②

Museo de las Momias

🏠Explanada del Panteón 🕙9am-6pm Mon-Thu (to 6:30pm Fri-Sun) 🌐momias-deguanajuato.gob.mx

Northwest of the center of Guanajuato is this macabre museum, which owes its

popularity to the Mexican obsession with death. In cavernous rooms it exhibits over 100 gruesome-looking mummies with gaunt and twisted faces, disinterred from a nearby cemetery where they had mummified naturally.

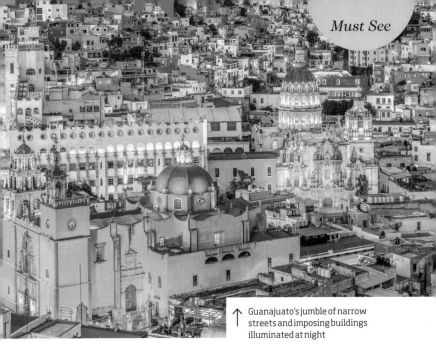

↑ Guanajuato's jumble of narrow streets and imposing buildings illuminated at night

③
Museo Ex-Hacienda de San Gabriel de la Barrera

◪ Marfil, 1.5 miles (2.5 km) SW of city ◷ 9am-6pm daily ☎ (473) 732 06 19

This restored hacienda was built in the late 17th century for the wealthy Barrera family. It is now a museum displaying European furniture from the 17th to the 19th centuries. The grounds have been converted into 17 gardens, each beautifully landscaped in a range of international styles, including English, Italian, Roman, Arabic, and Mexican.

 GREAT VIEW
El Pípila

For an awe-inspiring view of the city, take the funicular from behind Teatro Juárez up to the Monumento al Pípila, a statue honoring a local independence hero. The view is magical at sunset.

④
Museo del Pueblo

◪ Positos 7 ☎ (473) 732 29 90 ◷ 10am-7pm Tue-Sat, 10am-3pm Sun

The former home of a wealthy mine owner is one of the city's finest buildings. The building now exhibits art pieces from pre-Hispanic to modern times, concentrating on colonial-era religious objects.

⑤
Mercado Hidalgo

◪ Juárez, at Mendizábal ◷ 8am-9pm daily

Guanajuato's main indoor market, the Mercado Hidalgo, is a huge iron-framed construction completed in 1910. If it seems reminiscent of Victorian train stations that's because it was originally supposed to be one (the rail project was never completed). Today, it's packed with all sorts of produce and is a great place to eat, with numerous stalls selling cheap Mexican street food.

⑥
Basílica de Nuestra Señora de Guanajuato

◪ Calle Ponciano Aguilar 7 ☎ (473) 732 03 14

This 17th-century church houses a sculpture of the city's patron saint, the Virgin Mary. It was given to the city by Charles I and Philip II of Spain in 1557. Reputed to date from the 7th century, it is thought to be the oldest piece of Christian art in Mexico.

The church interior is striking in the evening when it is lit by Venetian chandeliers.

→ The basilica's impressive sculpture of the Virgin Mary

Mural by José Chávez Morado, a highlight at Alhóndiga de Ganaditas, and *(inset)* the building's central courtyard

(9)

Museo Iconográfico del Quijote

⌂ Manuel Doblado 1 ☎ (473) 732 67 21 ⏰ 9am-7pm Tue-Sat, noon-7pm Sun

Art pieces relating to Don Quixote, from postage stamps to murals, are displayed here. The collection includes works by Dalí, Picasso, and Daumier.

(7)

Alhóndiga de Granaditas

⌂ Mendizábal 6 ☎ (473) 732 11 12 ⏰ 10am-6pm Tue-Sat, 10am-3pm Sun

This former granary, built at the end of the 18th century, was the site of the first major rebel victory of the War of Independence. In 1810, revolutionaries burned down the gates and killed most of the government troops barricaded inside. Reminders of the battle are the bullet-scarred walls and the hooks dangling from the building's four top corners, where the heads of four rebellion leaders were later hung.

The imposing building was later used as an armory and as a prison for 80 years. Today, it houses a regional museum covering art, ethnography, and archaeology. The staircase is decorated with murals by José Chávez Morado that depict the city's history.

(8)

Museo Palacio de los Poderes

⌂ Juárez 75 ☎ (473) 102 27 00 ⏰ 9:30am-5pm Thu-Sat, 9:30am-4pm Sun

This absorbing history museum occupies the opulent Palacio Legislativo, completed in 1903 to a design by English-born architect Louis Long. Visitors can view the beautifully preserved rooms, such as the Salón del Pleno (Plenary Hall) and the Salón Verde (Green Room), with ornate decor and original wooden furniture.

(10)

Casa Diego Rivera

⌂ Positos 47 ☎ (473) 732 11 97 ⏰ 10am-7pm Tue-Sat, 10am-3pm Sun

The house where Diego Rivera was born is now a museum dedicated to his life. His art fills the upstairs rooms, while the ground floor preserves the living area with its late 19th-century furniture and relics.

PARTY ON, GUANAJUATO

A fun way to explore the back alleys of Guanajuato is to join a *callejóneadas* tour. Students dressed as medieval minstrels play tunes and joke their way through the side streets, audience in tow. Most start at 8:30pm – tickets are required for drinks (you'll get a *porrón*, a drinking vessel, which is topped up as you walk). The spectacle is fun, but you'll need to speak Spanish to appreciate the jokes.

La Valenciana

📍 **Privada Cerro del Erizo, Valenciana 36230, 3 miles (5 km) N of city center**
📞 **(473) 101 54 20**
🕐 **10am-6pm Thu-Tue**

Silver and gold mining began here in the mid-1500s and boomed two centuries later after prospectors struck it rich at a shaft just to the west. The Bocamina de Valenciana, the original 1557 entrance shaft, is cut 330 ft (100 m) straight down into the rock. Visitors can climb down to half its depth on steep stairs over which miners once hauled up loads of ore-rich rocks on their backs. A small museum at the entrance tells the mine's history.

Museo Olga Costa-José Chávez Morado

📍 **Pastita 158, Torre del Arco** 📞 **(473) 731 09 77**
🕐 **9:30am-5pm Thu-Sat, 9:30am-4pm Sun**

The Mexican muralist José Chávez Morado (1909–2002) and his wife, German painter Olga Costa, once lived in the 17th-century Hacienda de Guadalupe, which is now a museum dedicated to their memory. The house contains some fine 18th-century majolica ceramics and glassware, 17th-century French furniture, and Persian wall hangings, but there's actually little of the couple's work on show. However, Morado's quirky stained-glass windows remain intact.

⑬
Templo de San Cayetano

📍 **Calle San José s/no, Mineral Km 1.5, Valenciana**
📞 **(473) 732 35 96**

Near La Valenciana mine is the city's most spectacular church. Also known as "La Valenciana," it was built between 1765 and 1788 with funds donated by the Count of Valenciana, owner of the nearby mine. Its pink limestone facade abounds with Churrigueresque pilasters. The Baroque interior has three splendid gold and polychrome altars and a pulpit inlaid with tortoiseshell and ivory.

EAT

Casa Mercedes
A cozy, candle-lit dining room helmed by lauded chef Jesús Cárdenas. An innovative menu of gourmet Mexican food features delights such as duck tacos and chicken in pistachio mole sauce. Book ahead.

📍 **Arriba 6, San Javier**
🌐 **casamercedes.com.mx**

$$$

DRINK

One Bar & Lounge
This stylish rooftop bar has enchanting views over the city, especially at night. Expect minimalist decor, exquisite cocktails, and DJs on weekends.

📍 **Jardín de la Unión 7**
📞 **(473) 732 27 95**

↑ One of three gold and polychrome altars in the Templo de San Cayetano

A SHORT WALK
GUANAJUATO

Distance 0.5 miles (1 km) **Time** 15 minutes
Nearest bus stop Guanajuato

Most of Guanajuato's main sights are located near the center of the city, and one of the pleasures of visiting this historic gem is strolling around its twisting streets on foot, while marveling at the ornate architecture. Rich mine owners studded the narrow, winding streets with stately Spanish Colonial mansions and imposing churches, and a later silver bonanza led to splendid 19th-century touches. The unique result is a center devoid of traffic lights and neon signs that was made a UNESCO World Heritage site in 1988.

Casa Diego Rivera (p198), *the house where Rivera was born in 1886, is now a museum exhibiting over 100 samples of his work, including sketches of his murals.*

Converted from a riverbed in 1965 to alleviate traffic problems, this subterranean street, **Calle Hidalgo**, *winds under the city center.*

Plaza de los Angeles *is a popular spot for students to gather.*

START

FINISH

Callejón del Beso *(Alley of the Kiss) is only 2 ft (69 cm) wide in places.*

Casa Rul y Valenciana, *a beautiful late 18th-century mansion, is now the courthouse.*

Did You Know?

Callejón del Beso is named for a legend about two secret lovers who were caught kissing here.

| 0 meters | 50 | N |
| 0 yards | 50 | ↑ |

↑ The striking Basilica de Nuestra Senora de Guanajuato

GUANAJUATO

Locator Map
For more detail see p196

Museo del Pueblo (p197) *houses a fine collection of regional art in a 17th-century mansion.*

The **University** *was remodeled in Moorish style in 1945. It was originally a Jesuit seminary, founded in 1732.*

The Neo-Classical dome of **Templo de la Compañía** *replaced one that had collapsed in 1808. It is now a city landmark. The facade is an early example of the Churrigueresque style.*

Plazuela del Baratillo *was once a busy marketplace. The fountain was a gift from Emperor Maximilian.*

LASCURÁIN DE RETANA

PLAZA DE LA PAZ

AYUNTAMIENTO

EL TRUCO

OBREGÓN

ALLENDE

The colorful **Basílica de Nuestra Señora de Guanajuato** (p197) *is an iconic city landmark.*

Laid out in 1861, the laurel-shaded **Jardín de la Unión** *is the heart of the city and a favorite meeting place. The municipal band plays here several times a week.*

Doric columns, giant statues, and an auditorium hung with velvet set the tone at the lavish **Teatro Juárez** (p196).

PLAZUELA DE LA CONSTANCIA

Iglesia de San Diego

3

ZACATECAS

⌖B3 **🏠Zacatecas** **✈🚌** **ℹAvenida Hidalgo 403; www.zacatecas.gob.mx**

The town of Zacatecas overflows with lavish Spanish Colonial architecture. Founded in 1546, shortly after the discovery of metal deposits in the area, Zacatecas was soon supplying silver to the Spanish crown. The city is remarkable for its Baroque limestone buildings that fill a narrow valley between steep, arid hills.

Aristocratic patrons of this silver mining town built many stately mansions, convents, and churches in Zacatecas. Its pink quarry stone buildings and elegant streets seem as if they have been plucked straight out of classical Spain. The best way to appreciate these treasures is by gliding over its red-roof tops by cable car. Silver financed the city's rapid rise in the 18th century, and its mines are now mostly tourist attractions, but it's the legacy of colonial-era wealth that today provides the real allure: a magnificent cathedral, grand mansions, and a cache of fine art museums. A lively market, fine restaurants, and good hiking opportunities add to the town's appeal.

Cathedral

🏠Avenida Hidalgo 617

The profuse decoration on the impressive three-tiered facade of the city's cathedral is considered the prime example of the Churrigueresque, or Ultra-Baroque architectural style (p42) in Mexico. Apostles, angels, flowers, and fruit adorn the pillars, pedestals, columns, and niches in excess. This exuberant exterior of the cathedral contrasts strangely with an interior whose treasures were lost in the turmoils of the Reform (p56) and, later, the revolution (p58). Most of the building was constructed between 1730 and 1775, but the northernmost of the two towers was not completed until 1904. The cathedral's two lateral facades are both comparatively sober. A crucified Christ adorns the one that faces north toward the Plaza de Armas.

---

②

Museo Rafael Coronel

🏠Cnr of Abasolo and Matamoros **☎(492) 922 81 16** **🕐10am-5pm Thu-Tue**

Another Coronel collection, this one by Pedro's brother Rafael, is held in the restored

↑ Ritual mask, part of a collection held at the Museo Rafael Coronel

Zacatecas with its colorful buildings and grand Churrigueresque cathedral

ruins of the Ex-Convento de San Francisco. An artist and a lover of folk art, Rafael Coronel amassed 10,000 ritual and dance masks from all over the country. About one-third of the collection is exhibited beside a mass of other fine examples of Mexican popular art, pre-Hispanic and colonial-era pottery, and architectural drawings and mural sketches by Diego Rivera.

---

③ 🖼

Museo Francisco Goitia

🏛 Enrique Estrada 102
☎ (492) 922 02 11
🕙 10am–5pm Tue–Sun

Paintings, silkscreens, and sculptures by the Coronel brothers and other Zacatecan

artists are exhibited in a Neo-Classical villa. On two floors connected by a breath-taking marble staircase, the amazing work of Francisco Goitia catches the eye. Until 1962, the house was used as the official residence of state governors. Allow time to stroll through the formal gardens, which overlook the Parque Enrique Estrada. This hilly park drops down to the remains of an 18th-century aqueduct and the Quinta Real hotel, which is built around the old bullring.

---

④ 🖼

Museo Pedro Coronel

🏛 Plaza de Santo Domingo
☎ (492) 922 80 21
🕙 10am–5pm Tue–Sun

The Zacatecan painter and sculptor, Pedro Coronel, is responsible for this unique art collection spanning a number of civilizations and continents, from Egyptian mummy cases to works by Goya and

Hogarth. All this is housed on the upper floors of a former Jesuit seminary. There is also a library of 25,000 volumes dating from the 16th to the 19th century.

Next to the museum stands the Templo de Santo Domingo. Its sober facade conceals a rich interior containing eight altarpieces of wood gilded in gold foil. In the octagonal sacristy, eight 18th-century paintings from the painter and gilder Francisco Martinez represent the most dramatic scenes from the Via Crucis (Stations of the Cross).

Must See

Did You Know?

Mexico is the world's leading producer of silver, thanks in large part to Zacatecas.

Stunning view of from Cerro de la the Bufa, and *(inset)* a cable car making its way up the hill

EAT

La Plaza

The incredible setting makes eating at this posh hotel restaurant truly memorable - it overlooks the historic bullring. It is known for its *zacatecano* - usually meaning a dish smothered with chilis and cream.

🏠 Hotel Quinta Real, Ignacio Rayón 434
📞 (492) 922 91 04

$$$

SHOP

Centro Platero de Zacatecas

The best place to buy silver lies within this former hacienda, south of central Zacatecas. Students and graduates of the on-site silversmith school create original silverwork designs to sell here.

🏠 Ex-Hacienda de Bernardez, Lomas de Bernardez, Guadalupe
🌐 centroplatero-dezacatecas.com

⑤
Museo Toma de Zacatecas

🏠 Cerro de la Bufa
🕐 10am–4:30pm daily
📞 (492) 922 80 66

The hill northeast of the city center, Cerro de la Bufa, was the scene of a bloody battle in 1914. The Museo Toma de Zacatecas at the summit exhibits items from the victory, which was won by Francisco "Pancho" Villa *(p184)*.

Cerro de la Bufa also offers splendid views from the *Teleferico* (cable car), which stretches around 650 m (2,130 ft) from here to the nearby hill Cerro del Grillo.

---

⑥
Eden Silver Mine

🏠 Antonio Dovali Jaime s/no 📞 (492) 922 30 02
🕐 10am–6pm daily

The main attraction at Cerro del Grillo hill is a tour of three of the seven levels of the legendary Eden Silver Mine, which includes a ride in a mine train through 2,000 ft (600 m) of tunnel.

⑦
Museo de Arte Abstracto Manuel Felguérez

🏠 Colón, at Seminario
🕐 Wed–Mon 10am–6pm
🌐 useodearteabstracto.com

This large modern art gallery occupies a former prison – the cells have been turned into galleries. Most exhibits are by Manuel Felguérez himself (born 1928), a native of Zacatecas state and one of Brazil's most respected abstract artists. Notable works include *El Arco del Día*, a huge bronze tripod, and *Retablo de los Mártires*, a monumental abstract canvas.

---

⑧
Museo Zacatecano

🏠 Dr Hierro 307 📞 (492) 922 65 80 🕐 10am–5pm Wed–Mon

The old Zacatecas mint was operated until 1842, and has since been converted into a

> The old Zacatecas mint was operated until 1842, and has since been converted into a comprehesive regional history museum, Museo Zacatecano.

further when they were later turned into a hotel and casino. Presbyterian missionaries from the US purchased the church in the 1880s and proceeded to strip it of its Catholic decoration, tearing down the tower and ripping out the facade. Only the Plateresque side entrance was spared. Ornate blocks taken from the exterior are now piled up like giant jigsaw pieces inside, a reminder of the former grandeur that is now a blank, white wall. The church is now used as a convention center, while the former convent is now the seat of the Zacatecas bishopric.

⑩ Museo Regional de Guadalupe

🏛 Jardín Juárez Oriente, Guadalupe 📞 (492) 923 20 89 🕐 9am-6pm Tue-Sun

Just 6 miles (10 km) east of the city center lies the town of Guadalupe, whose imposing

Franciscan church and ex-seminary house a museum of colonial-era religious art second only in importance to that of Tepotzotlán (*p156*). The treasures include works by Miguel Cabrera, Rodríguez Juárez, Cristóbal Villalpando, and Juan Correa. The staircase is an example of Baroque magnificence, and conserves huge canvases by Miguel Cabrera. Beside the church is the jewel-like Capilla de Nápoles, built in the 19th century and considered to be the paragon of Mexican Neo-Classical expression.

> 💬 INSIDER TIP
> **Folklore Festival**
>
> In August, Zacatecas hosts the International Folklore Festival. This lively celebration of tradition draws groups from all over the world to share their culture and history through dance and costume.

comprehensive regional history museum, Museo Zacatecano. Murals by Antonio Pintor Rodríguez adorn the central stairwell, while videos, historic documents, dioramas of the silver mines, and examples of silverwork tell the story of Zacatecas from prehistoric times. Local art is displayed, beside 18th-century altarpieces and indigenous embroidery.

⑨ Ex-Templo de San Agustín

🏛 Plazuela de Miguel Auza 📞 (492) 922 80 63 🕐 10am-5pm Tue-Sun

This large Augustinian church and its adjoining convent were tragically sacked during the Reform years (*p56*). Their Baroque splendor suffered

→

Anuncion by Cristobel de Villalpondo at the Museo Regional de Guadalupe

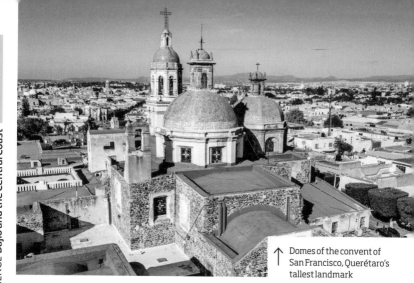

↑ Domes of the convent of San Francisco, Querétaro's tallest landmark

4

QUERÉTARO

🗺️ C4 🚍 Querétaro 🚌 ℹ️ Luis Pasteur Nte 4; (442) 238 50 67

Although a wealthy commercial city, Querétaro features a gorgeous historic core of opulent mansions and fine churches. The colonial-era center is especially charming at weekends, when street sellers and musicians fill the plazas, which are crammed with raucous cafés and bars.

① Cerro de las Campanas

🏛️ Centro Universitario

The barren hill where Emperor Maximilian was executed with two of his officers on June 19, 1867, is now a tree-filled municipal park. A broad stairway leads to the Neo-Gothic chapel that was donated by the emperor's family to commemorate the renewal of diplomatic

← Monument to Benito Juárez, standing on Cerro de las Campanas

relations between Mexico and the Austro-Hungarian Empire in 1900. Inside, three marble slabs mark the spot where the executions took place.

The whole site is dominated by a massive statue on the hilltop of the Mexican hero Benito Juárez, who was Maximilian's nemesis (p56).

② Museo Regional

🏛️ Corregidora Sur 3 📞 (442) 212 48 88 🕐 9am–6pm Tue–Sun

The state's regional museum is housed in the former convent of San Francisco, an impressive building noted for its cloisters, domes, and stone columns. The ethnographic, archaeological, and colonial sections are on the ground floor. The second floor has exhibits that feature weapons, furniture, and images tracing Querétaro's pivotal role in Mexican history since the fight for independence.

Both the convent and its adjoining church, the Templo de San Francisco, were begun by Franciscan missionaries in 1540, and the complex was finished in a blend of styles in 1727. The church has *trompe l'oeil* murals and the city's tallest tower.

③ Plaza de Armas

With its austere colonial-era fountain, bougainvillea-covered garden, and stately old mansions, this intimate 18th-century square is a corner of Spain transplanted to Mexico. Most of the former residences on the plaza, among them the sumptuous Casa de Ecala, now house government offices, including the state congress and court. The only white facade, with plain moldings and sober balconies, is the Casa de la Corregidora, which was built in 1700 for Querétaro's royal representatives. Completely restored in 1981, it is now the seat of the state government. A few prison cells have been preserved in its rear courtyard. The bronze statue crowning the square's fountain honors the Marqués de la Villa del Villar, the city's early 18th-century patron.

(4)

Museo de Arte

🏠 Allende Sur 14 ⏰ 10am-6pm Tue-Sun 🌐 cultura queretaro.gob.mx

This vast collection of 17th to 19th-century Mexican paintings is displayed alongside temporary art exhibitions and a smattering of contemporary paintings and photographs. They are housed in the 18th-century Ex-Convento de San Agustín, whose church captures the eye with its finely sculpted Plateresque facade and octagonal blue- and white-tiled dome. The real treasure here, however, is the supremely elegant Baroque main cloister, considered the finest of its kind in the Americas. Its richly carved details include caryatids supporting the arches.

(5)

Convento de la Santa Cruz

🏠 Independencia & Felipe Luna 📞 (442) 212 02 35 ⏰ 9:30am-2pm & 4:30-6pm daily

This plain convent started life in 1531 as a hermitage, on the site of the last battle between the Chichimecs (Nahua) and the Spanish. A 450-year-old replica of the cross that miraculously appeared in the sky, inducing the Chichimecs to surrender and embrace Christianity, is over the main altar of the church. By 1683, the hermitage had become the first missionary college in the Americas, and in 1848 the US invaders made the convent their headquarters. Emperor Maximilian was imprisoned here before his execution.

(6)

Museo Casa de la Zacatecana

🏠 Independencia 59 ⏰ 10am-6pm Tue-Sun 🌐 museolazacatecana.com

This 18th-century mansion has been converted into a fascinating house museum, which is filled with art and furniture shedding light on the lifestyles of the wealthy of the period. The Salon de los Rejoles is crammed with fine antique clocks, while the Salon de los Cristos contains 54 historic crucifixes. However, the house is most famous for the ghoulish legend of the woman from Zacatecas (the "Zacatecana") who once lived here, and is thought to have murdered her husband.

"LA CORREGIDORA" - MEXICO'S LADY LIBERTY

Celebrated for her role in Mexico's fight for independence, María Josefa Ortiz de Domínguez was dubbed "La Corregidora" after her governor husband ("Corregidor" in Spanish). In 1810, aware María had hosted independence meetings, her husband locked her up while he made plans to arrest her conspirators. She nevertheless managed to get a message to the rebels, who were able to flee town.

⑤

MORELIA

🅰B5 🏛Michoacán ✈🚌 ℹAvenida Francisco 1, Madero Pte 488; www.michoacan.gob.mx

Morelia's first settlers were Spanish nobility and religious orders, who laid out a city of magnificent palaces, convents, and churches along flagstone avenues. The center has retained its Spanish character, and even some new buildings sport Spanish Colonial facades.

①

Palacio Clavijero

🏛Nigromante 79
🕐10am-6pm Tue-Sun
🌐ccclavijero.mx

The grand proportions and Baroque styling of the former Colegio de San Francisco Javier, a 17th-century Jesuit college, are best appreciated from its vast main courtyard. Elegant arcades on the ground floor contrast with a closed upper cloister where 28 windows replace the arches below. Geometrical patterns in the stone pavement imitate the layout of gardens that once surrounded the central fountain. The building now houses government offices and the tourist information bureau.

②

Museo Regional Michoacano

🏛Allende 305 📞(443) 312 04 07 🕐9am-5pm Tue-Sun

For more than a century, the Regional Museum has collected objects relating to the state's ecology and history from pre-Hispanic to modern times.

About one fifth of its treasures are on public display in the Baroque mansion. Highlights include indigenous codices, a rare 16th-century Bible written in three languages, and a celebrated early 18th-century painting entitled *Traslado de las Monjas (The Moving of the Nuns)*, one of the few realistic portrayals of Mexican colonial-era society.

③

Palacio de Gobierno

🏛Avenida Francisco I Madero 63 📞(443) 313 07 07 🕐24 hours

The Spanish Colonial Government Palace opened in 1770 as the headquarters of the Tridentine Seminary, which was attended by key figures of the independence *(p56)* and Reform *(p58)* movements. It later became the seat of state government. In the 1950s, the grand staircase and first floor were adorned with beautiful murals that represent local themes.

↑ Alfredo Zalce murals that adorn the first floor of the Palacio de Gobierno

←

The majestic twin towers of Morelia cathedral, built in pink trachyte stone

④

Casa de Artesanías

📍Fray Juan de San Miguel 129 📞(443) 312 24 86 🕐8am-7:30pm Mon-Fri, 9am-3pm & 4-7:30pm Sat & Sun

The 16th-century Convento de San Buenaventura was restored in the 1970s and is now a showcase for Michoacán's rich craft tradition. The rooms around the arched courtyard contain a selection of items for sale, including pottery, textiles, and lacquerware. In the upstairs rooms, visitors can observe artisans at work.

⑤

Aqueduct and Calzada Fray Antonio de San Miguel

📍Avenida Acueducto

Water once flowed along this 18th-century aqueduct from a well 5 miles (8 km) away to the city's 30 public fountains and 150 private outlets. The final stretch consists of 253 arches, some of which reach a height of 33 ft (10 m). It is especially stunning when lit up at night.

The aqueduct was built by Bishop Fray Antonio de San Miguel, who also created the *calzada* (avenue) that bears his name. This pedestrian esplanade leads from the city end of the aqueduct to the Guadalupe Sanctuary. With its ash trees, Baroque benches, and 18th-century mansions, it recalls a long-gone era.

⑥

Museo del Estado

📍Guillermo Prieto 176 📞(443) 313 06 29 🕐9am-3pm & 4-8pm Mon-Fri, 10am-6pm Sat & Sun

Set inside an 18th-century mansion, high-quality changing exhibitions take up much of the space. However, there are permanent archeological displays, galleries on colonial history, some rare Tarascan jewelry, and ethnological exhibits on the major indigenous cultures of Michoacán, notably the Tarascan (Purépecha).

EAT

Cielo Cocina Fusión
Sublime meals that put a contemporary spin on Mexican dishes make this spot worth the taxi ride from the center. Expect anything from peanut chicken mole to salmon ceviche, served in a rooftop space.

📍Blvd García de León 700 📞(443) 427 03 23

$$$

Dulces Morelianas Calle Real
At this famous sweet shop, founded in 1840, sample Morelia's specialty *dulces* (sweets made of candied fruit or evaporated milk). Enjoy even more sweet stuff at the on-site café, El Patio de Atrás.

📍Madero Ote 440 🌐callereal.mx

$$$

A SHORT WALK
MORELIA

Distance 1 mile (1.5 km) **Time** 20 minutes **Nearest bus stop** Morelia

Starting from the Plaza de Armas, almost all of Morelia's important sights are within short walking distance. The colonial-era streets and captivating Spanish architecture make this a pleasant city to stroll around. Capital of the state of Michoacán, Morelia was founded in the mid-1500s under the name of Valladolid. The city's name was changed in 1828 to honor José María Morelos, the native son instrumental in leading Mexico toward independence.

The peaceful courtyard of the **Conservatorio de las Rosas** is enhanced by the sounds of practicing music students.

Teatro Ocampo

Templo de las Rosas

ZARAGOZA

SANTIAGO TAPIA

PRIETO

START

NIGROMANTE

MELCHOR OCAMPO

FRANCISCO I MADERO

FINISH

Government offices now surround the courtyard of **Palacio Clavijero**, a former Jesuit college. The austere Baroque building was named after a historian who taught here in the 1700s.

The **Templo de la Compañía de Jesús** was built in the 17th century. Since 1930 it has been home to the Public Library.

Colegio de San Nicolás is the alma mater of several illustrious Mexicans. It has been an educational institution since the 16th century.

Centro Cultural

Palacio Municipal

GALEANA

← Cafés lining the tiny park opposite the Conservatorio de las Rosas

A former seminary, **Palacio de Gobierno** (p208) has been the seat of the state government since 1867. Bright murals decorate the upper level.

Built in a mixture of styles between 1660 and 1774, the **cathedral** has two towers that soar to a height of more than 200 ft (60 m). Its monumental 4,600-pipe German organ is the main star of the annual International Organ Festival.

Locator Map
For more detail see p209

MORELIA

JUAREZ

MORELOS

ALLENDE

GARCÍA OBESO

HIDALGO

CORREGIDORA

ABASOLO

Plaza de Armas was laid out as the center of town in the 16th century. The bandstand dates from 1887.

↑ Inside the Morelia's cathedral on Plaza de Armas

Casa Natal de Morelos is where the Independence hero José María Morelos was born in 1765.

0 meters   50   N
0 yards   50   ↙

Palacio de Justicia

Museo Regional Michoacano (p208), one of Mexico's oldest museums, spans pre-Hispanic to modern eras.

Part of a 16th-century Augustinian ex-convent, **Iglesia de San Agustín** has a sober Plateresque facade. It is seen here through the arches of the courtyard in front of it.

Diners relaxing in the courtyard of El Parián restaurant in Tlaquepaque

Regional de la Cerámica. Located in a beautiful old mansion, the museum counts a 16th-century kitchen among its most interesting exhibits. Many of the items sold in Tlaquepaque are in fact made in workshops in the neighboring suburb of Tonalá. Like Tlaquepaque, this was once a village outside Guadalajara, and was originally an indigenous settlement. Its streets become an open-air craft market, Tianguis Tonala, on Thursdays and Sundays.

Museo Regional de la Cerámica

 Independencia 237 ☎ (333) 860 11 77 ⏰ 9am–5pm Tue

7

Cañada de la Virgen

🅱B4 🏛Guanajuato
ℹ Principal 14, Zona Centro; www.inah.gob.mx

The impressive ancient Mesoamerican pyramids of Cañada de la Virgen were opened to the public in 2011 after years of archaeological excavations. The site comprises several enormous structures associated with the

EXPERIENCE MORE

6

Tlaquepaque

🅱B4 🏛Jalisco ℹ Ayuntamiento, Calle Donato Guerra 160; (333) 562 70 50

Once a potters' village and weekend retreat for the residents of Guadalajara (p194), Tlaquepaque is now effectively a suburb of the city. However, it retains a village atmosphere.

The overwhelming selection of pottery, blown glass, textiles, metal, wood, and papier-mâché items in the crafts shops is the main factor that attracts large numbers of visitors to come here.

There are also many restaurants. A favorite meeting spot off the appealing, flower-filled central square is El Parián. Hailed as the world's biggest cantina, it gathers about 20 eating and drinking establishments around its giant courtyard. In the center is a bandstand where mariachi musicians often play.

The best ceramics pieces from Tlaquepaque and the surrounding region can be appreciated at the **Museo**

A giant sailfish statue on the waterfront plaza in Manzanillo ↑

> Once a separate potters' village and weekend retreat for the residents of Guadalajara, Tlaquepaque is now effectively a suburb of the city.

Otomí of the Toltec–Chichimec culture, constructed between AD 540 and 1050. The city was abandoned thereafter, though it's not known why.

Today the site features five sets of ruins, the most important of which is Complex A and its "13 Sky House," which is thought to have been some kind of celestial observatory. Complex B is centered around the "House of the Longest Night," a pyramidal structure that probably served a mixture of public and ritualistic functions. At the main entrance a visitor center and museum provide context.

8

Cuyutlán

🅰A5 📍Colima 🛈Blvd Miguel de la Madrid 875A; www.colima.gob.mx

Cuyutlán is a traditional resort on the central part of Colima's coast. It is characterized by black volcanic sand, pounding surf, and Mexican tourists who come here on weekends. It is situated at the southern tip of the immense Cuyutlán Lagoon, which extends south for 20 miles (32 km) from Manzanillo.

The tiny **Museo de la Sal** gives an insight into the salt economy, its workers, and harvesting methods. A spectacular phenomenon seen on the coast here is the *ola verde* (green wave), when waves up to 33 ft (10 m) in height gleam with phosphorescent marine organisms. It is most commonly seen in April and May. In the recent past, it has caused a number of deaths, so caution should be taken when coming to see the wave.

Around 2.5 miles (4 km) further along the coast from Cuyutlán, the **Centro Ecológico de Cuyutlán "El Tortugario"** is a turtle sanctuary dedicated to the conservation and protection of local wildlife. The sanctuary organizes boat trips into the wildlife-rich Laguna Cuyutlán, to help teach visitors about the importance of preserving the local wildlife and their habitats.

Museo de la Sal
🏠Calle Benito Juárez 📞(312) 326 40 14 🕐9am–6pm daily

Centro Ecológico de Cuyutlán "El Tortugario"
♿🚫 🏠Av Lopez Mateo 🕐9am–5pm Thu-Tue 🌐tortuga riocuyutlan.com

9

Manzanillo

🅰A5 📍Colima 🚆🚌 🛈Blvd Miguel de la Madrid 875A; www.colima.gob.mx

Mexico's main west coast shipping center, Manzanillo is also Colima state's foremost beach resort. Colorful houses of the old port cling to a hill overlooking the main harbor, while the newer part of town covers a sandbar separating the lagoon from the ocean. Most of the restaurants and hotels are along the sands of Las Brisas and Playa Azul.

Separating the Bahía de Manzanillo from the Bahía de Santiago is a peninsula, site of Las Hadas ("The Fairies"), a luxury Moorish-style hotel.

10 Paricutín

 B5 24 miles (38 km) NW of Uruapan, Michoacán

One of the youngest volcanoes in the world, Paricutín erupted in February 1943. Amid thunderous explosions, its cone grew to more than 1,100 ft (330 m) within one year. Ash and lava flows buried two villages and, while nobody was killed by the eruptions, more than 4,000 people had to flee their homes. The volcano's activity lasted until 1952, leaving behind a barren cone rising 1,391 ft (424 m) from a sea of black frozen lava.

The *mirador* (lookout) at Angahuan offers a dramatic view of the lava field and Paricutín behind it. The church tower that can be seen above the lava belongs to the buried village of San Juan Parangaricutiro. For a closer look, hire a guide and a horse to take you down the cliff and through the lava rock formations. The stiff 30-minute climb to the crater rim is rewarded with views of the lunar-like landscape.

The town of Angahuan has preserved its traditional character despite the influx of visitors to Paricutín, and most people here speak the Tarascan language, Purépecha.

11 Sierra Gorda

C4 Querétaro

One of the largest untamed regions in central Mexico, the semi-arid mountain range of the Sierra Gorda rises northeast of the city of Querétaro (*p206*) to over 10,000 ft (3,000 m). The lush green of its foothills is interrupted only by the massive monolith La Peña de Bernal, towering 1,460 ft (445 m) above the village of Bernal.

In the mountains beyond Cadereyta, with its square of colored churches, are the archaeological sites of Toluquilla and Las Ranas. These two sites are set on the rugged ridges near San Joaquín, to the east of Mex 120. Both feature pre-Hispanic ceremonial structures built between the 7th and 11th centuries AD. Farther north into the mountains, Mex 120 gets even steeper before descending to Jalpan. This town is the site of one of five Franciscan missions founded in the mid-16th century to convert the indigenous peoples of these mountains. The missions – the others are in Concá, Tilaco, Tancoyól, and Landa de Matamoros – all have scenic settings, and distinctive facades with strong indigenous touches in their profuse mortar decorations.

12   Santuario El Rosario

C5 Off Mex 15, 8 miles (13 km) E of Ocampo, Michoacán Nov–Mar: 9am–5pm daily mariposa monarca.semarnat.gob.mx

This UNESCO World Heritage site is one of two sanctuaries open to the public in the Monarch Butterfly Biosphere Reserve in the mountains west of Mexico City. The 60-sq-mile (160-sq-km) preserve is the winter home of an estimated 100 million monarch butterflies (*Danaus plexippus linneo*),

Did You Know?

Monarch butterflies cover up to 190 miles (300 km) a day to escape the winter in Canada and the US.

which migrate here each year. The annual migration of the monarch butterfly begins in early autumn. It is then that a special generation hatches, with a life cycle of up to nine months, four times that of spring and summer butterflies. These autumn-born insects fly south in groups of several hundred to reach the *oyamel* fir forests of central Mexico where they spend the winter. In spring they mate and head north again. En route, the females lay about 500 eggs each. Their offspring take up the baton and continue north to arrive in early June. None of the original migrants will survive to return to Mexico the following year.

The best time to visit is late February when rising temperatures encourage the insects to search for flowers or begin their journey back north. The hiking route will be well marked.

The nearby **Sierra Chincua Monarch Butterfly Sanctuary** sees fewer visitors than El Rosario, but is easier to reach and offers horses for its more rustic trails. Guides will accompany visitors on request.

Sierra Chincua Monarch Butterfly Sanctuary
⊛ ⊛ 🏠 Llano de las Papas, 6 miles (9 km) NE of Angangueo 🕒 Nov–Mar: 8am–5pm daily

← Tourists clamber around San Juan Parangaricutiro's buried church

↑ Palapa seafood restaurant on the Santa María del Oro lake, in the hills southeast of Tepic

Tepic

🏠 A4 🏠 Nayarit ✈ 🚌
🛈 Corner of Avenida México and Calzada del Ejército Nacional; www.riviera nayarit.com

A provincial town with an agreeable climate, Tepic was founded in the foothills of an extinct volcano. Not far from the Plaza Principal and the cathedral is the **Museo Regional de Nayarit**, where you will find shaft-tombs and displays about the Cora and Huichol people. The **Museo de Los Cinco Pueblos** (Museum of Five Peoples) has exhibits about the Huicholes, Tepehuanos, Mexicaneros, Coras, and *mestizo* cultures of the region (*mestizo* meaning people of mixed European and Mexican descent). One of Mexico's most beloved poets is commemorated at the **Museo Amado Nervo**, in the house where he was born.

Museo Regional de Nayarit
⊛ 🏠 Av México 91 Norte 📞 (311) 212 19 00 🕒 9am–6pm Mon–Sat (to 3pm Sat)

Museo de Los Cinco Pueblos
⊛ 🏠 México Norte 105, at Zapata 📞 (311) 212 17 05 🕒 9am–2pm & 4–7pm Tue–Sun

Museo Amado Nervo
🏠 Zacatecas Norte 284 📞 (311) 212 29 16 🕒 10am–2pm & 4–7pm Tue–Sat, 10am–2pm Sun

---

TOP 4 | **REGIONAL FIESTAS**

Fiesta de Año Nuevo
Purépecha dancers in Ihuatzio perform masked dances to Pirecua songs to mark the new year.

Easter
In both Tzintzuntzán and Tarímbarom, a volunteer performs a realistic re-enactment of the Crucifixion.

Feria de San Marcos
Mexico's largest fair is held in Aguascalientes, with parades, concerts, fireworks, bullfights, rodeo shows, and more.

Day of the Dead
On November 1, families gather to commemorate relatives who have passed (*p221*). There are particularly beautiful festivites on Janitzio Island in Lake Pátzcuaro.

14
Tequisquiapan

🅰C4 🏠Querétaro 🚌
ℹ️Independencia 1, Plaza
Miguel Hidalgo; (414) 273
08 41

Just 35 miles (57 km) east of
Querétaro lies the quaint spa
town of Tequisquiapan (aka
"Tequis"), a former Otomí
village that developed in the
Spanish period thanks to its
hot springs. Today its cobbled
lanes, folk art boutiques, and
spa hotels make it a popular
retreat. Lavish villas, all with
beautiful walled gardens,
are set around central Plaza
Miguel Hidalgo, itself ringed
by arched portals and the
handsome rose-colored
church of Santa María de la
Asunción. The Mercado de
Artesanías Tequezquicalli –
a crafts market – lies one
block from the plaza.

15
Colima

🅰A5 🏠Colima 🚌 ℹ️Palacio
de Gobierno, Reforma 37;
www.colima.gob.mx

The graceful provincial town
of Colima was the first Spanish
city on the west coast. It has

been rebuilt several times
since 1522 because of earthquakes, but the center still
has Neo-Classical buildings,
several museums, and the
main plaza Jardín la Libertad.
Ceramic vessels and human
and animal figurines from
early shaft-tombs can
be seen in the **Museo de las
Culturas de Occidente**. The
**Museo Universitario de Artes
Populares** exhibits regional
and national folk art, covering
both pre-Hispanic and more
recent periods. Colima's **Museo
Regional de Historia** features
pre-Hispanic ceramics and
artifacts, much of them found
in local tombs.

On the outskirts of town,
La Campana archaeological
site was an important pre-
Hispanic settlement between
AD 700 and 900, with the
earliest remains dating as far
back as 1500 BC.

Museo de las Culturas
de Occidente

🏠 Corner of Galván &
Ejército Nacional 📞(312) 313
06 08 🕙10am-6pm Tue-Sun

Museo Universitario
de Artes Populares

🏠 Manuel Gallardo
Zamora 99 📞(312) 312 22 28
🕙10am-2pm & 5-8pm Tue-
Sun (to 1pm Sun)

↑ The rose-colored church
standing on Plaza Miguel
Hidalgo, Tequisquiapan

Museo Regional
de Historia

🏠Portal Morelos 1
📞(312) 312 92 28 🕙9am-
6pm Tue-Sun

16
Mexcaltitán

🅰A4 🏠Nayarit

This tiny island, its name
meaning "Place of the Moon
Temple," is no more than
1,310 ft (400 m) across. It sits
in a lagoon in Mexico's largest
mangrove swamp area, and
in the rains of August and
September the streets
become canals. The island

GREAT VIEW
Twin Peaks

North from Colima, High-
way 54-D to Guadalajara
has views of the active
Volcán de Fuego and the
dormant El Nevado de
Colima behind. Hikes up
the latter are popular
and relatively easy to
arrange in Colima.

is thought to be the legendary Aztec homeland Aztlán, from where the tribe set out on their migration to the Valley of México around 1091 AD – from the air, it really does resemble a tiny version of Tenochtitlán, the final Aztec capital. According to legend the Aztecs slept here on the way to their promised land.

Although no Aztec artifacts have been found here, the archaeological pieces on display in the **Museo del Orígen** nonetheless emphasize the importance of the island of Mexcaltitán as "The Cradle of Mexicanism" (*Mexcaltitán* literally means "House of the Mexicans" in Náhuatl).

Museo del Orígen

⊛ 🅰 Porfirio Díaz 1 🅲 (311) 131 56 27 🅲 9am-2pm & 4-6pm Tue-Sun

---

 17

Mineral de Pozos

🅰 C4 🅰 Guanajuato
🅸 Centro de Atención al Visitante, Hwy 46; www. visitmexico.com

A rich and flourishing mining community in the 18th century, the semi-ghost-town of Mineral de Pozos was largely abandoned in the 1900s. Though it began experiencing a revival in the early 2010s, it still remains less developed than San Miguel de Allende (*p224*).

Today the heart is clustered around the white dome of Parroquia San Pedro and the Jardín Principal. The center is home to a handful of hip hotels, restaurants, and handicraft shops, selling everything from old-fashioned sweets to pre-Hispanic musical instruments and toys.

Crumbling ruins swamp the town's fringes, in between old mine workings and abandoned haciendas. Highlights include the ruins of the Hacienda de Cinco Señores, a vast mine complex, the three distinctive

16th-century Jesuit smelters (*hornos*) of Santa Brígida, and the newly opened Lavender Farms of Pozos.

 18

Uruapan

🅰 B5 🅰 Michoacán 🔀 🚌
🅸 San Miguel Arcángel; (452) 524 71 99

Uruapan is a busy agricultural center. Nestling against the Sierra de Uruapan, it links the cold upland region (*tierra fría*) to the humid lowlands (*tierra caliente*) that stretch toward the Pacific. Its subtropical climate supports exuberant vegetation, including vast avocado plantations.

The Spanish monk Juan de San Miguel founded the town in 1533 and divided it into nine neighborhoods (*barrios*), which still preserve their own traditions. He also built **La Huatápera**, a chapel and

hospital that now houses a fine museum of Michoacán crafts.

The **Parque Nacional Barranca del Cupatitzio** is a park on the edge of Uruapan's urban sprawl. It encompasses a lush, tropical ravine created by the Río Cupatitzio, which springs underground from a rock known as La Rodilla del Diablo ("the Devil's knee"). Cobbled footpaths weave between banana plants and palms to take in man-made cascades and fountains. Local trout is sold and served at restaurants and taco stands.

La Huatápera

🅰 Plaza Morelos 🅲 (452) 524 34 34 🅲 9:30am-1:30pm & 3:30-6pm Tue-Sun

Parque Nacional Barranca del Cupatitzio

⊛ 🍷 🍴 🅰 Calzada de San Miguel, 0.5 miles (1 km) from the plaza 🅲 8am-6pm Mon-Thu, 8am-7pm Fri-Sun
🔳 parquenacional.gob.mx

↑ Visitors diving off the rocks into a waterfall at the Parque Nacional Barranca del Cupatitzio

San Juan de los Lagos

B4 **Jalisco** **Fray Antonio de Segovia 10; (395) 785 09 79**

The imposing 18th-century cathedral in San Juan de los Lagos is one the most important Catholic sanctuaries in Mexico. An estimated nine million pilgrims travel here every year to venerate the Virgen de San Juan de los Lagos, a small 16th-century corn-paste statue enshrined in an altar originally made for the church of Santa Maria degli Angeli in Rome.

The cathedral, which reaches a height of 223 ft (68 m), has a sumptuous interior. In its vast sacristy is a group of large 17th- and 18th-century paintings, six of which have been attributed to Rubens. Touching votive pictures, expressing gratitude to the Virgin for favors granted, line the walls of a room beside the sacristy.

Tequila

A4 **Jalisco** **José Cuervo 33; (374) 742 00 12**

Everything in Tequila reminds the visitor of Mexico's most famous drink, especially the scent from the distilleries. Plantations of *Agave tequilana weber* surround the town, the cores (*piñas*) of which have been used to make tequila since the 16th century.

The biggest and oldest factories are La Perseverancia (home of Sauza Tequila since 1878) and La Rojeña (base of the José Cuervo brand since 1758) – both offer factory tours and tasyings. Learn more at the Museo Nacional del Tequila, or head 9 miles (15 km) southeast to the Herradura distillery. The three major distilleries also offer all-inclusive day tours (weekends only) from Guadalajara by train or bus.

Las Pozas

C4 **Off Mex 120, 2 miles (3 km) NW of Xilitla, San Luis Potosí** **9am–6pm daily** **xilitla.org**

High in the mountains south of Ciudad Valles, near the spectacularly situated town of Xilitla, is this extraordinary, dreamlike jungle estate created by the British artist, eccentric, and millionaire Edward James (1907–84).

According to his friend Salvador Dalí, James was "crazier than all the Surrealists put together. They pretend, but he is the real thing." Born into a wealthy English family, James was himself a moderately successful poet and artist, but excelled as a patron of the arts. He founded ballet companies, published books, financed large exhibitions, and amassed paintings by Dalí, Picasso, and Magritte.

In the 1940s, James started seeking to create his own Garden of Eden and, with the help of Yaqui guide Plutarco Gastelum, came upon the area of Xilitla in 1945. James first used the Las Pozas property to grow orchids and then as a private zoo, but over the next 30 years he continued to add fanciful buildings and structures to the estate. To complete his architectural fantasy, James again worked with Gastelum and many local artisans, sometimes numbering up to 150 at a time.

Slippery paths weave between the hundreds of Surrealist metal and concrete sculptures, scattered amid thick subtropical vegetation, springs, waterfalls, and pools. Much of James's work is not finished or already disintegrating, so exploring the estate can feel like stumbling upon the ruins of a long-lost, mythical civilization.

This fantastical estate is a popular sight, and with a limit of 800 visitors per day, it fills to capacity fast – especially on holidays and weekends. Try to arrive early, and be prepared for a wait to enter.

↑ Las Pozas, a "Garden of Eden" created by British artist Edward James

La Quemada

B4 **Mex 54, 35 miles (57 km) SE of Zacatecas, Zacatecas** **(492) 922 50 85** **9am–6pm daily**

The archaeological site at La Quemada stretches over a steep hill rising from a wide, arid valley. From around AD 350, La Quemada was an important religious and

Parroquia de la Asunción in Lagos de Moreno and *(inset)* its vibrantly colored interior

political center and the focal point for trade between the area and Teotihuacán *(p140).* After AD 700, La Quemada seems to have substituted trade with more bellicose activities. In around 1100, it apparently suffered a violent end, despite an 800-m (2,600-ft) long and 4-m (13-ft) tall defensive wall on its northern slope.

It takes about two hours to explore the site by following the steep, rocky path that leads from the lower Main Causeway and Hall of Columns all the way up to the Citadel.

Lagos de Moreno

▲B4 ☐Jalisco ▦ ⓘPedro Moreno 419, Centro; (474) 410 36 218

A lesser-visited architectural gem, Lagos de Moreno is known as the "Athens of Jalisco" thanks to the many famous writers who were born here. Once an important post on the silver road, it's a tranquil and graceful little city today, with cobbled streets climbing steeply from the Río Lagos to hilltop Templo del Señor del Calvario, a 19th-century church modeled on Rome's St. Peter's.

On central Jardín de los Constituyentes stands the magnificent Baroque church, the Parroquia de la Asunción. Just behind the church, the Museo de Arte Sacro contains a large collection of religious art from the 17th to the 19th centuries, while grand Teatro José Rosas Moreno opened in 1907 with a stunning mural on its dome depicting the Mexican Revolution *(p62).*

Ribera

▲B4 ☐Jalisco ▦ ⓘMadero 407 Altos, Chapala; (376) 765 31 41

The built-up Ribera has a near-perfect climate, and its proximity to some of Mexico's other big, central cities has resulted in streams of foreign visitors. It stretches for some 13 miles (21 km) from the old-fashioned resort of Chapala to the village of Jocotepec at the western end of a lake. Ajijic, an artists'

colony with cobblestone streets, crafts shops, galleries, and a 16th-century chapel, is the most picturesque village of the Ribera. Farther west, the spa resort of San Juan Cosalá offers the attractions of public swimming pools and a natural geyser.

Boat trips from Chapala head for two islands: the tree-covered Isla de los Alacranes, with its fish restaurants; and Mezcala, with the ruins of a 19th-century fort where independence fighters held out for four years before surrendering to the Spanish in 1816.

The scenic road that runs along the mostly undeveloped southern shore of the lake opens up splendid views.

> **A lesser-visited architectural gem, Lagos de Moreno is known as the "Athens of Jalisco" thanks to the many famous writers who were born here.**

25

Dolores Hidalgo

 B3 Guanajuato
Plaza Principal 2; www.
dolores-hidalgo.com

The battle for independence from Spain began in 1810 with Father Miguel Hidalgo issuing his famous *Grito* (cry) to arms *(p59)*. The beautifully laid-out Plaza Principal at the heart of Dolores is still dominated by the ornate facade of the 18th-century Nuestra Señora de los Dolores, the illustrious church where this portentous event took place. Learn more at the **Museo Histórico Curato de Dolores**, Father Hidalgo's home between 1804 and 1810, and the **Museo del Bicentenario**, which tells the history of the city.

Museo Histórico Curato de Dolores

Morelos 1, at Hidalgo
(418) 182 01 71 10am-5:45pm Tue-Sat, 10:am-4:45pm Sun

Museo del Bicentenario

Plaza Principal (418) 182 77 31 9am-4:45pm Tue-Sun

26

Pátzcuaro

 B5 Michoacán
Portal de Hidalgo 2;
(434) 342 02 15

Set amid the pastures and pine forests on the southern shore of Lake Pátzcuaro, this town was once an important center of the Purépecha people. Its later colonial-era grandeur was due to Michoacán's first bishop, who temporarily turned it into the civic, religious, and cultural seat of the state.

The ambitious Basílica de Nuestra Señora de la Salud was to boast five naves and accommodate thousands of people, but only one nave was completed. Fires and earthquakes ravaged the building over the centuries, and the church was finally finished in a jumble of styles in 1833.

Just to the south is the **Museo de Artes e Industrias Populares** craft museum. Among the exhibits is a cabin-like *troje* with Purépecha furnishings. Another crafts center can be found in the **Casa de los Once Patios**.

Huge ash trees shade the quiet, elegant Plaza Vasco de Quiroga. Many of the colonial-era mansions that face the square have been converted into restaurants, shops, and hotels, but the real commercial hub of the town is the nearby Plaza Gertrudis Bocanegra, named after a local independence heroine. On Fridays, the streets toward the Santuario de Guadalupe church fill with stalls, and pottery is sold in the Plazuela de San Francisco.

Museo de Artes e Industrias Populares

 Corner of Enseñanza and Alcantarilla (434) 342 10 29 9am-5pm Tue-Sun

Casa de los Once Patios

Madrigal de las Altas Torres (434) 342 43 79
9am-5pm daily

> INSIDER TIP
> **Island Hopping**
>
> Tours to the islands on Lake Pátzcuaro leave from the docks, which are located in the north of town. Isla Janitzio, with its monument to Morelos and quaint shops, is the most popular destination.

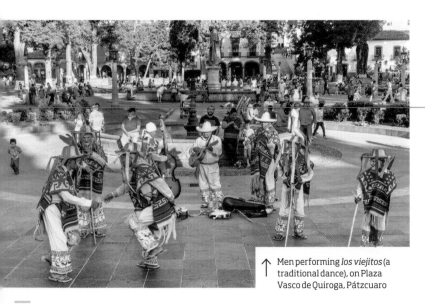

↑ Men performing *los viejitos* (a traditional dance), on Plaza Vasco de Quiroga, Pátzcuaro

↑ Dancers with painted skull masks during the Day of the Dead festivities

THE DAY OF THE DEAD

This Mexican celebration centers around the belief that the dead have divine permission to visit friends and relatives on Earth once a year.

A JOYFUL CELEBRATION

During the Day of the Dead, the living welcome the souls of departed loved ones with offerings of flowers, food, candles, and incense. This is not a morbid occasion, but one of peace and happiness. The souls of children are thought to visit on November 1, and adults on November 2. Skulls and skeletons abound in the imagery and decorations of this festival, but death is portrayed with humor and even affection by craftspeople and artists.

WHERE TO SEE THE DAY OF THE DEAD

Celebrations occur virtually everywhere in central and southern Mexico, with some areas adding their own local twist. The ceremonies around Lake Pátzcuaro, for example, are particularly impressive, largely because of the local Purépecha villagers' deep indigenous roots and the pretty settings. Throughout the night, boats decorated with candles and flowers and laden with chanting villagers travel between the Pátzcuaro docks and the island, and the air is filled with wafts of incense and the ringing of bells.

Afro-Mexicans, meanwhile, pay homage to the suffering of their enslaved ancestors with the *Danza de los Diablos* (Dance of the Devils) - through synchronized stomping, spinning, and comical theatrics, large ensembles tell the story of enslaved workers mocking a violent, white ruling class.

SYMBOLS OF THE DEAD

Personalized altars laden with symbolic offerings are set up in homes, and may also be displayed in public places.

 Sugar figures and other foods are displayed. The dead are believed to take the essence or the aroma of the offerings.

 A photo of the dead person is a common focal point for the altars. Holy pictures may also be added.

 The marigold (*cempasúchil*), often referred to in Mexico as "the flower of the dead," is used in profusion on altars and as festive decor.

 Papier-mâché skeletons are often displayed in public places, performing everyday activities in humorous scenes.

 La Catrina, a tall female skeleton drawn by José Guadalupe Posada, is widely associated with the day. It often appears in art.

 Skull masks and clothing painted with bones are sometimes worn by children on the day.

San Luis Potosí

C4 | **San Luis Potosí**
| **Manuel José Ottón 130; www.slp.gob.mx**

The mining wealth that the city of San Luis Potosí accumulated in the 17th and 18th centuries is evident in the historic buildings and three grand plazas at its core. The cathedral dominates the central square, the Plaza de Armas, along with the Palacio de Gobierno, the seat of Benito Juárez's government when he denied clemency to Emperor Maximilian in 1867. Behind it stands the Real Caja, or Royal Treasury, whose wide staircase enabled pack animals to reach the storage chambers above.

The second square is the Plaza de los Fundadores, the site of a former Jesuit college and two 17th-century churches, the Iglesia de la Compañía and the graceful Capilla de Loreto. On the eastern side of town is the third main square, the Plaza del Carmen, on which stand the church of the same name, the imposing Teatro de la Paz, and the **Museo Nacional de la Máscara**. The museum is housed in a restored former mansion where the walls are

HIDDEN GEM
Paradise on Earth

In the southeast of San Luis Potosí state is Huasteca Potosina: an area of stunning natural beauty known in pre-Hispanic times as Tamoanchán, or "Earthly Paradise."

adorned with over 1,000 decorative and ritual masks.

The Churrigueresque church of **Templo del Carmen**, built in the mid-1700s, is by far the most spectacular religious structure in the city, with a three-tiered facade, ornate tower, and multicolored domes. Even more fabulous is the interior, not least for Francisco Tresguerras' main altar and exuberant Altar de los Siete Príncipes. The latter is actually a floor-to-ceiling interior facade enclosing the entrance to a chapel, its white stucco surface dotted with polychrome statues of angels.

The Franciscans began work in 1686 on the ambitious **Ex-Convento de San Francisco** complex, which took over a century to complete. It now contains the Museo Regional

Potosino, which has colonial and pre-Hispanic exhibits. Upstairs is the splendid Capilla de Aranzazú, the lavish private chapel for the former occupants. A unique Baroque jewel despite the garish colors chosen by its restorers, it has a rare covered atrium and a carved wooden portal.

The city also has two other noteworthy museums. **Museo Federico Silva** pays homage to one of Mexico's most respected sculptors. Born in 1923, Silva is known for his modern interpretations of Mexico's pre-Hispanic art, and the museum displays many of his volcanic stone and steel creations. **Museo de Arte Contemporáneo** occupies the old 19th-century post office, and showcases high-quality traveling shows of contemporary art.

The former state prison, built in the 1890s, has been transformed into the stylish **Centro de las Artes** complex. The sympathetically restored buildings contain temporary art exhibitions, the cell where Francisco Madero was held in 1910, and the Museo

Leonora Carrington, which is dedicated to the English-born Mexican surrealist painter.

Museo Nacional de la Máscara

⊛ 🏠 Villerías 2 🕓 10am-6pm daily (to 5pm Sat, to 3pm Sun & Mon) 🌐 museonacionaldelamascara.com

Templo del Carmen

🏠 Manuel José Othón 410 📞 (444) 812 28 78 🕓 7am-1:30pm & 4-9pm daily

Ex-Convento de San Francisco

⊛ 🖐 🏠 Plaza de Aranzazú 📞 (444) 814 35 72 🕓 9am-6pm Tue-Sun

Museo Federico Silva

⊛ 🏠 Obregón 80 🕓 10am-6pm Mon & Wed-Sun (to 2pm Sun) 🌐 museofedericosilva.org

Museo de Arte Contemporáneo

⊛ 🏠 Morelos 235 🕓 10am-6pm Tue-Sun (to 2pm Sun) 🌐 macsanluispotosi.com

Centro de las Artes

⊛ 🏠 Calzada de Guadalupe 705 🕓 10am-2pm & 5-7pm Tue-Sun 🌐 centrodelasartesslp.gob.mx

↑ Perched high on the mountainside, the town of Real de Catorce, dominated by its Neo-Classical church

㉘
Real de Catorce

 C3 🏠 San Luis Potosí 🚌 🛈 Presidencia Municipal, Constitución 27; www.realdecatorce.info

The crumbling structures and ghost-town atmosphere of Real de Catorce testify to the rapidly changing fortunes of Mexican silver-mining centers. Hidden high in the mountains of the Sierra Madre Oriental, it is accessible only through a 1.5-mile (2.5-km) tunnel.

In the early 20th century the town boasted a population of 40,000, served by several newspapers, a theater, a grand hotel, and an electric tramway. Then, drastically hit by falling silver prices, its fortunes slumped until only a few families remained. Its semi-deserted feel has made it the chosen set for several Mexican cowboy films.

Only the Neo-Classical church, the Parroquia de la Purísima Concepción, with its reputedly miraculous statue of St. Francis of Assisi, was maintained for the sake of the pilgrims who flood here.

←
Plaza del Carmen, with its fountain and church, in San Luis Potosí

Opposite the church is the dilapidated Casa de Moneda (closed on Mondays and Tuesdays), a former silver warehouse and mint from the 1860s. The town's former glory can also be seen in the shells of ornate mansions and the ruined bullring.

STAY

Mesón del Refugio

This chic hotel in an old hacienda has a glass-covered courtyard and plenty of amenities.

 C3 🏠 Lanzagorta 55, Real de Catorce 🌐 mesondelrefugio.net

$$$

Mesón de la Abundancia

Built out of the ruins of the old Treasury. Expect rustic stone walls, beams, brick floors, and ancient doors.

 C3 🏠 Lanzagorta 11, Real de Catorce 🌐 mesonabundancia.com

$$$

↑ The picturesque El Jardín Principal, at the vibrant heart of San Miguel de Allende

❷⁹ San Miguel de Allende

 C4 ⬛ Guanajuato
ℹ Plaza Principal 8; (415) 152 09 00

A delightful colonial-era town overlooking the Río Laja, San Miguel has cobbled streets lined with handsome mansions and churches. The town's active cultural life combines traditional charm with a cosmopolitan and multi-cultural atmosphere.

El Jardín Principal, the main plaza, is dominated by a church built in 1880. Nearby, the birthplace of independence hero Miguel Allende now operates as the Museo Histórico de San Miguel de Allende. The Mercado Ignacio Ramirez (town market) is full of fruit, vegetables, and medicinal herb stalls, while the adjacent Mercado de Artesanías overflows with handicrafts. The notable Sala Quetzal inside La Biblioteca (library) is a gem, all four walls smothered with lavish murals by artist David Leonardo.

 HIDDEN GEM
Move Over Michelangelo

The Santuario de Jesús Nazareno de Atotonilco, just north of San Miguel, is the Sistine Chapel of Mexico. Founded in the 18th century, its walls and ceiling burst to life with exquisite paintings in the Mexican folk style.

❸⁰ Aguascalientes

 B4 ⬛ Aguascalientes
🚇🚌 ℹ Plaza de la Patria; (449) 910 20 88

Named after its hot springs, Aguascalientes still attracts visitors to its thermal baths but is today best known for its popular spring fair, the Feria de San Marcos (p215).

The Spanish Colonial Palacio de Gobierno has a spectacular maze of arches, pillars, and staircases around its main courtyard. A series of murals inside were painted by Osvaldo Barra Cunningham, a pupil of Diego Rivera. Across the Plaza de la Patria is the 18th-century cathedral, and the Neo-Classical Teatro Morelos. One of the most beautiful churches in Mexico, the Templo del Santuario Nuestra Señora de Guadalupe has an ornate Baroque facade, and a dazzling interior of intricate carvings.

Aguascalientes has a handful of fascinating museums. The **Museo de Arte Contemporáneo** displays prize-winning contemporary works, and the **Museo José Guadalupe Posada** has engravings by Mexico's best known satirical cartoonist. Mexico's obsession with images of death over the centuries is chronicled at the fascinating Museo Nacional de la Muerte, while the Museo de Aguascalientes is an art museum, with a primary focus on the naturalistic work of Saturnino Herrán.

Museo de Arte Contemporáneo
♿ ⬛ Morelos and Primo Verdad 📞 (449) 915 79 53
🕐 11am–6pm Tue–Sun Sun

Museo José Guadalupe Posada
♿♿🏠 ⬛ Jardín del Encino s/n 📞 (449) 915 45 56
🕐 11am–6pm Tue–Sun

❸¹ Puerto Vallarta

 A4 ⬛ Jalisco 🚇🚌
ℹ Independencia 123, Proyecto Escola; www.visitpuertovallarta.com

Hollywood stars discovered the tropical paradise of Bahía

de Banderas (Banderas Bay) in the 1960s. Since then, the areas main hub, Puerto Vallarta, has become one of Mexico's top Pacific resorts. Now 1.5 million tourists flock here annually to savor the beautiful beaches, the year-round pleasant climate, and the vibrant nightlife.

The various resort towns stretch for more than 25 miles (40 km) around the bay, but at the heart is Puerto Vallarta's old town, Viejo Vallarta. This area has managed to conserve some of the quaintness of a Mexican village, with its white-washed, tile-roofed houses and stone-paved streets stretching toward the jungle-clad mountains.

The Plaza Principal is backed by the pretty main church, the Templo de Nuestra Señora de Guadalupe, which is topped by its iconic crown.

Isla Río Cuale, a small island in the river dividing the town, is home to boutiques, cafés, and a botanical garden, and the **Museo del Cuale**, which displays pre-Hispanic artifacts from the region. On the other side of the river, the stalls of Mercado Municipal del Cuale are crammed with local jewelry, papier-mâché, clothes, and souvenir stalls.

Head to the *malecón*, the waterfront boardwalk, for water taxis serving other parts of the bay, such as the Zona Hotelera, the main hotel strip that extends to the seaport in the north. Farther north is Marina Vallarta, Mexico's largest marina, surrounded by luxury hotels, shopping malls, and a golf course. Beside the marina, although in another state (Nayarit) and even another time zone, is Nuevo Vallarta. This is the most recent development on the bay, and its miles of beach, river, and estuary frontage reach as far as the town of Bucerías. The tourist infrastructure then peters out, leaving a string of small, pristine beaches that stretch to the bay's northernmost point, Punta Mita.

The southern, more scenic arc of Banderas Bay begins with Playa de los Muertos (Beach of the Dead), the old town's most popular section of coastline. From here, the road winds past villa-dotted cliffs and sparkling blue coves to Mismaloya (the beach where John Huston filmed *The Night of the Iguana*), before turning inland at the village of Boca de Tomatlán. Beyond this point, the exotic coves and superb swimming and snorkeling beaches are accessible only by watertaxi. The best targets are the first stop of Las Ánimas, a large bay with a long, sandy beach, and languid Yelapa, some 30 minutes from Boca and the final water-taxi stop.

Museo del Cuale

🅰Isla Río Cuale 📞(333) 614 54 16 🕐9am–5pm Mon–Sat

Tourists flock to Puerto Vallarta annually to savor the beautiful beaches, the year-round pleasant climate, and the vibrant nightlife.

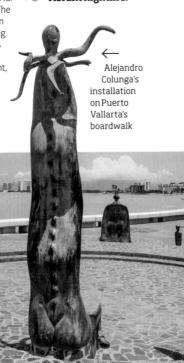

← Alejandro Colunga's installation on Puerto Vallarta's boardwalk

A SHORT WALK
SAN MIGUEL DE ALLENDE

Distance 1 mile (1.5 km) **Time** 15 minutes **Nearest metro** Central de Autobuses

San Miguel de Allende is filled with opulent mansions and old churches, all connected by narrow, cobbled streets. Once an important crossroads for mule trains, which carried silver and gold to the capital and returned with

European treasures, the city is now a popular tourist destination. The heart of the city is perfect for exploring on foot, as all the major sights are just a short stroll from the central Plaza Allende.

The **Escuela de Bellas Artes** *art school, located in a former convent, has an unfinished 1940s mural painted by David Alfaro Siqueiros (1896–1974).*

A huge dome from 1891 towers over the gilded altar of **Templo de la Concepción**.

Casa del Mayorazgo de la Canal, *the town's most sumptuous mansion, has Neo-Classical and Baroque styling.*

Casa Allende, *now a historical museum, was the birthplace of Ignacio Allende, a hero of Mexican independence.*

Casa del Inquisidor *once housed visiting representatives of the Spanish Inquisition.*

Casa de la Inquisición *served as the prison of the Inquisition.*

Notable for its fantastic Neo-Gothic facade, **La Parroquia** *was remodeled in the late 19th century by self-taught architect, Zeferino Gutiérrez.*

START

HERNÁNDEZ MACÍAS

CANAL

HIDALGO

UMARÁN

PLAZA ALLENDE

ALLENDE

JESÚS

CUNA DE LLENDE

CUADRANTE

↑ The elegantly odd concave facade of
Templo de Nuestra Señora de la Salud

FINISH

Iglesia de Santa Ana

Along with the Camarín de la Virgen, **Santa Casa de Loreto** *is one of two opulent side chapels of the Oratorio de San Felipe Neri. Its multi-tiered lantern illuminates the lavishly decorated octagonal space within.*

A series of 33 oil paintings inside **Oratorio de San Felipe Neri** *show scenes from the life of the Florentine St. Philip Neri. They are attributed to Miguel Cabrera (1695–1768).*

INSURGENTES

LLANOS

MESONES

RELOJ

SAN FRANCISCO

JUAREZ

Casa de las Postas

Templo de Nuestra Señora de la Salud *was the chapel for residents of the 18th-century college next door. Its early Churrigueresque entrance beneath a giant shell has strong indigenous influences.*

CORREO

The Neo-Classical tower of **Templo de San Francisco** *contrasts sharply with its two ornate Churrigueresque facades.*

Casa del Conde de Casa Loja

0 meters   75
0 yards   75

N ↑

A DRIVING TOUR
LAKE PÁTZCUARO

Length 55 miles (90 km) **Stopping-off points** There are plenty of good places to eat in Isla Janitzio and traditional family run restaurants in Santa Fe

The road around this idyllic lake bedded in rolling hills passes colonial-era and pre-Hispanic architectural gems, and towns with rich craft traditions. Pátzcuaro, Tzintzuntzán, and Quiroga are popular destinations, but the western shore and marshlands to the south see fewer visitors. Yet here the winding road offers spectacular vistas of the lake and rare glimpses of Purépechan (Tarascan) village life. To see the islands, take a boat from Pátzcuaro's Muelle General.

↑ Dusk falling over Janitzio island in Lake Pátzcuaro

El Guacapian
9,777 ft (2,980 m) △

Rancho de Oponguio

Puácuaro

Isla La Pacanda

Isla Yunuén

Erongarícuaro

Napízaro

Isla Tecuena

The town of **Erongarícuaro** *was a favorite hideaway of Surrealist André Breton.*

Isla Janitzio

San Francisco Uricho

Jarácuaro

Arocutín

Tocuaro
FINISH

Famous for its prize-winning wooden masks, **Tocuaro** *has a number of unmarked workshops selling these fantastic creations.*

San Miguel Nocutzepo

San Bartolo Pareo

Ajuno

14

14

Did You Know?

Tzintzuntzán's week-long La Fiesta del Señor del Rescate (February) celebrates a local 19th-century miracle.

Isla Janitzio *is a car-free island known for its fish restaurants, souvenir stalls and panoramic summit, crowned by an 160 ft (49 m) statue of José María Morelos.*

0 kilometers 5
0 miles 5

N ↑

BAJÍO AND THE
CENTRAL COAST

Lake Pátzcuaro

Locator Map

Santa Fe *has a fine 17th-century church, and roadside stalls selling the local black pottery.*

A busy market town, **Quiroga** *sells agricultural and handicraft products from all over Michoacán. Lacquerware, such as wooden bowls and trays painted with bright flowers, is a typical local product.*

San Jerónimo
Purenchecuaro

Chupícuaro

Santa Fe de
la Laguna

Quiroga

San Andrés
Tziróndaro

*Lake
Pátzcuaro*

Atzimbo

Ichupio

Patambicho

Tarerio

Tzintzuntzán

Yácatas de
Tzintzuntzán

△ Tarriaqueri
8,671 ft (2,643 m)

△ Yahuarato
8,277 ft (2,523 m)

The yácatas – multilevel temple bases – near the town of **Tzintzuntzán** *reveal its history as the former Tarascan capital. Also noteworthy are the 16th-century Franciscan convent and the market.*

Ucasanastacua

Colonia
Lázaro Cárdenas

Las Cuevas

Cucuchucho

Sanabria

Chapultepec

Buenavista

Ihuatzio

Tzurumútaro

Huecorio

El Manzanillal

△ Cerro Blanco
7,546 ft (2,300 m)

Pátzcuaro
START

The peaceful village of **Ihuatzio** *stands near massive Tarascan ruins, which overlook the lake. A stone coyote sculpture found at the ruins now graces the village church.*

→ The Tarascan *yácata* ruins outside Tzintzuntzán

SOUTHERN MEXICO

Southern Mexico's mild climate and fertile soils attracted some of the earliest recorded settlements in Mesoamerica, with the Oaxaca Valley first inhabited in the 7th century BC. Three centuries later, the Zapotecs built their capital at Monte Albán, which dominated the valley for hundreds of years, before giving way to other, smaller cities. Meanwhile, in the east, the Maya were reaching their cultural peak and building the magnificent city of Palenque. The Spanish conquered the region in the 16th century, but it remained a relative backwater for most of the colonial period. Even now, industry is limited beyond the cities, and much of the region remains underdeveloped, making the southern states some of the poorest in Mexico. Rural poverty helped fuel the 1994 Zapatista rebellion in Chiapas.

Geographically, the South is dominated by the mountains of the Sierra Madre del Sur, which make travel difficult but provide spectacular scenery. The Pacific coast is mostly unspoiled. Its sandy beaches are lined with palm trees and pounded constantly by surf.

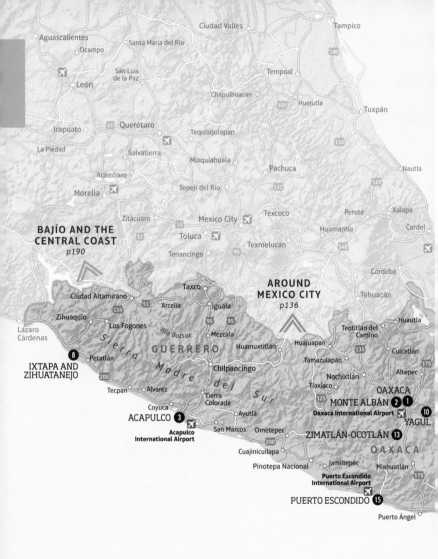

SOUTHERN MEXICO

Must Sees

1. Oaxaca
2. Monte Albán
3. Acapulco
4. Palenque

Experience More

5. Bonampak
6. Cascadas de Agua Azul
7. San Cristóbal de las Casas
8. Ixtapa and Zihuatanejo
9. Tuxtla Gutiérrez
10. Yagul
11. Cañón del Sumidero
12. Mitla
13. Zimatlán-Ocotlán
14. Comitán de Domínguez
15. Puerto Escondido
16. Chiapa de Corzo
17. Toniná
18. Yaxchilán

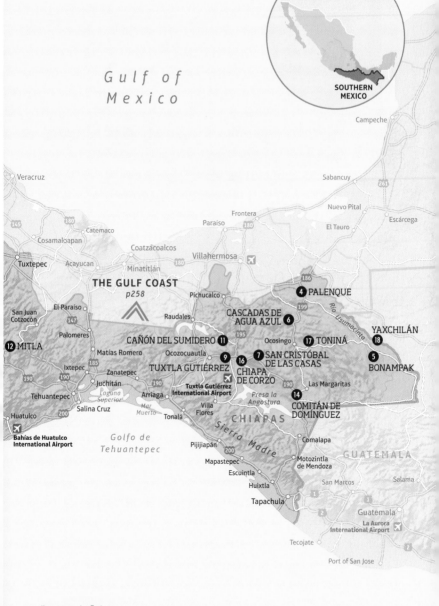

Gulf of
Mexico

SOUTHERN
MEXICO

Campeche

Veracruz

Sabancuy

Nuevo Pital

Frontera

Paraíso

El Tauro

Escárcega

145

180

Catemaco

Cosamaloapan

Coatzacoalcos

Villahermosa

186

Tuxtepec

Acayucan

Minatitlán

Pichucalco

4 PALENQUE

San Juan
Cotzocón

El Paraíso

147

Palomeres

THE GULF COAST
p258

Raudales

199

**CASCADAS DE
AGUA AZUL** **6**

Río Usumacinta

YAXCHILÁN

18

12 MITLA

Matías Romero

CAÑÓN DEL SUMIDERO **11**

195

Ocosingo

17 TONINÁ

185

Ocozocuautla

9

5

Ixtepec

Zanatepec

TUXTLA GUTIÉRREZ

16 **7** **SAN CRISTÓBAL
DE LAS CASAS**

BONAMPAK

190

190

Juchitán

*Laguna
Superior*

Arriaga

190

**CHIAPA
DE CORZO**

Las Margaritas

Tehuantepec

**Tuxtla Gutiérrez
International Airport**

*Presa la
Angostura*

Huatulco

200

Salina Cruz

Villa
Flores

14

**COMITÁN DE
DOMÍNGUEZ**

**Bahías de Huatulco
International Airport**

*Mar
Muerto*

Tonalá

Sierra Madre

CHIAPAS

*Golfo de
Tehuantepec*

Pijijiapán

Comalapa

GUATEMALA

200

Mapastepec

Motozintla
de Mendoza

Salama

Escuintla

San Marcos

Huixtla

1

Tapachula

2

Guatemala

**La Aurora
International Airport**

1

*Pacific
Ocean*

Tecojate

2

Port of San Jose

| 0 kilometers | | 150 | | N |
| 0 miles | | 150 | | ↑ |

A delightful cobbled street in Oaxaca, lined with brightly painted craft stores

❶

OAXACA

Oaxaca ✈🚌 🏛 Avenida Benito Juárez 703; www.oaxaca.travel

With its blend of elegant colonial-era architecture, a vibrant indigenous culture, and one of the richest culinary scenes in Mexico, it's easy to fall in love with Oaxaca. The city invites aimless wandering, its blossom-filled streets and cobbled alleys lined with crafts stores, galleries, markets, and excellent restaurants.

①

Museo de Arte Contemporáneo

🏛 Macedonio Alcalá 202
🕐 10:30am-7:45pm Wed-Mon 🌐 museomaco.org

The city's contemporary art museum is housed in a carefully refurbished 16th-century building, called the Casa de Cortés (House of Cortés) after the conquistador who is reputed to have commissioned it. Set around a central courtyard, the museum displays works of note painted by local and international modern artists, including Francisco Toledo and Rodolfo Morales. It is also a popular venue for holding temporary exhibitions and other cultural events.

②

Mercado Juárez

🏛 Corner of 20 de Noviembre & Las Casas
🕐 7am-9pm daily

Mercado Juárez was once the city's main market and is still a great place to pick up crafts made in surrounding villages. Traditional clothing, leather goods, and the famous Oaxaca pottery are all sold here.

③

Cathedral

🏛 Avenida de la Independencia 700

The cathedral is was originally constructed in 1553, but a series of earthquakes meant that it had to be rebuilt in 1730. The Baroque facade includes a fine relief of the Assumption of the Virgin Mary above the main door. Inside, the main feature is the splendid bronze altar, crafted in Italy.

④

Central Oaxaca

The Plaza de Armas, or zócalo, is the geographical and social center of the city. Closed to traffic, it bustles with vendors, students, tourists, and villagers from outside the city. It is a great place to watch the world go by, especially from the cafés around its perimeter. Just northwest of the zócalo is the Alameda de León, a lovely square with market stalls that specialize in arts and crafts.

⑤

Iglesia de Santo Domingo

🏛 Corner of Alcalá and Gurrión

Of the many churches in the city, this is the one most likely to take your breath away. Begun in 1572, it was completed over 200 years later

Museo Textil de Oaxaca

🏠 Hidalgo 917 📞 (951) 501 16 17 🕐 10am–8pm daily (to 6pm Sun)

Oaxaca's history of textile making is chronicled at this fascinating museum, with lots of colorful examples from the state's indigenous communities on display. Set in a renovated 16th-century convent, the museum is funded by Mexican billionaire Alfredo Harp Helú.

⑦ Casa de Juárez

🏠 García Vigil 609 📞 (951) 516 18 60 🕐 10am–7pm Tue–Sun

The house where Benito Juárez lived between 1818 and 1828 is now a museum devoted to his life and times. Around a shady patio, the rooms have been kept almost as they were when Juárez lived here, and provide fascinating insights into the lives of the middle classes in 19th-century Mexico.

BENITO JUÁREZ (1806–72)

Benito Juárez, one of Mexico's greatest liberal reformers, was born just north of Oaxaca. He was orphaned at the age of three, but was educated by priests and went on to become a champion of agricultural reform and indigenous people's rights. He was made president in 1858 and, after defeating the French, personally oversaw the execution of Emperor Maximilian in 1867 *(p58)*. He continued to pursue reform until his death.

at a total cost of over 12 million pesos in gold. Its misleadingly simple facade hides an interior that dazzles with gilded plaster and colored stucco, in a sublime combination of Romanesque, Baroque, Gothic, and Moorish styles. On the south side is the gilt-covered Capilla del Rosario, where there are numerous paintings of saints and Madonnas in varying sizes.

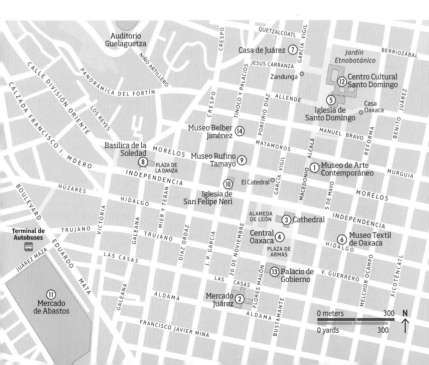

⑧

Basílica de la Soledad

 Avenida Independencia 107 (951) 516 50 76

The Basílica de la Soledad is noted for its 79-ft (24-m) high Baroque facade, which resembles a folding altarpiece, and for its gilded interior. It was built between 1682 and 1690 to house the image of the Virgin of Solitude, Oaxaca's patron saint. This figure can be seen inside, encrusted with 600 diamonds and topped with a 4-lb (2-kg) gold crown. There is a small religious museum round the back of the church crowded with stained glass, paintings. and depictions of the Virgin of Solitude.

⑨

Museo Rufino Tamayo

 Avenida Morelos 503
🕐 10am-2pm & 4-7pm Mon & Wed-Sat, 10am-3pm Sun
🌐 rufinotamayo.org.mx

This beautifully presented museum, which is housed in a charming 17th-century building, contains a wondrous collection of pre-Hispanic art once owned by the artist Rufino Tamayo (p108). It was

← Pre-Hispanic stone carving exhibited at the Museo Rufino Tamayo

OAXACA'S POTTERY

Distinctive black or dark green ceramics are seen all around Oaxaca. The black style, from San Bartolo Coyotepec, 6 miles (10 km) south, was popularized by Doña Rosa Real. The green pottery, which is made in Santa María Atzompa, 5 miles (8 km) northwest of Oaxaca, is beautifully decorated. It is best to buy both in the villages themselves.

partly Tamayo's intention in collecting the pieces to stop them from falling into the hands of illicit artifact traders. He left them to his native state to make his fellow Mexicans aware of their rich heritage. The fascinating displays are arranged according to aesthetic themes, in a series of rooms set around an attractive 17th-century patio.

⑩

Iglesia de San Felipe Neri

 Avenida de la Independencia 407

This charming church also has a facade shaped like an altarpiece, but its highlight is the gilt altarpiece itself, which is in the Churrigueresque style (p42). Benito Juárez, Mexico's most celebrated president, was married here.

⑪

Mercado de Abastos

 Cnr of Periférico and Juárez Maza 🕐 7am-9pm daily

Most of the serious trading happens at this huge market,

situated southwest of the center. Crafts including ceramics, jewelry, and painted wooden animals are sold here, but the real attraction is the chance to take in the noise, heat, smells, and color of one of the most vibrant markets in the country. The buyers and sellers chatter not in Spanish but mostly in the local Zapotec and Mixtec tongues, as they haggle at stalls laid out with the utmost care and attention. The liveliest day is Saturday.

⑫

Centro Cultural Santo Domingo

 Cnr of Alcalá & Gurrión (951) 516 97 41 🕐 10am-6:30pm Tue-Sun

Housed in the buildings of a former monastery attached to the Iglesia de Santo Domingo (p234), the Centro Cultural Santo Domingo incorporates a museum, a botanical garden, a university library with books dating from the 15th century, and a bookstore.

The Museo de la Culturas is dedicated to pre-Hispanic artifacts from the ancient cities of Oaxaca state. On display here are some of the remarkable treasures found at Monte Albán (p240), in particular the extraordinary cache of Mixtec art and jewelry discovered in Tomb 7. This hoard includes lovingly crafted pieces in alabaster, obsidian, jade, and

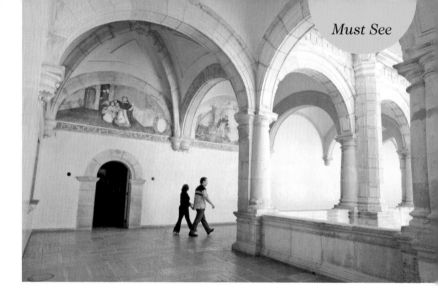

↑ The monastery complex, home to the Centro Cultural Santo Domingo

other precious materials, but is most famous for the objects in gold, regarded as the finest of their kind in the Americas.

Palacio de Gobierno

🏛 Plaza de la Constitución
📞 (951) 501 81 00 🕐 8am-3pm Mon-Sat

Oaxaca's Neo-Classical Palacio de Gobierno (the State Government building) occupies the zócalo's southern side. It was completed in 1884 and then remodeled in the 1940s.

The main reason for a visit today are the fabulous murals on the stairwells inside, which were created by Arturo García Bustos in the 1980s. They depict in detail key moments in Oaxacan history, as well as

famous locals such as Benito Juárez, José María Morelos, Porfirio Díaz, Vicente Guerrero (being shot at Cuilapan) and the 17th-century nun and love poet Juana Inés de la Cruz. Note that you need to sign in and pass through security to gain access to the building.

Museo Belber Jiménez

🏛 Matamoros 307 🕐 10am-7pm Wed-Mon 📞 (951) 514 49 96

This small museum – easy to spot thanks to its vibrantly blue exterior – displays the impressive private collection of local jeweller Francisco Jiménez and his wife Ellen Belber. Exhibits include rare gold Mixtec jewelry, an array of 20th-century silver work by William Spratling (p162), Oaxacan folk art, indigenous clothing, and local pottery.

Look out for the original Mexican flag, which was presented to President Díaz on a visit to Oaxaca. One of the key pieces on display is the necklace given to Frida Kahlo by her husband, Diego Rivera, engraved with the word "Amor" ("love").

 HIDDEN GEM
Cactus Paradise

Behind the Museo de las Culturas is a beautiful cactus garden, the Jardín Etnobotánico. It's a tranquil oasis, containing orchids, frangipani, and other native species. By guided tour only (www.jardinoaxaca.mx).

EAT

Oaxaca is a top foodie destination, and restaurant menus are bursting with local specialities, such as chocolate-based mole sauce and delicacies like fried maguet worms, ground with chilies as a seasoning.

Casa Oaxaca
🏛 Constitución 104-A
🌐 casaoaxacael
restaurante.com

💲💲💲

El Catedral
🏛 García Vigil 105 🕐 Tue
🌐 restaurantecatedral.
com.mx

💲💲💲

Zandunga
🏛 García Vigil 512
🌐 zandungasabor.com

💲💲💲

THE INDIGENOUS PEOPLES OF MEXICO

Over 25 million Mexicans identify as indigenous (20 percent of the total population). Indigenous communities are concentrated mainly in the south of the country, although some large groups are found in the north.

Though Spanish conquistadors destroyed the last of the great Mesoamerican civilizations *(p144)*, their people did not disappear, and today the ancestors of the Aztecs, Maya, Zapotec, and many other cultures remain. Official statistics show that around 6 percent of the country's population speak one of Mexico's 62 native language groups.

Many ethnic groups have multiple names: one they use to refer to themselves, and another that is a more common term used by the rest of Mexican society.

CONTEMPORARY COMMUNITIES

For centuries after the Spanish Conquest, indigenous peoples faired poorly in Mexico, suffering from European diseases, slavery, and discrimination. Though many communities remained poor as a result, things have improved in recent decades.

Many people have moved away from traditional dress and customs, but some – such as the Rarámuri *(p181)* - retain much of their pre-Hispanic way of life, and the legacy of their cultural roots is still evident. One of the most authentic indigenous markets in Mexico takes place every Thursday in the ancient Zapotec town of Zaachila *(p253)*. The open-air market full of fresh fruits and local produce is virtually unchanged since the pre-Hispanic era.

↑ A Rarámuri woman of northern Mexico weaving a traditional basket out of pine needles

→ A street market in Chiapas, a traditional meeting place for indigenous communities

Trique

▽ Living in Oaxaca state, the Trique (also known as the Triqui) are among the less numerous indigenous peoples.

Rarámuri

The Rarámuri (or Tarahumara; *p181*) of Chihuahua state play a tough endurance ball game called *rarajipari*, which can last for several days.

Yaqui

△ The Yaqui (or Yoeme) people of Sonora state put their own twist on Easter and the Day of the Dead with the Deer Dance.

Maya

△ The Mesoamerican Maya civilization went into decline before the arrival of the Spanish. The descendants of the Maya, who inhabit the state of Chiapas and the Yucatán Peninsula, speak a large number of Maya languages.

Huichol

▽ The Huichol (or Wixáritari) are famous for their dazzlingly colored handicrafts, especially beadwork. They live on the border of Jalisco and Nayarit states.

Mixtec

The early Mixtec civilization emerged in Oaxaca state in the 1100s. Mixtec people are renowned for their jewelry, ceramics, and mosaic art.

Zapotec

▽ The Zapotec population is concentrated around Oaxaca. Villages are often associated with a specific craft, such as black pottery or textiles.

Lacandón

The Lacandón (or Hach Winik) live in Chiapas state, and have retained one of Mexico's most traditional cultures.

Totonac

△ Totonac communities live in southern Mexico, where they have preserved their language and many of their traditional customs, including the Voladores "flying" dancers *(p262)*.

② ⊘ ⦿ ⑨ ⊡ ⑪

MONTE ALBÁN

🄰D6 🄰Off Mex 190, 5 miles (8 km) W of Oaxaca, Oaxaca 🚌From Oaxaca
🕙8am–5pm daily 🌐inah.gob.mx

Spectacularly situated on a mountain 1,315 ft (400 m) above the Oaxaca Valley, Monte Albán is the greatest of the Zapotec cities and one of the most important archaeological sites in Latin America.

In a triumph of engineering, the mountain top was leveled to allow for the creation of the ceremonial site. Its long history began with the Olmecs (p272) around 500 BC. The city came to dominate the cultural, religious, and economic life of the region. Falling under the influence of Teotihuacán (p142) during the height of its power, Monte Albán declined in later years and by AD 800 was largely abandoned. It was subsequently adopted by the Mixtecs, primarily as the site for some magnificent gold-laden burials.

The South Platform has stelae at its northeast and northwest corners showing prisoners of war with their arms and legs bound.

Mound III

Mound M

Los Danzantes gallery contains carvings of humans in tortured positions, thought to be prisoners of war.

Gran Plaza

Thought to have been built as an observatory, or to celebrate victory in battle, this structure has glyphs carved on its walls.

Palace

Building P

Altar

Mound II

Buildings G, H, and I, which served as temples, were found to contain several tombs. A tunnel leads from the Palace to Building H.

Stela

← An uncovered tomb on show in the museum at Monte Albán

A typical ballcourt, this I-shaped structure was used for playing the ceremonial ballgame.

The North Platform, the largest structure at Monte Albán; *(inset)* detail of carvings

System IV is almost identical to Mound M. Both are well-preserved pyramids that would once have been surmounted by one-room wooden temples.

The Sunken Patio has an altar at its center.

Building B

When Tomb 104 was opened in 1937, a vaulted burial chamber containing a single skeleton, surrounded by urns, perfuming pots, and other offerings, was discovered.

Tomb 103

A staircase leads up to the North Platform. At the top are two rows of broken columns that once supported a flat roof.

Museum, Tomb 7 and entrance

Illustration of the archaelogical site at Monte Albán

PICTURE PERFECT
Monte Albán at Sunset

The best time to photograph Monte Albán is in the late afternoon, as the sun sinks into the valley. The classic view is from the top of the Platforma Norte, which looks down on the main plaza.

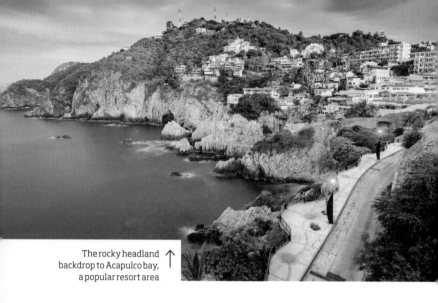

The rocky headland backdrop to Acapulco bay, a popular resort area ↑

ACAPULCO

 C6 Guerrero 🛫🚌 ℹ️ Avenida Costera Miguel Alemán 603; www.guerrero.travel

With its dazzling bay and long swathe of golden sands, backed by high-rise hotels and the green foothills of the Sierra Madre, Acapulco is the grande dame of the Mexican tourist industry. It's a sub-tropical city-by-the-sea, popular with inhabitants of the capital, who flock here for the nightlife, culinary scene, and attractions.

① Centro Cultural La Casa de los Vientos

📍 Inalámbrica 6, Cerro de la Pinzona (off La Quebrada) 📞 (744) 482 11 61 🕐 10am–6pm Mon–Fri

La Casa de los Vientos (aka "Exekatlkalli" or "House of the Winds"), is where Diego Rivera spent the last two years of his life, living with his former model and partner, Dolores Olmedo Patiño. Rivera worked on five large murals here between 1955 and 1957; from the street you can view the sensational work that covers the entire outside wall, made of seashells and colored tiles; the 66 ft (20 m) snake on the

right depicts the Aztec god Tlaloc, while the 42 ft (13 m) feathered serpent on the left is Quetzalcoatl, another important Mesoamerican deity. There's more artwork inside, but since it's often closed for renovation, check the latest at the tourist office.

② Fuerte de San Diego

📍 Calle Hornitos y Morelos 📞 (744) 482 38 28 🕐 9am–6pm Tue–Sun

Today, one of the few reminders of the city's history is the star-shaped Fuerte de San Diego, a 17th-century fort housing the Museo Historico

de Acapulco. It details the city's history from pre-Hispanic times to independence, with special emphasis on its importance as a commercial center.

③   La Quebrada

📍 Avenida Adolfo López Mateos 340, Las Playas 📞 (744) 483 12 60 (hotel) 🕐 1pm, 7:30pm, 8:30pm, 9:30pm & 10:30pm daily

The death-defying cliff divers (clavadistas) of La Quebrada provide Acapulco's most spectacular attraction. The performance starts with the young men climbing a 125-ft (38-m) cliff. On reaching the top, they offer a prayer at a small altar before launching themselves into the shallow

> 💬 INSIDER TIP
> **Two Sides**
>
> Acapulco can be divided in two. To the west is the Centro Histórico, with historic remnants. To the east is the main beach, anchored by La Costera Miguel Alemán, lined with hotels, restaurants, and nightclubs.

waters below. Each dive must coincide with an incoming wave if the diver is to avoid being dashed on the sharp rocks below. The shows and the rest of the evening can be seen from a viewing platform off the Plazuela de Quebrada (for a small charge), or more comfortably from Hotel El Mirador, where you can enjoy a drink while watching the divers. To view for free, keep walking further up to López Mateos. The last two shows are performed holding flaming torches.

Bahia de Acapulco

Much of the town stretches out along the shores of Acapulco Bay, which are broken up into a number of separate beaches.

Playa Caletilla and Playa Caleta are situated on the peninsula south of the Centro. Smaller and more intimate than the other beaches, they are popular with local families who enjoy the calm, clean waters. Boat trips can be taken from here for the ten-minute journey to Isla la Roqueta, a small offshore island featuring thatched-roof restaurants, a small zoo, and several more beaches.

Playa Honda, Playa Larga, and Playa Manzanillo, on the northern side of the same peninsula, were popular in the 1930s and 40s, but now serve mainly as departure points for charter fishing trips.

Playa Hornos and Playa Hornitos occupy a central position on the bay. They have a family atmosphere but can get busy on the weekends. They also have the advantage of several beachside restaurants and nearby Papagayo Park, which has boating, rides, and other children's activities.

Farther east, Playa Condesa is the best known and most crowded of all the beaches. It is considered by those in the know to be the resort's "hot-spot" and is a favorite with younger visitors. On the eastern side of the bay, Playa Icacos runs from the Presidente Hotel to the naval base and is generally less crowded than the other beaches.

Just east of the city, Puerto Marqués is a large bay with luxury hotels, food stands on the beach, and safe swimming.

EAT

Pitiona del Mar
This restaurant is known for its fresh and contemporary take on traditional Oaxacan cuisine. Expect imaginatively prepared dishes and cocktails giving a delicious taste of Oaxaca.

 Avenida Costera de las Palmas s/n, Granjas del Marqués (744) 980 06 76

$$$

El Pescador
Watch the sunset over the Pacific while you enjoy drinks and the day's catch in this rightfully popular seaside restaurant.

 Calle M. F. Maury 1, Fracc Costa Azul, Costa Azul (744) 469 12 34

$$$

PALENQUE

🅰 F5 **🅰 5 miles (8 km) SW of Palenque town, Chiapas** **🚌 From Palenque town** **🕐 8am–4:45pm daily** **🌐 inah.gob.mx**

The dense jungle covering the hills and the echoing sound of howler monkeys forms an evocative backdrop to the mighty Maya temples of Palenque, deservedly one of the best examples of Maya architecture in Mexico.

① The Palace

Standing on a raised platform some 328 ft by 262 ft (100 m by 80 m) and 33 ft (10 m) high, the palace, a complex of courtyards and corridors, is the product of many kings. The earliest buildings date to the time of Pakal, but the basal platform conceals earlier phases, some preserved as underground galleries. The palace was the home of the royal family and their imme-diate entourage. Carvings and stucco decorations can be seen in parts of the building. Particularly interesting are the sculptures of captives in the courtyard, where visitors could be suitably impressed by the might of the Palenque kings. The Oval Tablet depicts the accession of Pakal, who receives the emblems of office from his mother, a short-reigning queen.

② Temple of the Jaguar

A short path behind the Temple of the Inscriptions leads to this ruined structure. Its name derives from the image of a king seated on a jaguar throne inside, now destroyed. Unexcavated and overgrown, it gives an idea of what the site must have been like when it was first explored in the late 18th century.

Temple of the Inscriptions

This impressive pyramid was constructed during the 68-year reign of Pakal (AD 615–83) and later contained his funerary crypt, a fact that was revealed only by the dramatic

Did You Know?

In the Classic Maya era, the temples would have been covered with plaster and painted red.

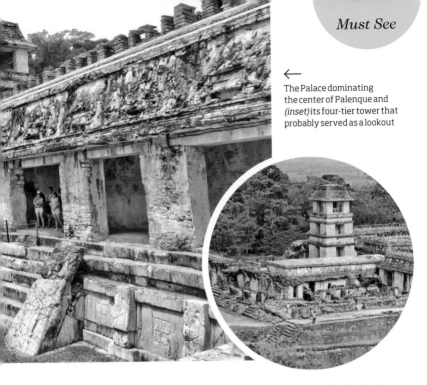

← The Palace dominating the center of Palenque and *(inset)* its four-tier tower that probably served as a lookout

discovery of his tomb by Alberto Ruz Lhuillier in 1952. The lid of the sarcophagus is decorated with a symbolic scene of Pakal's resurrection from the jaws of the underworld. Many of the artifacts and jewelry found in the tomb are on display in the Museo Nacional de Antropología in Mexico City *(p100)*.

④
Outlying Temples

Two clearly marked paths that set off from in front of the Temple of the Sun lead to Temples XVIII and XXI, and other isolated buildings that are nearby but hidden by trees. More buildings can be reached by the path from the site to the museum, which passes through Group B and the Group of the Bats. Branches off this path lead to Group C, Group I, and Group II. There are hundreds of similar but less accessible structures at Palenque that are hidden by the surrounding jungle.

⑤
The Museum

🕐 9am–4:45pm Tue–Sun

This modern building on the road between Palenque town and the archaeological site provides an overview of the development of the Maya city. Many artifacts found on the site are on display here, including the so-called Tablet of the Slaves.

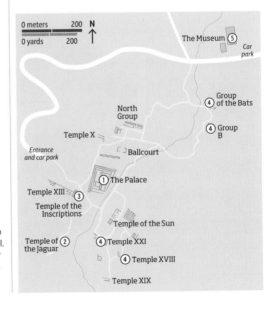

| 0 meters | 200 | N |
| 0 yards | 200 | ↑ |

The Museum ⑤ — Car park

Group ④ of the Bats

North Group

Group ④ B

Temple X

Entrance and car park

Ballcourt

① The Palace

Temple XIII ③

Temple of the Inscriptions

Temple of the Sun

Temple of ② the Jaguar

④ Temple XXI

④ Temple XVIII

Temple XIX

Exploring Palenque

Palenque is everything that an archaeological site should be: mysterious, solemn, well preserved, and imposing in its beautiful jungle setting. The Maya first settled here as early as 100 BC, and the city reached its apogee between AD 600 and 800, when it served as a regional capital. It fell into a precipitous decline in the early 10th century and was abandoned to the ever encroaching jungle. Hundreds of ruined buildings are spaced out over a huge area, but only a fairly small central area has been excavated, which has uncovered some ruins emblazoned with fine sculpture and splendid stuccowork.

The most interesting and best preserved buildings are in the Principal Group. The tallest and most imposing of these is the Temple of the Inscriptions. The entrance to the tomb is by way of two flights of steep stone steps that descend 82 ft (25 m). A few lesser-known temples can be reached by easy paths through the jungle. Another path leads from the Principal Group past a series of waterfalls to the site museum.

Did You Know?

The Temple of the Count was, in the 1830s, the home of an eccentric European nobleman.

The Temple of the Foliated Cross is named after a panel showing a cruciform corn plant.

Inside the Temple of the Cross are carvings and a striking roof comb.

Although badly damaged, Temple XIV has been largely reconstructed. It contains some well-preserved glyphs and carvings.

Ballcourt

The North Group consists of five temples on a single platform. At the base of the platform is this carving of the god Tlaloc.

Path to Groups B and C, waterfalls, and museum (p245)

↑ Detail of an unspoiled fresco uncovered in Temple XIV

The Temple of the Count

→

Temple of the Sun, one of the best-preserved buildings on the site

The Temple of the Sun is a four-level pyramid crowned with a prominent roof comb, a massive carved stone slab. Inside are glyphs and stucco friezes, one of which shows the sun.

Water Channel

Path to Temple of the Jaguar (p244)

Temple of the Inscriptions (p245)

Temple XIII

Temple of the Dying Moon

Tomb of Alberto Ruz Lhuillier

Entrance

The Palace (p244)

This stone slab carved with a figure is one of nine that can be seen in the courtyard of the palace.

Temple X

←

Illustration of the ancient archaeological site of Palenque

OTHER THINGS TO DO IN PALENQUE

The town of Palenque, 4 miles (7 km) east of the ruins, is the best place to stay overnight when you're planning a visit here. Most activity in town occurs around Parque Central, the main plaza, which is lined with handicraft stalls, bars, restaurants, and an old colonial-era church.

EXPERIENCE MORE

5

Bonampak

🅰F6 🏠95 miles (153 km) SE of Palenque, Chiapas 🕐8am–5pm daily 🌐inah. gob.mx

The Maya site of Bonampak reached its apogee under its ruler Yahaw Chan Muwan (AD 776–90). The subject of three fine stelae at the site, Yahaw Chan Muwan commissioned Bonampak's remarkable Temple of the Paintings. The walls and vaulted ceilings are decorated with vividly colored murals. These give insights into the life of the nobility of Bonampak and the pageantry surrounding Maya warfare. Murals in the two outer rooms show noblemen in elaborate headdresses. Below are musicians and dancers, and on the ceiling animals and figures representing constellations of the Maya cosmos. The two main paintings in the middle room depict a battle where Maya warriors are defeating their enemy.

6

Cascadas de Agua Azul

🅰F5 🏠Off Mex 199, 78 miles (125 km) NE of San Cristóbal de las Casas, Chiapas 🕐8am–6pm daily 🌐visitachiapas.com

The Parque Nacional Agua Azul has a series of stunning waterfalls – over 500 in all, ranging from 10 to 100 ft (3–30 m) in height.

It is possible to swim in some of the park's aquamarine-colored rock pools, which brings welcome relief from the heat and humidity of the lowlands. The falls are best visited outside of the

Ruins of a Maya temple at Bonampak with *(inset)* striking murals inside

rainy season (Jun–Sep), during which the waters become murky. Do not swim where there are signs warning of dangerous currents, and bring shoes that you are happy to wear in the water, which will make it easier and safer to step on the rocky ground underwater.

Some 14 miles (22 km) before the road from Agua Azul reaches Palenque *(p244)* is the spectacular, 100-ft- (30-m-) high waterfall at Misol-Ha. Set within the lush surroundings of a tropical rainforest, this is another good place to stop for a swim.

↑ A memorial cross erected in the square outside the cathedral of San Cristóbal de las Casas

---

San Cristóbal de las Casas

A F6 **B** Chiapas **C** **D**
E Eje vial s/n, Los Pinos;
(967) 678 65 70

Founded by the Spanish in 1528 and marked by centuries of geographical isolation, San Cristóbal is now a popular tourist spot. Its pedestrianized streets are lined with a blend of adobe houses, colonial-era churches, and cosmopolitan bars and restaurants. It's a great base for exploring highland Chiapas, a scenic region rich in Maya history and culture.

Situated 7,550 ft (2,300 m) above sea level, San Cristóbal has a refreshingly cool climate. The town's main square, Plaza 31 de Marzo, is dominated by the Palacio Municipal and the cathedral. The latter was started in the 16th century, but construction and alterations continued until the beginning of the 19th century. Its lavish interior contains an elaborate gold-encrusted pulpit and notable altarpieces. A few blocks north is the 16th-century Dominican Templo de Santo Domingo, the most impressive church in the city. It has an intricate pink facade, a gilded Baroque interior with magnificent altarpieces, and a pulpit carved from a single piece of oak. Next door, the **Museo Centro Cultural de los Altos** records the history of the city. On General Utrilla is the main market, Mercado José Castillo Tielemans, where indigenous people from the surrounding hills come to trade.

Cutting through the heart of the city is the Andador Eclesiástico, a pedestrianized thoroughfare, lined with shops, restaurants, and cafés.

The **Na Bolom** museum and research center is devoted to studying and preserving the culture of the Lacandón Maya. Here visitors can learn more about the Lacandón culture through the museum, or with visits to their community in the rainforest.

The Iglesia de San Cristóbal to the west, and the Iglesia de Guadalupe to the east, offer excellent views over the city from their hilltop positions.

The ruined Maya ceremonial site of Moxviquil lies 1 mile (1.5 km) north of the center, and is accessed by a tranquil loop trail through the forest. There are also several villages 6 miles (10 km) or so from San Cristóbal, including San Juan Chamula, which has a beautiful church. A trip here provides an insight into the mix of Christian and pre-Hispanic traditions of the Tzotzil-speaking inhabitants. The village's fiestas and markets are among the best in Mexico. Visitors are warned not to take photos, especially in religious buildings, as this may cause serious offense.

Museo Centro Cultural de los Altos
⊗ **C** 9am-6pm Tue-Sun
C (967) 678 2809

Na Bolom
⊗ ☺ ☺ **A** Avenida Vicente Guerrero 33 **C** 9am-7pm daily **W** nabolom.org

---

> ### THE ZAPATISTA UPRISING
>
> On January 1, 1994, the EZLN (Zapatista Army of National Liberation) seized the town of San Cristóbal de las Casas. Their aims - taken from those of Emiliano Zapata *(p62)* - were a redistribution of power and resources from the wealthy few to the poor majority. Forced out of the town by the army, the Zapatistas fled into the jungle. A ceasefire was agreed in 1995. While the EZLN have now joined mainstream political parties, relations are tense, and visitors to the jungle area they occupy are cautioned to be discreet.

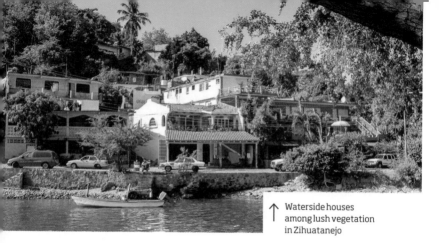

↑ Waterside houses among lush vegetation in Zihuatanejo

⑧ Ixtapa and Zihuatanejo

🅰B5 🅰Guerrero
🛈 Ayuntamiento; www.
zihuatanejodeazueta.
gob.mx

Ixtapa and Zihuatanejo are two resorts in one. Ixtapa is glitzy and full of luxury high-rise hotels. It is located along an attractive curving beach, Playa Palmar, which backs onto a broad, palm-lined avenue packed with restaurants, shops, and nightclubs.

Zihuatanejo is more intimate, and still has the feel of a fishing community. Set in a scenic, sheltered bay, fishermen come here to sell their daily catch. Both resorts offer world-class deep-sea fishing, and excellent scuba diving.

⑨ Tuxtla Gutiérrez

🅰E6 🅰Chiapas
🛈 Andrés Serra Rojas 1090,
Edificio Torre Chiapas;
www.chiapas.gob.mx

Tuxtla Gutiérrez is a modern, working city, and a major gateway for visitors. Plaza Cívica, the main square, bustles with life and is

---

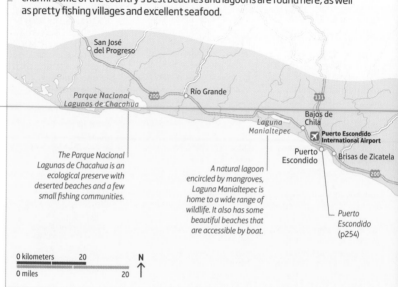

OAXACA'S COAST

This area has seen limited development and so still retains a sense of undisturbed charm. Some of the country's best beaches and lagoons are found here, as well as pretty fishing villages and excellent seafood.

San José del Progreso

Parque Nacional Lagunas de Chacahua — 200 — Río Grande — 131

Bajos de Chila

Laguna Manialtepec

Puerto Escondido International Airport

Puerto Escondido — Brisas de Zicatela

The Parque Nacional Lagunas de Chacahua is an ecological preserve with deserted beaches and a few small fishing communities.

A natural lagoon encircled by mangroves, Laguna Manialtepec is home to a wide range of wildlife. It also has some beautiful beaches that are accessible by boat.

Puerto Escondido (p254)

0 kilometers 20
0 miles 20

N ↑

regularly used for music and street theater performances. On its south side is the cathedral, built at the end of the 16th century and refurbished in a more modern style in the 1980s. Twelve carved wooden figures of the apostles appear from the bell tower as the bells chime out the hour.

Just east of the plaza, the **Museo del Café** charts the history of coffee production in Chiapas. After exploring the museum, head west from the plaza along Avenida Central to Parque de la Marimba, a café-rimmed plaza that is Tuxtla's true social center. For another side of the cultural scene, the **Museo de la Marimba** showcases the history of the eponymous musical genre.

The **Museo Regional**, located northeast of the center, provides information on the geography and history of Chiapas. Nearby, the Jardín Botánico contains a range of plants native to the state, including beautiful orchids.

Museo del Café

⊛ 🏛 2a C Oriente Norte 236 🕒 Mon-Sat 9am-5pm 🅦 museodelcafe.chiapas. gob.mx

Museo de la Marimba

🏛 9a Calle Poniente Norte 🅲 (961) 600 01 74 🕒 10am-10pm Tue-Sun

Museo Regional

⊛ ⊛ ⊜ 🏛 Calzada de los Hombres Ilustres 885 🅲 (961) 613 43 75 🕒 Tue-Sun

---

🔟 ⊛

Yagul

🅰 D6 🏛 Mex 190, 22 miles (36 km) SE of Oaxaca, Oaxaca 🅲 (951) 513 33 46 🕒 8am-5pm daily

The city of Yagul was first inhabited by the Zapotecs in around 500 BC. However, it gained real religious and political influence in the region only after the decline of Monte Albán (p240), at the end of the 8th century AD, and most of the buildings at the site date from this period. Yagul was subsequently taken over by the Mixtecs and was finally abandoned after the arrival of the Spanish.

Dramatically set on and around a rocky outcrop, the city had a good defensive position. It is divided into two main areas. The lower level, called the Acropolis, includes a large ballcourt, more than 30 tombs, and a labyrinthine complex of buildings known as the Palace of the Six Patios. On the summit of the outcrop is the Fortress, surrounded by a strong defensive wall and offering superb views.

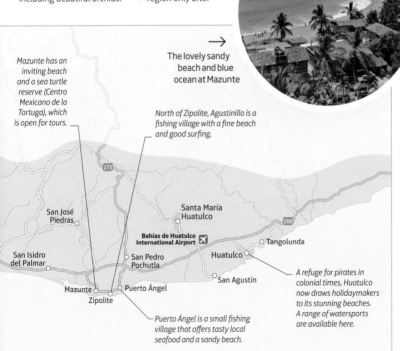

→ The lovely sandy beach and blue ocean at Mazunte

Mazunte has an inviting beach and a sea turtle reserve (Centro Mexicano de la Tortuga), which is open for tours.

North of Zipolite, Agustinillo is a fishing village with a fine beach and good surfing.

San José Piedras

Santa María Huatulco

Bahías de Huatulco International Airport 🛪 Tangolunda

San Isidro del Palmar

San Pedro Pochutla

Huatulco

San Agustín

Mazunte

Puerto Ángel

Zipolite

Puerto Ángel is a small fishing village that offers tasty local seafood and a sandy beach.

A refuge for pirates in colonial times, Huatulco now draws holidaymakers to its stunning beaches. A range of watersports are available here.

11

Cañón del Sumidero

E5/6 **Chiapas**

The breathtaking Sumidero Canyon forms the heart of a beautiful national park. Legend has it that in the mid-16th century, several hundred indigenous warriors chose to hurl themselves down its precipitous sides after a defiant last stand, rather than submit to the invading Spanish forces.

Nearly half a mile (a kilometer) deep, and around 9 miles (14 km) in length, the canyon was carved by the Grijalva river over the course of millions of years. This important river stretches from Guatemala to the Gulf of Mexico.

Excellent views of the sheer-sided canyon are available from a series of five lookout points along its western rim. Alternatively, visitors can enjoy a two-hour boat trip along the river. Boats leave daily from two embarkation points, one at Cahuaré (on the west bank of the Grijalva, on Mex 190), and the other at the docks in Chiapa de Corzo (call 961 616 06 80 for more information). The trip takes in caves and waterfalls. It also provides an opportunity to see a variety of unusual plants, and many animals and birds, including monkeys, crocodiles, iguanas, herons, and kingfishers.

12

Mitla

D6 **Off Mex 190, 27 miles (44 km) SE of Oaxaca, Oaxaca** **(951) 513 33 52** **8am–5pm daily**

An important Zapotec city-state after the decline of Monte Albán (p240), Mitla was home to approximately 10,000

people at its height. The city was later occupied by the Mixtecs, who had a significant influence on the architecture and decoration of its buildings.

Many of Mitla's temples were destroyed by the Spanish when they invaded, and the stonework was used

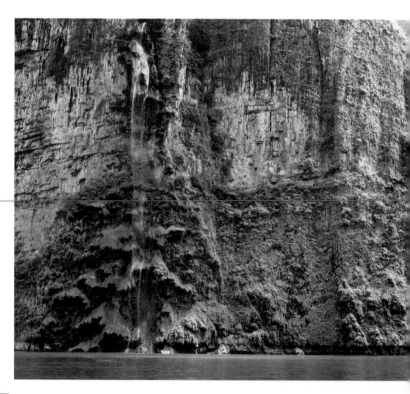

to build the Iglesia de San Pablo, the huge Catholic church that dominates the site.

Five main groups of buildings remain, two of which are accessible to visitors. The Grupo de las Columnas, in the east of the site, is a former palace. It consists of three large rooms set around tombs and a courtyard. The palace walls are decorated with the distinctive geometric mosaics that characterize Mitla's buildings. Each frieze is made of up to 100,000 separate pieces of cut stone. One of the rooms, the Salón de las Columnas, houses six monolithic pillars that once supported the roof.

To the north is the Grupo de la Iglesia, centered around the colonial-era church. The pre-Hispanic buildings that survived its construction are of similar design to those in the Grupo de las Columnas, but on a smaller scale. They still retain traces of paintwork.

↑ Part of the substantial ruins still standing at the archaeological site of Mitla

Zimatlán-Ocotlán

🅐D6 🅐Oaxaca ⊞
🅘Murguia 206; www.oaxaca.travel

The Central Valleys of Oaxaca state comprise several distinct regions. Zimatlán and Ocotlán sit in the heart of the Valles Centrales, south of Oaxaca city. These districts abound with interesting sights that make perfect day trips from the busy city. One such place is San Antonio Arrazola, which produces carved wooden figures of animals painted in vivid, multicolored designs. San Bartolo Coyotepec is another good place to discover local crafts, as this is where the gleaming black pottery (barro negro brillante), which is commonly found in souvenir shops, is made.

The former convent at Cuilapan de Guerrero, on Mex 131, was established on the site of a Zapotec pyramid in 1550. It was abandoned two centuries later, but today still retains some impressive architectural features and murals. The roofless chapel

←

Cañon del Sumidero's Christmas tree falls, so named for its color and shape

has a Renaissance facade, an elegant columned nave, and thick earthquake-proof walls. Vicente Guerrero, hero of the War of Independence, was imprisoned here before being executed on Valentine's Day 1831. A monument to his memory stands at the convent. Zaachila, also on Mex 131, is the site of the last Zapotec capital. A pyramid and two impressive tombs are open to the public.

AFRO-MEXICANS IN COSTA CHICA

Stretching from Acapulco (p242) to Juchitan, the Costa Chica region is home to a large population of Afro-Mexicans, especially in the city of Cuajinicuilapa. It's a great place to explore this aspect of Mexico's culture and history. Start with the Museo Nacional de la Cultura Afro-Mestiza (Cuauhtémoc s/n, Centro, Cuajinicuilapa), for an interactive look at the cultural legacy of Afro-Mexican people. Look out for local culinary specialties, too, such as caldo de res rojo (red beef stew).

Comitán de Domínguez

🗺 F6 🏛 Chiapas
ℹ 1a Av Norte; www.
turismochiapas.gob.mx

Set on a rocky hillside, this city (known simply as Comitán) has an elegant, colonial-era core and a small but absorbing market. At its heart lies the spacious Plaza Central, and the 17th-century Templo de Santo Domingo. Just east of the plaza, the Museo de Arqueología displays artifacts from local Maya sites.

To the south, the **Casa Museo Belisario Domínguez** preserves the former home of the local doctor and liberal politician who was assassinated in 1913 after criticizing President Huerta. Of the city's historic churches, the twin-towered, all-white Templo de San José is especially attractive, while the 19th-century Iglesia de San Caralampio features a flamboyant red and peach-colored stucco facade.

Casa Museo Belisario Domínguez

 🏛 Avenida Central Sur Belisario Domínguez
📞 (963) 632 13 00 🕐 10am–7pm Mon–Fri, 9am–1pm Sat & Sun

SHOP

Comiteco Nueve Estrellas

Comitán is famed for *comiteco*, a local spirit made from agave and flavored with tropical fruits. This shop sells its own top-quality bottles.

🗺 F6 🏛 1a Avenida Poniente Sur, Comitán de Domínguez
🌐 facebook.com/comiteco.nueveestrellas

Puerto Escondido

🗺 D6 🏛 Oaxaca ✈ 🚌
ℹ Blvd Benito Juárez; www.oaxaca.travel.index.php

Puerto Escondido, literally the "undiscovered port," lived up to its name until discovered by hippies in the 1970s and has since become a significant tourist destination. Although showing some signs of the strain of development, it retains much of the fishing-village character that originally made it popular.

Playa Marinero, the main beach, is popular with locals and tourists alike. Shaded by palm trees, it faces a small cove dotted with fishing boats and fed by an endless supply of gentle surf. Playa Zicatela is a larger beach to the west and is very popular with surfers, especially in the late summer months when the waves are at their highest.

At the end of November, the town comes alive for an international surfing festival. A popular local fiesta with music and dancing takes place at the same time. Puerto Escondido is also a good base for trips to the nearby freshwater lagoons, such as Laguna Manialtepec.

Just southeast of Puerto Escondido, the village of Barra de Navidad guards the mouth of the Río Colotepec, home to mangrove swamps, crocodiles, and bird species. Locals offer various tours.

 TOP 3 REGIONAL FIESTAS

Guelaguetza
Groups from all over the state gather in Oaxaca to reenact traditional dances on the last two Mondays of July.

Feria de San Cristóbal
On July 25, a torchlit procession takes place to honor the patron saint of in San Cristóbal de las Casas.

Noche de los Rábanos
Oaxaca locals compete to carve vegetables into people, animals, and plants on December 23, also known as the Night of the Radishes.

Chiapa de Corzo

🗺 F6 🏛 Chiapas ℹ Corner of 5 de Febrero and Vicente López; www.turismo-chiapas.gob.mx

Overlooking the Río Grijalva, Chiapa de Corzo is Tuxtla's smaller and more elegant neighbor. Officially founded in 1528, it was the first Spanish city in Chiapas – today it's also the starting point for Cañón del Sumidero boat rides *(p252)*.

The central Plaza Ángel Albino Corzo is dominated by the Fuente Colonial, an ornate

↑ Fuente Colonial, the main feature of Plaza Ángel Albino Corzo, Chiapa de Corzo

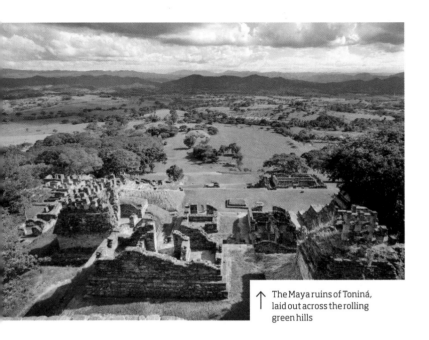

↑ The Maya ruins of Toniná, laid out across the rolling green hills

16th-century fountain that appears on Chiapas licence plates. South, behind the *portales* (arcades), stands the handsome church, Templo de Santo Domingo de Guzmán, and the Centro Cultural, a series of galleries in an old convent. Northeast of the plaza, the pre-Hispanic ruins of Chiapa de Corzo originated as a farming settlement in the early pre-Classic period (1400–850 BC).

17 Toniná

F6 66 miles (106 km) E of San Cristóbal, Chiapas (961) 612 83 60 8am-5pm daily

In its prime, the Classic-period Maya city of Toniná is thought to have been a great regional power – like all the big Maya centers, it was mysteriously abandoned after 900 AD. The main focus of the ruins today is known as the Acrópolis, featuring seven artificial terraces set into the hillside and incorporating dozens of buildings and temples. Several carved stucco reliefs survive, including the massive Mural de las Cuatro Eras, which tells the story of Maya cosmology with plenty of decapitated heads and a skeletal Lord of Death. The temple at the summit provides stellar views across the valley. The museum at the main entrance adds context with scale models, artifacts, and sculptures from the site.

---

18 Yaxchilán

F6 80 miles (130 km) SE of Palenque, Chiapas 8am-5pm daily inah. gob.mx

The city of Yaxchilán, set 66 ft (20 m) above the Usumacinta river in the heart of the Lacandón rainforest, is one of the most dramatic of all Maya sites. It can only be reached by air from Palenque, or by taking a boat along the river from Frontera Corozal.

Built between AD 350 and 800, it rose to prominence during the 8th century under the command of its most famous kings, "Shield Jaguar", and his son "Bird Jaguar." Yaxchilán is rich in glyphs, stelae, carved lintels, stucco roof combs, and temples. One of the best-preserved buildings is Temple 33.

→ Detail on a lintel at Yaxchilán's Maya archaeological site

A DRIVING TOUR
THE TLACOLULA VALLEY

Length 55 miles (90 km) **Stopping-off points** The town of Santiago Matatlán is a traditional center of the local mezcal industry, from one-man artisan distilleries to large factory operations. You can visit most of them and enjoy free samples.

This region is a great place for history lovers to explore multiple Mesoamerican sites in one easy road trip. The area around Oaxaca, and in particular the Tlacolula Valley, has been an important cultural and historical center since the 10th century BC. Over 2,500 years of civilization can be explored here, from the early Zapotecs to the final Mesoamerican empire of the Aztecs. Today, the valley is crammed with diverse attractions reflecting its Zapotec, Mixtec, Aztec, and Spanish heritage.

Reputed to be over 2,000 years old, the **Arbol del Tule** *in Santa Maria del Tule is one of the world's largest trees.*

San Agustín Yatareni

Tlalixtac de Cabrera

START

Oaxaca

Santa Lucia del Camino

San Francisco Tutla

Santo Domingo Tomaltepec

Santa Maria del Tule

San Antonio de la Cal

Alongside the valley's ancient ruins are some colonial-era sites, such as the 16th-century **San Jerónimo Tlacochahuaya**, *which was decorated by Zapotec artisans.*

San Jerónimo Tlacochahuaya

Dainzú

Rio Salado

Santa Cruz Papalutla

San Sebastián Teitipac

San Juan Teitipac

↑ Santa Maria del Tule's 2,000-year-old *Arbol del Tule* (Tree of the Tule)

Once a Zapotec city, **Dainzú** *has a tiered pyramid, a ballcourt, several tombs, and a unique collection of carved stone reliefs depicting ballgame players. Parts of the site date from 350 BC.*

← The ruins of the Yagul, with gorgeous views of the valley

SOUTHERN MEXICO • The Tlacolula Valley

Locator Map

The oldest town in the Tlacolula Valley, **Teotitlán** is known for its Zapotec rugs, made with natural dyes. It also has a small museum and some Zapotec ruins.

The Zapotec site of **Lambityeco** was settled around AD 700 after the decline of Monte Albán. The site has well-preserved stucco and stone carvings, and several tombs.

Santa Ana del Valle is a tiny village known for its high-quality, locally produced textiles and rugs. Zapotec weavers have been making them here for centuries.

Perched on top of a rocky outcrop, the fortified city of **Yagul** (p251) was built by the Zapotecs and later occupied by the Mixtecs.

Teotitlán del Valle

Macuilxóchitl

190

Lambityeco

San Juan Guelavía

Santa Ana del Valle

Villa Díaz Ordaz

Yagul

Tlacolula de Matamoros

San Bartolomé Quialana

San Lucas Quiavini

Tanivet

Río Salado

San Pablo Vila de Mitla

FINISH

190

190

Santiago Matatlán

Tlacolula de Matamoros village has the area's main market, which sells pottery, woven goods, food, and the local specialty, mezcal, a distilled alcoholic beverage.

Complex geometric stone mosaics adorn the facades of the fabulous pre-Hispanic buildings in **Mitla** (p252).

0 kilometers   5

0 miles   5

N ↑

257

THE GULF COAST

The tropical plains fringing the Gulf of Mexico were once home to three major Mesoamerican cultures – the Olmecs, the Totonacs, and the Huastecs. In 1519 this coast was once again at the fulcrum of Mexican history, when Cortés disembarked here on his conquest of the Aztec empire. Over the next 300 years, the region's colonial-era towns prospered due to their startegic coastal position. The Port of Veracruz was particularly important to the colony of New Spain; no less than 200,000 enslaved Africans were forced into the country here, while vast quantities of gold and silver were shipped to Europe. International trade from Veracruz slumped between independence and the revolution, but picked up again in the mid-20th century. Today, Veracruz is once again a bustling port city, while the rest of the Gulf Coast produces much of Mexico's sugarcane, citrus fruits, vanilla, and coffee.

This green and fertile region is full of outdoor adventures, from the snowcapped Pico de Orizaba to the humid, low-lying jungle in the south. The Gulf Coast is also a cultural hotspot, with fascinating indigenous traditions like the flying *voladores* performances and the mix of Mexican and African culture in the Costa Chica region.

THE GULF COAST

Must Sees

1. El Tajín
2. Museo de Antropología de Xalapa

Experience More

3. Xalapa
4. Coatepec
5. Quiahuiztlan
6. Cempoala
7. Papantla
8. Córdoba
9. Veracruz
10. Orizaba
11. San Andrés Tuxtla
12. Santiago Tuxtla
13. Tapijulapa
14. Comalcalco
15. Malpasito
16. Villahermosa
17. Laguna de Catemaco
18. Tlacotalpan
19. Xico

Gulf of Mexico

Chenkán

Sabancuy

Nuevo Progreso

Frontera

THE YUCATÁN PENINSULA
p276

Paraíso

Reforma

Sanchez Magallanes

COMALCALCO 14

TABASCO

Coatzacoalcos

Cunduacán

Cárdenas

VILLAHERMOSA

16 ✈ Villahermosa International Airport

Jonuta

El Triunfo

Chablé

Minatitlán

Las Choapas

Huimanguillo

Río Grijalva

Macuspana

Emiliano Zapata

VERACRUZ

Chontalpa

Teapa

Palenque

Tenosique

Cerro Nanchital

Pichucalco

13 TAPIJULAPA

Istmo de Tehuantepec

15 MALPASITO

Raudales

CHIAPAS

Parque Natural Montes Azules

SOUTHERN MEXICO
p230

Ocozocuautla

0 kilometers   100

N

Cintalapa

Tuxtla Gutiérrez

0 miles   100

1

EL TAJÍN

D4 Off Mex 180, 7 miles (12 km) SE of Poza Rica, Veracruz
 From Papantla or Poza Rica   9am–5pm daily   inah.gob.mx

An outstanding example of the grandeur and importance of the pre-Hispanic cultures of Mexico, the mysterious El Tajín site displays some unique structures, but the Pyramid of the Niches takes center stage.

Developed from an earlier settlement, the city of El Tajín was a political and religious center for the Totonac civilization. Many of its buildings date from the early Postclassic period, between AD 900 and 1150. Decorated with relief panels and sculptures, they would have been painted in strong colors such as red, blue, and black. The excavated nucleus of this spectacular ancient city covers about 0.4 sq miles (1 sq km), but the entire urban area once spread over 4 sq miles (10 sq km) and had a population of 25,000.

Originally crowned by a temple, the Pyramid of the Niches has 365 niches, representing the days of the year. Each niche may have held an offering.

Building 12

Building 10

The small Statue of Dios Tajín probably represents Tajín, god of thunder and lightning, an important deity to the people of El Tajín.

The four pyramids that surround the massive Plaza del Arroyo stand at the cardinal points. They are some of the oldest structures in the city.

Six relief panels on the side walls of the southern ballcourt illustrate rituals of the game (p296), including the sacrifice of one or more players.

The well-preserved ruins of the El Tajín settlement set against a jungle backdrop

El Tajín Chico

Northern Ballcourt

Plaza Oriente and Gran Xicalcoliuhqui

Illustration showing the layout of the El Tajín archaelogical site

Ballcourt 13/14

LOS VOLADORES

This ancient ritual of the Totonac people from the Papantla region takes place daily at the site entrance. Five men climb to the top of a pole reaching as high as 100 ft (30 m). While one plays a drum and a pipe on a platform at the top, the other four *voladores* (fliers) launch themselves from the top of the pole and descend as the ropes round the pole unwind. In total, the *voladors* circle the pole 52 turns, symbolizing the cycles of the Mesoamerican calendar.

→

Olmec heads displayed
inside the museum and
(inset) the museum's exterior

2 ⬡ ⬡ ⬡ ⬡

MUSEO DE ANTROPOLOGÍA DE XALAPA

🅐 D5 🏠 Avenida Xalapa, Xalapa 🚌 CAXA Central de Autobuses, Avenida 20 de Noviembre Oriente 271 🕒 9am–5pm Tue–Sun 🌐 uv.mx/max

Housed in a beautifully light and airy modern complex, these stunning treasures, spanning some 3,000 years of pre-Hispanic history, include some of the most important ancient artifacts in the country. The galleries are presented around tranquil gardens and patios.

Known commonly as MAX, the Xalapa Anthropology Museum is second in importance only to the anthropology museum in Mexico City *(p100)*. Its outstanding collection is displayed in spacious marble halls and open-air patios. It consists of sculptures and artifacts from the Gulf Coast's major pre-Hispanic civilizations, found at various sites

within the region. The first halls are dedicated to the Olmec civilization (p272), which include a terracotta funerary urn that, when discovered in Catemaco, contained the remains of a small child. Central Veracruz and the Totonacs follow, and the final room exhibits the highly stylized sculptures of the Huastec culture. Guided tours are free, and should be reserved in advance.

EXPERIENCE MORE

3

Xalapa

🅐 D5 🅐 Veracruz 🚍
🅘 Avenida 20 de Noviembre
376; www.veracruz.mx

The capital of Veracruz state, Xalapa (or Jalapa) is known for its university and cultural life, and the second most important anthropology museum in Mexico after the Museo Nacional de Antropología (p100) in Mexico City. The city enjoys a beautiful setting: on a clear day there are splendid views of the 13,940-ft (4,250-m) Cofre de Perote peak from Parque Juárez, the main plaza. To one side of this square is the Neo-Classical **Palacio de Gobierno**, which has a mural by Mario Orozco Rivera (1930–98) on its stairs. Opposite the Palacio is the 18th-century cathedral. Uphill from the city center, colored houses with sloping tiled roofs and wrought-iron balconies line pretty, cobbled streets around the market.

It is a good base to explore the remote Filobobos archaeological zone. This consists of several Meosamerican sites, only two of which have been throughly explored. The main site, **El Cuajilote**, was founded around AD 200 by the Totonacs, and was in use until AD 800. Access to the site is via an 5-mile (8-km) scenic walk. It is worth the effort of getting there, however, because the ruins are truly spectacular.

You can also reach El Cuajilote through an organized rafting trip along the Rio Filobobos (Filobobos river). These tours can be booked in Xalapa (p264) or Tlapacoyan, through companies such as Aventurec (www.aventurec. com). Other river tours are also available. Whitewater rafting offers a challenge through the steep-sided river gorge to the east of Tlapacoyan.

GALLERY GUIDE

The exhibits are displayed in a descending series of halls and patios with steps and wheelchair ramps linking each level. Beginning at the main entrance, the items are arranged chronologically. The gardens contain flora representative of different areas of Veracruz state.

Palacio de Gobierno

🅐 Avenida Enriquez 📞 (228) 841 74 00 🕐 Mon–Fri

El Cuajilote

⊘ 🅐 Off minor road from Tlapacoyan to Plan de Arroyos, 68 miles (110 km) NW of Xalapa 🕐 Tue–Sun

EAT & DRINK

Café Chiquito

Great buffet breakfasts and set lunches are served in this pretty café, with outdoor tables in a plant-filled patio. There is also live music.

🅐 D5 🅐 Nicolás Bravo 3, Xalapa ⓦ cafechiquito. com

$ $ $

La Parroquia de Veracruz

The place for serious coffee drinkers. Also serves excellent Mexican cuisine for lunch and dinner.

🅐 D5 🅐 Calle Juan de la Luz s/n, Xalapa ⓦ laparroquia-deveracruz.com

$ $ $

Café Lindo

This is a great spot for breakfast, with fantastic coffee. Laidback during the day but gets going at night with live bands.

🅐 D5 🅐 Calle Primo Verdad 21, Xalapa 📞 (228) 841 91 66

$ $ $

Carnival
Across the Gulf Coast,
pre-lent celebrations
start with the burning
of a huge figure, who
represents "bad temper,"
followed by floats,
parades and dancing.

Candelaria
In the fortnight leading
up to February 2, the
Christian festival of
Candlemas features
street stalls, dancing
and music on the Gulf
Coast. In Tlacotalpan
the local Virgin is taken
on a river procession
with hundreds of boats.

**Feria de
Santiago Tuxtla**
Gigantic *mojiganga*
dolls are taken around
Santiago Tuxtla in
this elaborate saint's
celebration on the
week of July 25.

**④
Coatepec**

🅐D5 🅐Veracruz
🅘Matias Rebolledo 1; (228)
203 19 58

The lovely town of Coatepec
is famous for its culinary
offerings, including coffee,
fruit, liqueurs, and seafood.

The town's elegant houses
were built with the proceeds
of the early 20th-century
coffee boom. In the center of
town is the attractive Basílica
Menor de Nuestra Señora de
Guadalupe. The **Casa de la
Cultura**, off the main square,
hosts exhibitions, plays,
concerts, and workshops. The
town's biggest festival is the
Feria del Café y la Orquídea,
held every May. Hundreds
of Mexican and international
coffee and orchid growers
display their products, with
food stalls, live music, and
traditional dances.

Casa de la Cultura
🅐Jiménez del Campillo 4
🅞9am-7pm Mon-Sat
📞(228) 816 67 57

**⑤
Quiahuiztlan**

🅐D4 🅐Mex 180, 15 miles
(24 km) N of Cempoala,
Veracruz 🅞8:30am-5pm
Tue-Sun 🅦sic-gob.mx

Once inhabited by 15,000
people, the Totonac city of
Quiahuiztlan was a hilltop
stronghold. It was constructed
in the late Classic period, when
raids by warlike nomads from
the north forced sites like El
Tajín (p262) to be abandoned.
Despite originally being
ringed by defensive walls,
it was twice conquered, first
by the Toltecs in the 9th
century and then by the
Aztecs in the 13th century.

Today the only part of
the terraced site that can
be visited is the cemetery.
Here some 100 tiny tombs
were discovered, each
resembling a pre-Hispanic
temple. Many had human
bones and skulls in burial
chambers in their bases.
Small holes in the backs of
the tombs may have been
for relatives to communicate

←
The cemetery at
Quiahuiztlan, a Totonac ruin
from the late Classic period

↑ Ruins of Cempoala, where the Totonacs joined forces with Cortés against he Aztecs

with the dead. Across the main road from Quiahuiztlan is Villa Rica de la Vera Cruz, which was the first Spanish settlement in Mexico, now a fishing village.

6

Cempoala

⬛ D5 ⬛ Francisco del Paso y Troncoso, Zempoala, Veracruz ⬛ 9am-6pm daily ⬛ inah.gob.mx

Shortly after their arrival in Mexico (p57), Cortés and his men sheltered in the Totonac city of Cempoala (also known as Zempoala). Like many other cities, it was subjugated by the Aztecs, and the Totonacs were forced to pay them large tributes of food and prisoners. This led Cempoala's governor to collaborate with Cortés in return for protection.

The walled archaeological site containing the ruins of the former Totonac city adjoins Cempoala town. Around a central plaza are buildings faced with smooth, rounded stones. Straight ahead from the entrance is the Templo Mayor, a 13-tier pyramid topped by a sanctuary, which was originally thatched with palm leaves. In Las Chimeneas

(The Chimneys) – named for its hollow columns – archaeologists found a *chacmool*-like figure (p144), suggesting the Maya were associated with the site. The east-facing Gran Pirámide was a temple dedicated to the sun.

7

Papantla

⬛ D4 ⬛ Veracruz ⬛ ⬛ Calzada Jose Garcia Payon s/n; (784) 842 82 34

Best known as the home of the pole-plunging Totonac *voladores*, Papantla is the center for Mexico's vanilla industry, which has been cultivated here since pre-Hispanic times. The city is also the gateway to El Tajín (p262), but is worth a visit for its own attractions. It has a lively cultural scene, several museums, and many murals adorning public buildings, including one on the Palacio Municipal on the main *zócalo*. The most interesting museum in town is the **Museo Teodoro Cano**, with a collection of the founder's murals as well as regional history exhibits.

Besides the Totonac *voladores*, several other traditional dances are celebrated

here, including the Danza de los Guaguas, which is dedicated to the sun.

Museo Teodoro Cano
⬙ ⬛ Calle Rodolfo Curti 101 ⬛ (228) 156 71 83 ⬛ 10am-7pm Tue-Sun

EAT

Naku
A bustling venue that offers live music and a range of local specialties, including great bean tamales.

⬛ D4 ⬛ Heroico Colegio Militar, Col. Libertad, Papantla ⬛ (784) 842 31 12

$⬤$$⬤$$⬤$

Plaza Pardo
Regional favorites, such as tamales and shrimp dishes, plus city views from the balcony.

⬛ D4 ⬛ Juan Enríquez 105, Papantla ⬛ (784) 842 00 59

$⬤$$⬤$$⬤$

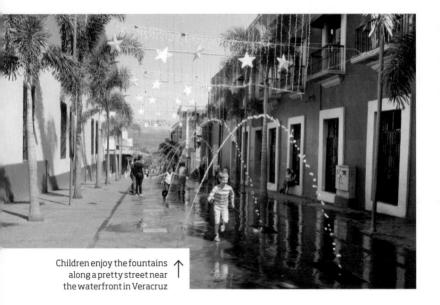

Children enjoy the fountains along a pretty street near the waterfront in Veracruz

8

Córdoba

 D5 ⚑ Veracruz 🚌
ℹ Palacio Municipal; (271) 717 17 00

Córdoba is a busy, modern town, although traces of its colonial-era heritage are still to be found around the central Plaza de Armas.

Historically, Córdoba's most significant building is the 18th-century Portal de Zevallos, an arcade on the north side of the Plaza de Armas. The Treaties of Córdoba, endorsing Mexican independence, were signed here in 1829. Also on the plaza are the Neo-Classical Palacio Municipal and the Catedral de la Inmaculada Concepción, which houses a lifelike image of the town's patron saint, the Virgen de la Soledad (Virgin of Solitude). Just off the plaza is the **Museo de Córdoba**, a history museum about the city and its pre-Hispanic roots. Housed in a beautiful mansion, its small collection includes Olmec sculptures and the 1821 Treaty of Córdoba.

West of Córdoba is the Barranca de Metlac, a spectacular gorge spanned by four bridges. One of these, a 19th-century railroad bridge, features in several paintings by artist José María Velasco.

Museo de Córdoba
🖼 ⚑ Calle 3 305-A
📞 (271) 712 09 67 🕐 10am–7pm Tue–Sun

9

Veracruz

 D5 ⚑ Veracruz ✈🚌
ℹ Palacio Municipal, Zaragoza s/n, Col Centro; www.disfrutaveracruz.mx

Veracruz is a place of fun. The life of the city revolves around the Plaza de Armas and the *malecón* (waterfront promenade), an enjoyable place to stroll and watch the ships come and go.

The tree-lined Plaza de Armas is flanked by the elegant 17th-century Palacio Municipal and the cathedral. The dome of the cathedral is decorated with Puebla tiles (*p148*) and crowned with a lantern and a small cross.

Standing opposite the cathedral, the *portales* (arcades) are filled with hotels and cafés. Musicians play here all day and most of the night, and most evenings there is also dancing to watch, whether it is a frenetic *zapateo* or a poised, serene *danzón*. The entertainment reaches a high point during the city's celebrated carnival.

→

The arcaded Palacio Municipal on Plaza de Armas in Veracruz

A FUGITIVE, A FREEDOM FIGHTER

Born in Gabon in 1545, Gaspar Nyanga - known also as Yanga - escaped slavery in Veracruz in the late 1500s, and established a *palenque* (maroon community). For survival, the colony farmed, hunted, and raided Spanish caravans and plantations. Yanga's fierce army defeated Spanish militia for over 30 years. On January 6, 1609, the settlement became the first free black town in the Americas. A statue of Gaspar Yanga still stands in the town of Yanga, Veracruz.

Son jarocho could be called the sound of Veracruz – a rhythmic folk music with Afro-Mexican roots. Veracruz once housed a major slave port and today many Afro-Mexicans call the city home. On weekends, tap your toes to *son jarocho* in the Plaza Mayor and the Plazuela de Campaná. Or stroll the Paseo de José Martí to be serenaded while stopping off in the area's bars and restaurants.

Situated on the *malecón* (waterfront esplanade) is the Gran Café de la Parroquia. This lively, convivial café opened in 1808 and is an institution. Boat trips from the *malecón* run past the Isla de los Sacrificios and around the harbor to the fortress of **San Juan de Ulúa**. Fortified in 1692, it was home to the last Spanish garrison to accept Mexican independence (*p58*) and has since seen several foreign invasions, the last by the US in 1914. It also became the country's most notorious prison during the Porfiriato era (*p61*).

The tiny Isla de los Sacrificios was the first place the conquistadors landed, and is named after the remains of human sacrifices they found.

The best of several museums in Veracruz, the **Museo Histórico Naval** is housed in the former Naval Academy in the city center. It tells the maritime history of the port. Exhibits include over 300 types of knots, and some intricate models of ships.

In 1880, the fortified wall around Veracruz was torn down leaving only one of the nine original bastions, the **Baluarte de Santiago** (Santiago Bastion). This small fort, built in 1635, now houses a good collection of pre-Hispanic gold jewelry.

South of the town are the hotel-filled suburbs of Playa de Oro and Mocambo. The beaches here are cleaner and less crowded than in Veracruz, but not very appealing. Boca del Río, farther along the coast, is famous for its seafood.

San Juan de Ulúa
⊗ ⊗ 🏛 Calle Pedro Sainz de Baranda 🕐 Jul & Aug: 9:30am-4:30pm Tue–Sun 🌐 sanjuandeulua.inah.gob.mx

Museo Histórico Naval
⊗ 🏛 Calle Arista 418 📞 (229) 931 40 78 🕐 10am-5pm Tue–Sun

Baluarte de Santiago
⊗ 🏛 Calle Francisco Canal 📞 (229) 931 10 59 🕐 9am-4pm Tue–Sun

> *Son jarocho* is the sound of Veracruz - a rhythmic folk music with Afro-Mexican roots. Veracruz once housed a major slave port and today many Afro-Mexicans call the city home.

←
The city of Orizaba, with the highest peak in Mexico rising above it

11 San Andrés Tuxtla

🅰E5 🚩Veracruz
🚌 ℹ️Palacio Municipal, Plaza Zaragoza, Tlacotalpan; (294) 947 93 00

San Andrés Tuxtla is a sprawling commercial town famous for its cigars. There are fields of tobacco everywhere, and the roadside is lined with stalls selling the finished products. You can also watch cigars being hand-rolled in the **Santa Clara Cigar Factory**.

The city center is anchored by the Parque Lerdo and its Catedral de San San José y San Andrés, built in 1870 with two bell towers and a sober Neo-Classical facade.

A 2-mile (3-km) walk from San Andrés Tuxtla along a dirt track leads to the Laguna Encantada (Enchanted Lake).

10 Orizaba

🅰D5 🚩Veracruz 🚌 ℹ️El Palacio de Hierro; (272) 728 91 36

Home to an Aztec garrison, and then to Spanish soldiers, Orizaba stood in what was a strategic position on the trading route between Veracruz and Mexico City in the 15th and 16th centuries. Dominated by the Cerro del Borrego hill, Orizaba today is mostly an industrial city, but still has plenty of character.

The Ex-Palacio Municipal, on the main plaza – the Parque Apolinar Castillo – is an ornate Art Nouveau construction. Built in Belgium in the late 19th century, it was brought over in pieces and reassembled here.

The Neo-Classical Palacio Municipal, on Calle Colón, was the base for a workers' education center after the revolution. It has a 1926 mural, *Reconstrucción*, by artist José Clemente Orozco (1883–1949). Orizaba's **Museo de Arte del Estado** features a fine collection of paintings housed in 10 beautifully restored rooms. Its collection also includes 37 rare works by artist Diego Rivera.

A cable-car ride up the Cerro del Borrego offers spectacular views over the city below. At its summit is a museum telling the story of the battle against French forces in 1862.

Museo de Arte del Estado
🚫🚫 🏠Corner of 4 Oriente and 23-25 Sur 📞(272) 724 32 00 🕐10am-6pm Mon-Fri

CLIMBING PICO DE ORIZABA

Rising to a massive 18,856 ft (5,747 m), Pico de Orizaba earns the title of Mexico's highest mountain. It is also one of the toughest but most popular challenges for climbers. A dormant volcano that last erupted in 1546, the mountain lies 14 miles (23 km) northwest of Orizaba. The best time to climb it is from November to March, which is the driest season. Climbers must take a guide, who can be hired from the nearest town, Tlachichuca.

It is so-named because its water level mysteriously rises in the dry season and falls when it rains.

Santa Clara Cigar Factory
⊛⊛⊛ ⬛ Blvd 5 de Febrero 10 ☎ (294) 947 99 06 🕐 8am-7pm Mon-Fri, 8am-5pm Sat & Sun

---

Santiago Tuxtla

🔺 E5 🔻 Veracruz 🚌
ℹ Palacio Municipal, Plaza Zaragoza, Tlacotalpan; (294) 947 93 00

The town of Santiago Tuxtla is a gateway to the world of the ancient Olmecs (p273),

> One pre-Hispanic custom that lives on in Santiago Tuxtla is the *danza de los liseres*, in which the dancers don the mask of a jaguar deity.

who lived more than 3,000 years ago. A colossal stone head, typical of the Olmec culture, stands in the middle of the town's main square. It is the only one of the heads yet discovered to have closed eyes, and lacks the realism of the others.

The **Museo Tuxteco**, on one side of the plaza, has an interesting collection of pieces from nearby sites. They include a head called "El Negro," the legendary powers of which were formerly tapped by local witch doctors. Other exhibits include examples of the Olmec practices of skull deformation and tooth sculpting (probably expressions of beauty and class), another colossal head (this one from San Lorenzo Tenochtitlán), and ceremonial and domestic objects made out of jade and stone.

One pre-Hispanic custom that still lives on in Santiago Tuxtla is the *danza de los liseres*, in which the dancers don the mask of a jaguar deity. It can be seen being performed during summer fiestas.

Did You Know?

The Olmec head in Santiago Tuxtla's main square is the largest one ever found.

A 12-mile (20-km) drive east through lush, tropical vegetation, leads to Tres Zapotes. This archaeological site was the center of Olmec culture around 400 BC, after La Venta (p273) had been abandoned. The site itself is now just a series of mounds, but several of the finds are displayed in the museum in Tres Zapotes village nearby.

Museo Tuxteco
⊛⊛ ⬛ Parque Juárez ☎ (294) 947 01 96 🕐 9am-5pm Tue-Sun

↓ The picturesque Salto de Eyipantla waterfall, near San Andrés Tuxtla

13 Tapijulapa

E5 **Tabasco**
Retorno Vía 5 122, Los Rios, Villahermosa; (993) 310 97 00

When exploring picturesque Tapijulapa, with its white-washed facades, terracotta roofs, and narrow, cobble-stoned streets, you might think you were in Andalucia. With its quintessentially Mexican charm and heritage, the village was designated a *pueblo mágico* – one of the "Magical Towns" promoted by the Security of Tourism for the rich experiences visitors can enjoy there.

Tapijulapa's well-preserved architecture includes the Templo de Santiago Apostol, a late-17th-century church built on a hilltop with lovely views over the town.

The village comes alive during Semana Santa (the week of Easter). Festivities include a fishing contest for the sightless sardines that live in caves just to the south of the village. The caves form part of the Parque Natural Villaluz, which also has good hiking trails leading to waterfalls, boat trips, and hot springs.

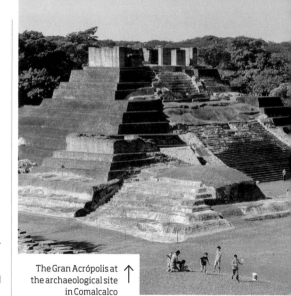

↑ The Gran Acrópolis at the archaeological site in Comalcalco

14 Comalcalco

E5 **Off Mex 187, 36 miles (58 km) NW of Villahermosa, Tabasco** **8am–4pm Tue–Sun**

Set in the lush, green, cocoa-producing area northwest of Villahermosa are the Maya ruins of Comalcalco. Dating mainly from the late Classic period of Maya civilization (AD 700–900), the architecture differs quite markedly from that found at Palenque (*p246*), which was occupied around the same time. Unlike Palenque, Comalcalco has structures built from bricks, which are held together with oyster-shell mortar. The bricks were sometimes incised with figures and glyphs when wet.

Comalcalco's principal structures are two pyramids, the Gran Acrópolis and the Acrópolis Este, and the North Plaza. Originally many of the site's structures would have been covered in high-relief stucco carvings. Of those that survive today, the most distinctive is a mask of the god El Señor del Sol, which is visible near the base of the Gran Acrópolis.

15 Malpasito

E5 **Hwy 187, Huimangillo, Tabasco** **(993) 352 10 30** **8am–5pm daily**

Beautifully located in rugged, mountainous countryside, the ceremonial site of Malpasito

↑ The tiny village of Tapijulapa, nestled in jungle-covered mountains

> **Malpasito is located within the Agua Selva ecotourism park, a natural playground of rivers, waterfalls, and hiking trails.**

a fascinating outdoor park and museum, has an informative display in English and Spanish on Olmec archaeology as you pass through the sculpture trail, the start of which is marked by a giant ceiba (the sacred tree of the Olmec and Maya). The **Museo Regional de Antropología Carlos Pellicer Cámara** is home to over 700 artifacts from the Olmec, Maya, and other Mesoamerican cultures, which include beautiful pottery and jade carvings.

Parque-Museo de la Venta

Avenida Ruíz Cortines
(993) 314 16 52 8am-4pm daily

Museo Regional de Antropología Carlos Pellicer Cámara

Avenida Carlos Pellicer Cámara 511 (993) 312 63 44 9am-5pm Tue-Fri, 9am-7pm Sat & Sun

was built and inhabited by the Zoque people during the late-Classic era, around AD 700–900. The site features terraced platforms and a ball-game court, but is most noteworthy for more than 100 exquisitely carved petroglyphs decorating over 100 boulders that are scattered around the Malpasito area. The carvings represent people, birds, monkeys, deer, and other animals, as well as elaborate geometric designs.

Malpasito is located within the **Agua Selva** ecotourism park, a natural playground of rivers, waterfalls, and hiking trails. There are even log cabins and a campsite so you can enjoy an extended stay.

Agua Selva

Ejido, 86449, Malpasito
Daily aguaselva.com.mx

16

Villahermosa

E5 Tabasco
Retorno Vía 5 122, Los Rios; (993) 310 97 00

Now the capital of the state of Tabasco, Villahermosa was originally founded in the late 16th century by a community forced to move inland by repeated pirate attacks.

Situated on the banks of the Grijalva river, Villahermosa is surrounded by exuberant natural beauty, and walking through the jungle is rewarded with waterfalls, sulphurous waters and even caves.

Today the city itself is a friendly, bustling place with two excellent museums. The **Parque-Museo de La Venta**,

THE OLMECS

The Olmecs were one of Mexico's foremost Mesoamerican cultures, with a great influence on later civilizations. However, the rise and fall of their own population remains a mystery. Today the most impressive reminders of the ancient Olmec culture are the colossal carved stone heads, fashioned from basalt blocks weighing up to 20 tons, which the Olmecs moved large distances, probably using river rafts. Ten of the 17 heads so far discovered were found at San Lorenzo Tenochtitlán - an area that comprises the three archaeological sites of San Lorenzo, Tenochtitlán, and Potrero Nuevo in the state of Veracruz. This great Olmec ceremonial center flourished from 1200 to 900 BC, when it was destroyed. Some of the pieces found here are on show at Potrero.

The highly decorated interior of Iglesia del Carmen, in the town of Catemaco

⑰ Laguna de Catemaco

🅰E5 🅰 Veracruz
🚌 *i* Palacio Municipal, Avenido Carranza, Catemaco; www.catemaco. info

This picturesque freshwater lake lies in the crater of an extinct volcano. It was formed millennia ago, when lava flow from Volcano San Martin Tuxtla blocked its current northern end, and stands now at 1,115 ft (340 m) above sea level. Its hot, humid climate suits many birds, including parrots and toucans, and its waters also contain a few crocodiles. Boat trips round the lake leave from the wharf in the town of Catemaco and circle the island of Tanaxpillo, which is home to a colony of macaque monkeys.

Two ecological parks on the north shore of the lake are accessible by boat or car. The more interesting of these, **Nanciyaga**, is a large swath of tropical rainforest with a great diversity in species of flora and fauna. Visitors to the park can take part in pre-Hispanic rituals, such as the *temazcal* (steam bath), or swim in spring-fed pools.

The Isla de Agaltepec, another island in the lake, supports a colony of Mexican howler monkeys. The monkeys are most vocal in the morning, and boat tours also include this island on their circuit.

The town of Catemaco itself is dominated by the Iglesia del Carmen, a brightly painted church with twin bell towers. The statue of the Virgen del Carmen inside is dripping with jewelry and trinkets left by the many pilgrims who come here.

Nanciyaga

🌀😊🅰 🅰 4.5 miles (7 km) NE of Catemaco 🅲 (294) 943 01 99 🅲 9am-2pm & 4-6pm Mon-Fri, 9am-2pm Sat

⑱ Tlacotalpan

🅰D5 🅰 Veracruz
🚌 *i* Palacio Municipal, Plaza Zaragoza; (288) 884 33 05

Exploring this delightful town is like turning the clock back 100 years. Its peaceful streets are lined with striking houses fronted by colonnades and painted in a flamboyant range of colors. As the Mexican writer Elena Poniatowska once put it, "when we want to smile, we think of Tlacotalpan."

The town is on the banks of the Río Papaloapan ("River of Butterflies"), which is over 984 ft (300 m) wide. Most of the elegant houses, with their Mozarabic-style portals, date from the second half of the 18th century, when large sugar and cotton plantations were established here. Important shipyards were also moved here from Cuba as a direct result of an English blockade of Havana, another Spanish possession, in 1762.

During this era, Tlacotalpan was the principal town in southern Veracruz and an important international port, often more in touch with Europe and Cuba than with the rest of Mexico. However, the building of railroad lines left Tlacotalpan without a commercial role. Paradoxically, the isolation that caused its decline has helped preserve this picturesque town.

Located in a typical 19th-century house in the heart of Tlacotalpan, the **Museo Jarocho Salvador Ferrando** is named after a local artist, and houses many of his portraits

WITCH DOCTORS

Witch doctors still practice in the state of Veracruz, around San Andrés Tuxtla *(p270)* and Catemaco. Using an assortment of medicinal plants, charms, effigies of saints and devils, and other traditional items, they will undertake to help their clients with all manner of issues, whether it's curing diseases, helping them find a better job, or resolving their marital problems. The practice is hereditary and can be traced back to a distant pre-Hispanic past.

Did You Know?

The macaques on Tanaxpillo island in the Laguna de Catemaco were introduced for research.

and landscapes painted in the 19th century. Locally made furniture and crafts from the same period are also on display in the museum.

Museo Jarocho Salvador Ferrando

🅰 Manuel María Alegre 6
📞 (288) 884 24 95 🕐 8am-7pm Tue-Sun

Xico

🅰 D5 🅰 Veracruz
🚌 ℹ Miguel Hidalgo 76, Centro; (228) 129 66 97

Located on the slope of the Cofre del Perote volcano, the attractive town of Xico is well worth a visit for the impressive colonial-era architecture lining the cobbled streets, and its bustling Sunday market. It's also a coffee production center and a gastronomic hot spot, with specialties that include *tamal canario* (sweet tamales) and spicy mole sauce.

The Xiqueños are renowned for their colorful dance costumes, worn for the town's lively carnival, held annually in February or March. The **Museo del Danzante Xiqueño**, situated a couple of blocks from the main square, has an excellent exhibition of such costumes and local customs. The tradition of mask-carving is explained, as well as the role of every masked character in each dance – the bull, the clown, the *negro separado*.

If you follow the path that leads to the Cascada de Texolo you'll be rewarded with spectacular views, and a waterfall that cascades down a sheer rock face. An exciting activity that involves rappeling through the torrent can be organized by local tour companies – an adrenaline-fueled way to take in the stunning scenery.

Museo del Danzante Xiqueño

🅰 Miguel Hidalgo 76
📞 (228) 129 66 97
🕐 10am-6pm Tue-Sun

SHOP

La Tia Celsa

Xico is a great place to buy local delicacies. This store sells a rainbow of spicy local sauces, including mole - one of Mexico's most ubiquitous sauces.

🅰 D5 🅰 Vicente Guerrero 182, Xico
🌐 latiacelsa.com

La Casa de Los Tesoros

Translating as "House of Treasures", this popular spot is just that. Inside is a used book store, a cafe, a restaurant, and a gift stop selling local crafts.

🅰 E5 🅰 Aldama 4, Centro, Catemaco
📞 (294) 943 29 10

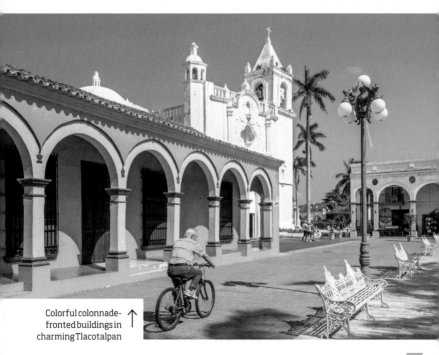

Colorful colonnade-fronted buildings in charming Tlacotalpan ↑

THE YUCATÁN PENINSULA

This tropical peninsula is home to some of the finest archaeological sites in the Americas. From around 2000 BC to the 16th century, the region's Maya population grew to become one of Mesoamerica's most advanced civilizations. But when the Spanish arrived in 1517, they had scant regard for the Maya, swiftly conquering their city states and destroying most of their historical records. The Spanish founded cities here to act as bastions in their fight for control of the Caribbean, against English, French, and Dutch pirates. In 1847, after Mexico had achieved independence, civil war erupted on the peninsula between settlers of European origin and the much-exploited descendants of the ancient Maya – a conflict which ended in defeat for the Maya. In the late 19th century, the production of henequen and sisal (for rope and fabric making) led to a period of prosperity in the Yucatán, while tourism has long been a major industry in this beautiful region of jungles, Maya ruins, and white-sand beaches.

The Riviera Maya, on the east coast, is one of Mexico's great holiday hotspots, sprinkled with grand resorts. Away from the coasts, meanwhile, traditional life continues much as it has done for years, with the indigenous Maya preserving their own language, customs, and culture.

THE YUCATÁN PENINSULA

Must Sees

1 Riviera Maya
2 Uxmal
3 Tulum
4 Mérida
5 Chichén Itzá

Experience More

6 Edzná
7 Ekbalam
8 Chetumal
9 Campeche
10 The Puuc Route
11 Celestún
12 Grutas de Loltún
13 Cobá
14 Dzibilchaltún
15 Izamal
16 Valladolid
17 Maní
18 Río Lagartos Biosphere Reserve
19 Progreso
20 Río Bec Sites
21 Sian Ka'an Biosphere Reserve

Gulf of Mexico

PROGRESO
19

Sisal

DZIBILCHALTÚN 14
Hunucmá

MÉRIDA 4
CELESTÚN 11   Umán
                    Mérida
Real de Salinas   **International Airport**
                    Yaxcopoil
Maxcanu
                    Muna
Halachó   Ticul
Calkiní   UXMAL 2
            Kabah
Jaina   THE PUUC ROUTE 10
                    Sayil *Labná*
Orizaba   Chunyaxnic
Tinum   261

CAMPECHE 9   Chencoyi
Lerma   Cayal   Hopelchen
Campeche
International Airport
Seybaplaya   Iturbide
            Hool 6 EDZNÁ
Haltunchen   Lubna
                    Dzibalchen
Champotón   Arellano
        El Zapote   269
            El Desempeno

Sabancuy   CAMPECHE

Isla Aguada
Nuevo   Ciudad del   Chicbul
Progreso   Carmen
        Laguna   Constitución
        de Términos Francisco   *Balamkú* *Becán*
                Escárcega   Conhuás *Chicanná*
El Vapoor   20
                                RÍO BEC
        Buenavista   SITES
THE GULF
COAST   Candelaria   Monclova   *Reserva*
p258   La Esperanza *Calakmul* *Biosphere*
                                    Calakmul
TABASCO   Nueva Coahuila

        Balancán
Macuspana   Emiliano Zapata
                Parque
                Nacional
    Palenque   Tenosique   *Laguna*
                        del Tigre
Tila   **CHIAPAS**
                    GUATEMALA
            El Naranjo

❶

RIVIERA MAYA

🅰 G4 🄰 Quintana Roo 🚗🚌🚢 ℹ️ Avenida Yaxilan s/n, 17M Lote 6, Cancún; www.visitmexico.com

Stretching along the coast from Puerto Morelos in the north to Tulum in the south, the 100-mile (160-km) Riviera Maya is the most touristy part of the Yucatán peninsula. Encompassing major resorts such as Cancún and Playa del Carmen, it is known for its beaches, warm waters, and range of hotels, restaurants, bars, and clubs. Just offshore is the world's second largest coral reef (a prime spot for diving) and inviting islands.

HIDDEN GEM
Remote Escape

A 40-minute drive from Cancún *(p282) is* Puerto Morelos, one of the least developed places on the riviera. It is a small, laidback resort built around a fishing village that offers excellent snorkeling and diving.

①

Isla Mujeres

🄰 Quintana Roo
🚢 Passenger ferry from Puerto Juárez, car ferry from Punta Sam ℹ️ Avenida Rueda Medina 130; www. isla-mujeres.net

This small island is just half a mile (1 km) wide by 5 miles (8 km) long. Its name, meaning "The Island of Women," prob-ably derives from Maya female statuettes found here and destroyed by the Spanish. It has developed considerably

since first becoming popular in the 1960s, but there are few high-rise buildings, and its small town is still quiet, especially in the evening when the day trippers from Cancún have left.

The best way to explore the island is on a bike or scooter. Its middle part is taken up by a brackish lagoon and an air-strip for small planes from the mainland. Also in the center is the ruined Hacienda Mundaca, said to have been built by the pirate Fermín Mundaca to impress an island beauty. Playa Los Cocos, just to the

north of the island's only town, has clean white sand and warm shallow water.

Located at Isla Mujeres' rather rugged southern tip are Garrafón Park and Playa de Garrafón. The coral reef offshore is now mostly dead, but there are lots of activities on offer, including ziplining and kayaking. The beach is pleasant, but gets crowded in the middle of the day. Nearby are the ruins of what is said to be an old Maya lighthouse. At the southern edge of the island is the Templo de Ixchel, a modest ruin that marks the easternmost point in Mexico.

A popular day trip from Isla Mujeres is to visit Isla Contoy, a tiny island 19 miles (30 km) away, off the northern tip of the Yucatán Peninsula. It is located at the northernmost part of the barrier reef, where the waters of the Caribbean Sea and Gulf of Mexico meet. The mingling currents create ideal conditions for plankton – food for the many fish, which in turn support an abundant bird life. Over 90 species of birds, including large flocks of egrets, pelicans, frigate birds, and flamingos, nest on the island, which is now a protected nature preserve.

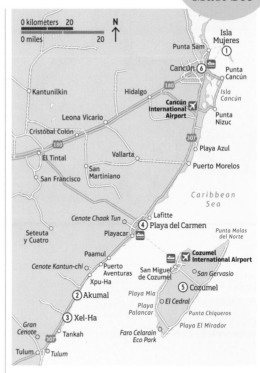

②
Akumal

🏠 Quintana Roo

Akumal is a small, uncrowded resort based around what was once a coconut plantation. Its beautiful beach is a breeding ground for green turtles (Akumal is Maya for "place of the turtle"), and migrating whale sharks can sometimes be spotted swimming past in December and January. Since the 1990s, this lovely sheltered bay's warm water has increasingly become popular with windsurfers, divers, and snorkelers.

③ 🤿 🍴
Xel-Ha

🏠 Puerto Juarez Federal Highway, Km 240, Quintana Roo 🕘 9am-6pm daily 🌐 xelha.com

Very popular with families and nature lovers, this aquatic adventure park is based around a series of interconnecting lagoons set among spectacular rocks and caves. Creating a natural aquarium, a huge variety of tropical fish swim in the park's beautifully clear waters, and the diving and snorkeling are wonderful. You can immerse yourself in *cenotes* or underground rivers, and ziplining and inner-tubing are among the many other activities on offer here.

←

Isla Mujeres, surrounded by calm, crystal-clear, turquoise waters

CENOTES

The Riviera Maya is famous for its *cenotes*, water-filled sinkholes that are great for a swim. Some have been turned into waterparks, while others are untouched. Cenote Chaak Tun and Gran Cenote are two of the best to visit in the region: the former, outside Playa del Carmen, is made up of two stalactite-filled caverns; the latter, close to Tulum, is great for snorkeling.

④

Playa del Carmen

🏠 Quintana Roo 🚌�
ℹ Parque Los Fundadores;
(984) 873 28 04

Playa del Carmen is the second biggest resort on the coast after Cancún. The town has a relaxed atmosphere and Quinta Avenida, the main street, is lined with small shops, coffee bars, and traditional

---

DIVING IN THE MEXICAN CARIBBEAN

Stretching for over 620 miles (1,000 km) down the eastern coast of the Yucatán peninsula to Belize, Guatemala and Honduras, the great Mesoamerican Reef System's crystal clear, marine life-rich waters are ideal for snorkelling and scuba-diving. The finest dive sites are scattered around the island of Cozumel, and there are options suitable for every level of ability. It is also possible to dive with whale sharks off the coast of Isla Holbox.

---

restaurants. Ferries to Cozumel leave from a pier close to the lively central square.

---

⑤

Cozumel

🏠 Quintana Roo 🚗🚢 Car ferry from Calica, passenger ferry from Playa del Carmen ℹ 5a Avenida Sur 51; www.cozumel.travel

Just off the east coast of the Yucatán Peninsula, Cozumel is Mexico's largest island, 9 miles (14 km) wide by 31 miles (50 km) long. Known to the Maya as Cuzamil, the "place of the swallows," it was an important center for the cult of Ixchel, goddess of fertility, pregnancy, and childbirth. The ruins of two of the main settlements are at El Cedral and San Gervasio. Both are overgrown, but visiting them provides an opportunity to see some of Cozumel's varied birdlife in the jungle habitat. San Gervasio, the larger site, has several restored buildings. The Spaniards also came to Cozumel. The first Mass in Mexico was said here in 1518, and Hernán Cortés, warmly received by the local inhabitants, planned his conquest of mainland Mexico from the island.

↑ Arched sculpture framing the white-sand beach at Playa del Carmen

Today, Cozumel is a tourist resort and diving hotspot. Ferries from the mainland arrive at San Miguel, the island's only town. Tourist shops, restaurants, and bars dominate the surrounding area, but a few blocks away, the town is quieter and more traditional.

Cozumel is ringed by stunning beaches, many only accessible by 4X4. Those on the eastern, windward side are beautiful, but not safe for swimming. The sheltered western side has safe swimming beaches, notably Playa Palancar, with a restaurant-bar and within striking distance of a Maya ruin, El Cedral. The best diving sites are here too, particularly around the Colombia, Palancar, San Francisco, and Santa Rosa reefs, as is the touristy Chankanaab Park, which has a lagoon and many varieties of tropical plants. At the southern tip of Cozumel is the more worthwhile Faro Celarain Eco Park, which has pretty beaches, bird-filled mangroves, and El Caracol, which is thought to have been a Maya lighthouse.

> **An underwater sculpture park off the coast of Cancún, the Museo Subacuático de Arte (MUSA) has a collection of 500 artworks.**

 (6)

Cancún

Before 1970, Cancún was little more than a sandy island and a fishing village of barely 100 inhabitants. The government decided to turn it into a resort, and in the late 1960s building began. Since then the population has soared to hundreds of thousands, and over 12 million (mainly non-Mexican) visitors flock here every year to enjoy the sandy beaches and perfect weather.

There are, in fact, two Cancúns. The downtown area, on the mainland, has very few hotels and no beaches, while the Cancún that most visitors see has plenty of both. The latter, known as Isla Cancún or the *Zona Hotelera* (Hotel Zone), is a narrow, 14-mile (23-km) L-shaped island connected to the mainland by two bridges.

Although many of the hotels appear to command private stretches of sand, all beaches in Mexico are public and can be enjoyed by anybody. The ones in front of the Hyatt Cancún and Sheraton hotels are particularly beautiful. If the resort beach scene and constant presence of hotel staff do not appeal, however, head for the equally attractive "public" beaches. Playa Linda, Playa Langosta, and Playa Tortugas, on the northern arm of the island, offer relaxed swimming in the calm Bahía Mujeres, while bigger waves and fine views can be found at Playa Chac-Mool, Playa Marlín,

and Playa Ballenas, which face the open sea on the eastern side. The protected Laguna Nichupté, between Isla Cancún and the mainland, is perfect for watersports.

Toward the southern end of the island is the small Maya site of El Rey (The King), occupied from AD 1200 until the Conquest. Here, a low pyramid and two plazas provide a quiet, cultural retreat from the beachfront action.

Some ferries for Isla Mujeres (p280) leave from a dock near Playa Linda, but the majority depart from Puerto Juárez or Punta Sam, both just to the north of Cancún.

The highlight of the resort's limited cultural scene, the **Museo Maya de Cancún** has Maya artifacts from across the region, as well as temporary exhibits. Its grounds contain the remains of a small Maya site known as San Miguelito.

An underwater sculpture park off the coast of Cancún, the **Museo Subacuático de Arte (MUSA)** has a collection of 500 artworks. You can see MUSA in a glass-bottom boat or on a snorkeling or scuba-diving trip.

Museo Maya de Cancún

⊘ 🏠 Blvd Kukulcán Km 16.5 ☎ (998) 885 38 42 ⏰ 9am–6pm Tue–Sun

Museo Subacuático de Arte (MUSA)

⊘⊘ 🏠 See website for tour times 🌐 musamexico.org

Visitors enjoying the nightlife in Cancún's *Zona Hotelera* (Hotel Zone) ↓

UXMAL

2 🤿 🚵 🖥 🛍

⚑F4 🚗Mex 261, 48 miles (78 km) S of Mérida, Yucatán
🚌Tours from Mérida 🕗8am–5pm daily 🌐inah.gob.mx

On entering the vast Maya ruins at Uxmal, the eye
is immediately drawn to its most awe-inspiring
structure, the Magician's Pyramid, but there are
many other fascinating structures to admire, too.

The late-Classic Maya site of Uxmal is one of the most complex
and harmonious expressions of Puuc architecture (p302). The
city's exact origins are uncertain, but most of the buildings date
from the 7th–10th centuries AD, when Uxmal dominated the
region. The real function of many of the structures is unknown,
and they retain the fanciful names given to them by the
Spanish. Unlike most Yucatán sites, Uxmal has no *cenotes*
(p280), and water was collected in manmade cisterns
(*chultunes*), one of which can be seen near the entrance.
The scarcity of water may explain the number of depictions
of the rain god Chac on the buildings.

20,000

A rough estimate of
the population of the
Maya settlement.

Illustration showing
the layout of the Maya
↓ ruins at Uxmal

Cemetery Group

Great Pyramid

The Dovecote

South Temple

Distinctive hooked noses of Chac
masks stand out against the mosaic
frieze that runs the length of the
Governor's Palace.

←

Stone latticework
and carvings on the
Nunnery Quadrangle

Nunnery Quadrangle

The stone latticework, ornate masks of Chac, and carved serpents on the walls are remarkable examples of closely fitting mosaic.

Magician's Pyramid

This spectacular pyramid is made up of multiple temples (p286).

Highlights of Uxmal

Dovecote

△ Named after its unusual roof comb, this ruined palace faces a rectangular garden, and is one of Uxmal's most peaceful spots.

Great Pyramid

A stairway climbs the 100-ft (30-m) pyramid to a temple that is decorated with Chac masks and macaws.

House of the Turtles

△ A frieze of turtles around the building, suggests that it might have been dedicated to a water god.

Governor's Palace

A masterpiece of Puuc architecture, the 9th–10th-century palace is actually three buildings linked by Maya arches.

The upper level of the elegant House of the Turtles is simply decorated with columns.

This impressive Nunnery Quadrangle was given its unlikely name because the Spanish thought that the 74 small rooms set around a central courtyard looked like the cells of a nunnery.

Entrance to site

At 115 ft (35 m), the Magician's Pyramid is the tallest structure at Uxmal.

Ballcourt

The Jaguar Throne is carved as a two-headed jaguar, an animal associated with chiefs and kings.

Pyramid of the Old Woman

↑ The well-preserved ruins of Uxmal, ornamented with Chac masks

The Magician's Pyramid

Tall, steep, and set on an unusual oval base, the Magician's Pyramid is the most striking of Uxmal's monuments. Legend tells that it was built in one night by a dwarf with supernatural powers – the magician – but, in fact, it shows five phases of construction from the 6th–10th centuries AD. At each phase a new temple was built, either on top of or obscuring the previous one. There are thus five temples on the pyramid. Unfortunately, visitors are no longer allowed to climb to the summit, to prevent further erosion.

↑ Visitors approaching the Magician's Pyramid

The facade of Temple IV is actually an expressive Chac mask with large rectangular eyes and a curling moustache. Its wide-open, toothed mouth forms the entrance. Temple III is behind Temple IV.

Entrance to Temple IV

Temple V is part of the final phase of construction – which took place around AD 1000 – and appears to be a small-scale reproduction of the nearby Governor's Palace (p285).

→ Reconstruction of the Magician's Pyramid

The east staircase provides access to Temple II, which is just a dark room today.

Chac masks on facade of Temple I

Entrance to Temple I (now blocked)

The west staircase, at the front of the pyramid, is flanked by representations of Chac, the rain god. The staircase is extremely steep and ascends the pyramid at an angle of 60°, meaning that the climb to the summit was very difficult.

Temple I was built in the sixth century AD, according to the results of radiocarbon dating, and is now covered by the pyramid. Partially collapsed, it cannot be visited.

⊙ **PICTURE PERFECT**
Best Views

To capture the unique curve of the Magician's Pyramid, take a photo at the base as you enter. For pictures of the best views, head to the top of the Great Pyramid, or the platform on the Governor's Palace.

GODS OF ANCIENT MEXICO

The civilizations of Mesoamerica *(p144)* worshiped multiple gods and goddesses. Gods were passed from one civilization to another and renamed over time.

Deities were often feared as much as revered. If they had created the world, it was believed that they could also destroy it. Ancient civilizations therefore thought it essential to appease them as much as possible, sometimes through human sacrifice.

CREATOR GODS
Mesoamerican societies had differing accounts of creation. According to one myth from central Mexico, Tonacatecuhtli and Tonacaciwhuatl resided in the 13th, or uppermost, heaven and from there sent down souls of children to be born on earth.

GODS OF THE UNDERWORLD
In Aztec mythology, the soul was thought to pass through a series of hazards in the nine levels of the underworld before reaching the deepest part, ruled over by Mictlantecuhtli and Mictecacihuatl.

THE SUN GOD
This deity was associated with the jaguar in ancient Mexico, an animal that evoked the vigor and power of the rising sun.

RAIN GODS
Abundant rainfall was vital to farming communities, and rain and lightning gods were venerated in all the civilizations of ancient Mexico.

QUETZALCOATL
Quetzalcoatl (or Kukulcan), the feathered serpent, appears in many cultures. Some revered him as a god of nature, while others considered him a creator god.

↑ Mictlantecuhtli, the Aztec god of the underworld

↑ Kinich Ahau, a sun god in the Classic Maya culture

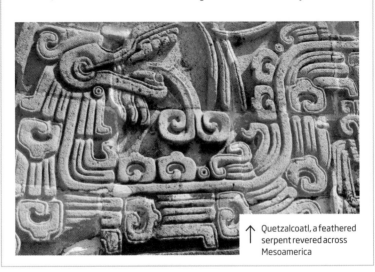

↑ Quetzalcoatl, a feathered serpent revered across Mesoamerica

❸ ✍

TULUM

🗺 G4 🏠 Mex 307, 80 miles (128 km) S of Cancún, Quintana Roo
📞 (983) 837 24 11 🚌 From Cancún 🕐 8am–5pm daily

What sets Tulum aside from other archaeological sites is its beautiful setting on a cliff by the Caribbean Sea. Its the perfect spot to enjoy the Yucatán's stunning scenery, as well as the region's ancient history.

Tulum is a Maya site that was at its height from around AD 1200 until the arrival of the Spanish in the mid-17th century (p57). The name, which means "enclosure" or "wall," is probably modern. It is thought that the site was originally called Zama, or "dawn," reflecting its location on the east coast, and the west-east alignment of its buildings. Its inhabitants traded with nearby settlements at Cozumel and Isla Mujeres, as well as farther afield with Guatemala and central Mexico.

If you want to beat the crowds, arrive early. There is not much shade at the site so bring plenty of sunscreen and a hat, and remember your swimming gear so you can enjoy the tempting beach after exploring the site.

Did You Know?

From its spectacular clifftop vantage point, El Castillo served as a landmark for seafarers.

OTHER THINGS TO DO IN TULUM TOWN

Although most famous for its Maya ruins, the town of Tulum has plenty more to offer travelers. Its long, sandy beach is one of the finest in the region. It also has a flourishing culinary scene, with a string of excellent places to eat and drink on the beach and in the town itself. Highlights include innovative restaurants Hartwood (www.hartwoodtulum.com) and Cetli (www.facebook.com/cetlitulum), and the casual mojito bar Batey (www.facebook.com/bateytulum).

The House of the Cenote is so named because it stands above a cenote, a subterranean well.

House of the Northeast

A wall runs along three sides of the site, 16 ft (5 m) thick and pierced by five gates.

House of the Halach Uinic, or Overlord

House of Chultún

Entrance

Illustration of the late-Maya site at Tulum ↑

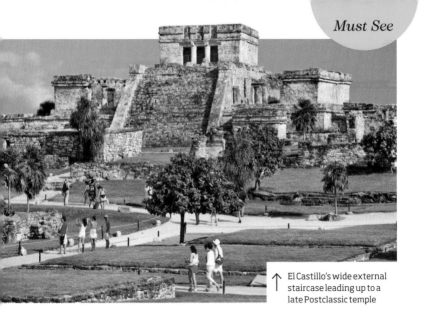

↑ El Castillo's wide external staircase leading up to a late Postclassic temple

Temple of the Wind

The Temple of the Descending God has a carving over its door showing a swooping or falling figure.

The temple that crowns El Castillo has three niches above the doorway.

Temple of the Initial Series

↘ To Temple of the Sea

El Castillo is the largest and most prominent building on the site.

Ceremonial platform

House of Columns or Grand Palace

Inside the Temple of the Frescoes, the walls are adorned with paintings.

→ Temple of the Frescoes, once an observatory for tracking the sun

EXPERIENCE The Yucatán Peninsula

❹

MÉRIDA

🅰F4 🄰Yucatán ✈🚌 ℹCalle 62 (Palacio Municipal); www.merida.gob.mx/turismo

Founded in 1542, the capital of Yucatán is one of the great cities of Latin America. In the early 1900s, Mérida was said to have had more millionaires per capita than anywhere else in the world, due to the booming sisal industry. This prosperity resulted in grand mansions, municipal buildings, squares, and parks, making the city an architectural treasure trove. Not stuck in the past though: Mérida is a thriving business and cultural hub.

① Teatro Jose Peon Contrera

🄰Calle 60, between calles 57 and 57 🕐Daily 🌐sinfonicadeyucatan.com.mx

Mérida prides itself on being the cultural capital of the Yucatán Peninsula, and the José Peón Contreras Theater is one of its main showcases. Built at the turn of the 20th century, it is a grand Neo-Classical creation

 in beige and white, with elaborate chandeliers in its massive foyer.

② Palacio de Gobierno

🄰Plaza Mayor 📞(999) 930 31 00 🕐Daily

The Government palace houses the Yucatán state authorities. It is remarkable for the numerous large murals adorning its courtyard, stairs, and first floor lobby. They were painted in the 1970s by Fernando Castro Pacheco, a local artist, and show his vision of Yucatán history from the time of the Maya to the 19th century.

③ Parque Santa Lucia

🄰Calle 60 476A

Santa Lucía Park is used for dancing and cultural events, and has a flea market on Sundays. Bronze busts placed on tall, white columns lining one corner of the park honor Yucateco musicians.
    Across the street, the small Iglesia de Santa Lucía, one of the earliest and most harmonious of the city's churches, is where the local Maya villagers were encouraged to come and worship.

④ Parque Cepeda Peraza

🄰Corner of Calle 60 and Calle 59 🕐Daily

Just off Calle 60, one of the city's major roads, is Parque Cepeda Peraza (Parque Hidalgo), a small

Did You Know?

Mérida's nickname, La Ciudad Blanca (White City) is from the white limestone buildings.

Map labels:
- Gran Museo del Mundo Maya 5 miles (8 km) (7)
- Museo Regional de Antropología (8)
- Paseo de Montejo (6)
- CALLE 45
- CALLE 47
- Parque de Santa Ana
- PASEO DE MONTEJO
- CALLE 45
- CALLE 49
- CALLE 51
- Hotel Julamis
- Parque Santa Lucía (3)
- Iglesia de Santa Lucía
- CALLE 53
- La Chaya Maya
- Teatro Jose Peon Contrera (1)
- CALLE 55
- Palacio de Gobierno
- Parque Cepeda Peraza (4)
- Parque de la Mejorada
- CALLE 57
- Dulcería and Sorbetería Colón (2)
- Cathedral
- Iglesia La Mejorada
- Plaza Grande (5)
- Museo Casa Montejo (9)
- CALLE 61
- CALLE 65
- Mercado Lucas de Gálvez
- 0 meters 400, 0 yards 400, N

but bustling square. Visitors can watch the many musicians and street merchants, or relax in one of the openair cafés. The imposing Jesuit church, the Templo de la Tercera Orden (Temple of the Third Order), on the north side of the square, dates from the 17th century. It has a huge entrance and two narrow bell towers. Inside, the gold altar and friezes of biblical scenes are the only decoration.

(5) Plaza Grande

Mérida is built on a grid system based around the main square, the Plaza Grande (also known as the Plaza Mayor or Plaza de la Independencia). In the evenings, and on Sundays, dancing and concerts take place outside the city hall, the Palacio Municipal. This building is in a mix of styles and has a notable 1920s clock tower.

The Museo Casa de Montejo (p292) on the south side of the plaza is now a bank, but was orignally built as the palace of the first Spanish governors.

East of the Plaza Mayor lies Mérida's historic post office, now the Museo de la Ciudad with exhibits on the city's colonial past as well as contemporary artworks.

Opposite the city hall is the cathedral, the oldest in the Americas. It was begun in the early 1560s, and finished in 1598. Three arched doors in the imposing facade lead to a soaring interior with a barreled roof and crisscross arches. A wooden sculpture, *Cristo de las Ampollas* (Christ of the Blisters), stands in a small chapel on the right. It is a copy of a statue that was brought to Mérida after miraculously surviving a fire. The original, which was later destroyed, is said to have developed blisters, as skin would, instead of burning – a miracle which is celebrated every year in Mérida (p305).

← The Palacio Municipal and its clock tower, a major landmark on Plaza Grande

⑥
Paseo de Montejo

The Paseo de Montejo stretches for several miles through the middle of the city. It is lined with the elegant town mansions of rich plantation owners and the private banks that prospered in the late 19th century. Many of the houses were built by Italian architects and are a medley of Neo-Classical elements. At the northern end of the Paseo de Montejo is the *Monumento a la Patria* (Monument to the Fatherland), an elaborate 20th-century work by Colombian sculptor Rómulo Rozo. The striking monument shows historical figures and animal sculptures, and encloses an eternal flame, a symbol of Mexico's independence.

⑦
Gran Museo del Mundo Maya

🏠 Calle 60 Norte 299
🕐 Wed-Mon 🌐 granmuseo-delmundomaya.com.mx

Housed in an eye-catching modern building north of

💬 INSIDER TIP
Hammocks

Mérida is one of the best places in Mexico to buy a hammock. A common sight in the markets, they are made from twine produced from henequen, a fibrous agave plant. Modern hammocks are often made from cotton or silk.

the city center, the Maya World Museum of Mérida is an excellent place to visit before heading out to explore the Yucatán's Maya sites. It provides an insight into the architecture, religious beliefs, scientific achievements, and everyday life of this fascinating ancient civilization.

The museum has more than 1,000 artifacts from sites across southern Mexico, as well as Belize, Guatemala, and Honduras, where the Maya also lived.

⑧
Museo Regional de Antropología

🏠 Paseo de Montejo 485
📞 (999) 923 05 57
🕐 Tue-Sun

One of the finest mansions on the elegant Paseo de Montejo is the Palacio Cantón, which houses the excellent Regional Museum of Anthropology. Its pre-Hispanic exhibits include a jaguar throne from Uxmal (p284), a chacmool from Chichén Itzá (p294), and fine examples of Mayan funerary offerings.

⑨
Museo Casa Montejo

🏠 Plaza Mayor 📞 (999) 923 06 33, ext 25565 🕐 Tue-Sun

A palace built between 1543 and 1549 for conquistador Francisco de Montejo, the founder of Mérida, the Museo

→
The striking exterior of the Gran Museo del Mundo and *(inset)* one of the exhibitions inside

↑ Decadent gold-embellished furniture displayed inside the Museo Casa Montejo

Casa Montejo is now owned by the National Bank of México. The plateresque architecture is majestic, with a blend of classical, Moorish, Gothic, and Renaissance elements. It still has its original portico, with the Montejo family coat of arms. Several of the rooms are open to the public and feature historic furnishings and decor. There are also a few halls that host temporary exhibitions.

EAT

Dulcería and Sorbetería Colón

There are few better ways to cool down on a hot day than at this Mérida institution. Here you'll find delicious pastries and refreshing sorbets and ice creams, with flavors ranging from tamarind to watermelon.

🏠 Plaza Grande
🌐 dulceriaysorbeteria colon.wordpress.com

La Chaya Maya

This is the place to come for traditional Yucatecan dishes such as *poc-chuc* (citrus-marinated pork), *sopa de lima* (tangy chicken soup), and *salbutes* (crisp tortillas topped with turkey, onion, avocado, and radish). There's also another branch at Calle 55.

🏠 Corner of calles 62 and 57 🌐 lachayamaya.com

STAY

Hotel Julamis

A few blocks from the Plaza Mayor, this boutique hotel is in a 200-year-old building that has been impeccably decorated by its Cuban owners. There's a rooftop terrace and hot tub, and the breakfast is delicious, too.

🏠 Calle 53 #475b
🌐 hoteljulamis.com

⑤ 🏛 🎭 🖥 🛍

CHICHÉN ITZÁ

🅰 G4 🏠 Mex 180, 25 miles (40 km) W of Valladolid, Yucatán 📞 (985) 851 01 37 🚌 From Valladolid, Mérida, or Cancún ⏰ 8am–5pm daily

Chichén Itzá was once an important site to the advanced Maya civilization. Even as ruins, the buildings here are still an awe-inspiring sight, and are now one of Mexico's most popular attractions.

The best preserved Maya site on the Yucatán Peninsula, Chichén Itzá confounds historians. The date of first settlement in the southern part of the site is not certain, but the northern section was built during a renaissance in the 11th century AD. Similarities with Tula (p154), and myths that tell how exiled Toltec god-king Quetzalcoatl (p287) settled at Chichén Itzá, suggest that the renaissance was due to a Toltec invasion. However, other theories hold that Tula was influenced by the Maya, not vice versa. In its heyday as a commercial, religious, and military center, which lasted until about the 13th century, Chichén Itzá supported over 35,000 people. In 2007 it was voted one of the New Seven Wonders of the World.

Chichén Itzá's ballcourt was the largest in Mesoamerica. You can still see the rings that the ball had to pass through.

↑ The large Nunnery, thought to have been a residential palace

Main entrance

Pisté and Mérida

Tomb of the High Priest

The slits in the walls of the Observatory correspond to the positions of celestial bodies on key dates in the Maya calendar.

The Church, or Iglesia, is decorated with fretwork, masks of the rain god Chac, and the bacabs – four animals who, in Maya myth, held up the sky.

The Nunnery is so named because it reminded the Spanish of a convent.

Chichén Viejo

Nunnery

▼ The facade of this building's east annex has some particularly beautiful stone fretwork and interesting carvings.

El Castillo

Built on top of an older structure, the building's height and striking geometric design dominate the site *(p296)*.

Ballcourt

Ballcourts *(p297)* have been found at all main pre-Hispanic sites, the largest being here.

Timeline

Observatory

▲ Also called El Caracol (The Snail) because of its spiral staircase, this building served as an astronomical observatory.

Temple of the Warriors

The raised temple is made even more impressive by the Group of a Thousand Columns surrounding it on various sides.

Sacred Cenote, a huge natural well, is thought to have been revered as the home of rain god Chac, and used for human sacrifice.

The Tzompantli is a low platform whose perimeter is carved with grinning skulls.

Platform of the Jaguars and Eagles

This 24-m (79-ft) high pyramid, El Castillo, was dedicated to Kukulcan, the Maya representation of the god Quetzalcoatl.

Set on a small pyramid, the Temple of the Warriors is decorated with sculptures of the rain god Chac and the plumed serpent Kukulcan.

The Group of a Thousand Columns, with colonnades on two sides of a huge plaza, may have been used as a market.

Entrance

↑ Illustration showing the layout of the ruins at Chichén Itzá

 PICTURE PERFECT
Equinox at El Castillo

Two serpents' heads at the foot of the north staircase are thought to represent the god Kukulcan, the Maya Quetzalcóatl *(p287)*. At the equinoxes, the play of light and shadow makes them appear to crawl up the pyramid.

El Castillo

The most awe-inspiring structure at Chichén Itzá is El Castillo (The Castle), a pyramid built around AD 800. It has a perfect astronomical design: four staircases face the cardinal points, various features correspond with aspects of the Maya calendar (p298), and, twice yearly at sunrise, a fascinating optical illusion occurs on the north staircase (p295). Continuing excavations on the eastern side allow visitors to watch the process of archaeology as it reveals that the pyramid was built on the remains of a much older settlement. Since the site was designated as one of the New Seven Wonders of the World, climbing the staircases is no longer permitted.

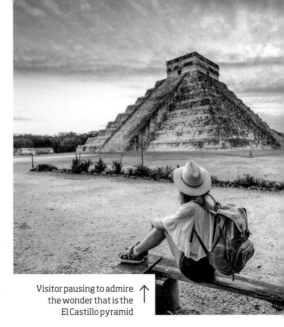

Visitor pausing to admire the wonder that is the El Castillo pyramid ↑

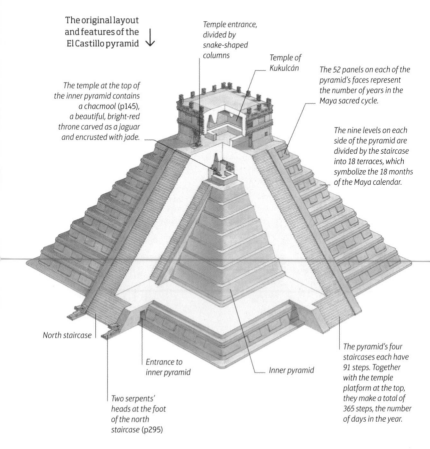

The original layout and features of the El Castillo pyramid ↓

Temple entrance, divided by snake-shaped columns

Temple of Kukulcán

The 52 panels on each of the pyramid's faces represent the number of years in the Maya sacred cycle.

The temple at the top of the inner pyramid contains a chacmool (p145), a beautiful, bright-red throne carved as a jaguar and encrusted with jade.

The nine levels on each side of the pyramid are divided by the staircase into 18 terraces, which symbolize the 18 months of the Maya calendar.

North staircase

Entrance to inner pyramid

Inner pyramid

The pyramid's four staircases each have 91 steps. Together with the temple platform at the top, they make a total of 365 steps, the number of days in the year.

Two serpents' heads at the foot of the north staircase (p295)

Must See

EXPERIENCE MORE

6 Edzná

F4 Mex 180 and 186, 37 miles (60 km) SE of Campeche, Campeche (981) 816 91 11 8am-5pm daily

A sophisticated canal system radiates out from the center of this Maya settlement to the agricultural areas beyond. The canals were primarily used for transporting goods, but may also have served a defensive purpose. Edzná was founded in around 600 BC, and in its heyday it is thought to have had a population of 25,000. The main structure is the Gran Acrópolis, dominated by the Edificio de los Cinco Pisos (Building of the Five Levels). Another building of interest is the Templo de los Mascarones (Temple of the Masks), named after its notable stucco mask.

7 Ekbalam

G4 Off Mex 295, 16 miles (25 km) N of Valladolid, Yucatán (988) 944 40 68 8am-5pm daily

Excavation work has revealed Ekbalam (Black Jaguar) as an important Maya city and religious center. It dates predominantly from AD 700 to 1000, is quite compact, and has an unusual double perimeter wall for fortification. The real highlight is the Tower – a 98-ft- (30-m-) high tiered pyramid that visitors can climb. On each of the pyramid's tiers, pits sunk into the structure are thought to be *chultunes* (Maya cisterns). From gaps in the surrounding walls at the cardinal points, Maya white roads, or *sacbeob*, radiate out to a distance of over 1 mile (1.5 km).

↑ Detail of a serpent's head at the foot of the staircase, El Castillo

THE BALLGAME

More than a sport, the ballgame that was played throughout Mesoamerica had a ritual significance. Two teams would compete to manipulate a large ball through a stone ring set high on the wall at the side of the court. It is thought that the losers of the game were subsequently put to death. The cities of Cantona *(p160)* and El Tajín *(p262)* each had a great number of ball-courts. A version of the game, called *ulama*, is still played today.

↑ The Tower and other ruins of Ekbalam archaeological site

THE MAYA

Unlike other Mesoamerican civilizations, the Maya did not have a large, centralized empire. Instead they lived in independent city-states in the Yucatán Peninsula, and parts of Guatemala, Belize, Honduras, and El Salvador. This did not impede them in developing a complex system of writing and counting, profound knowledge of astronomy, and an incredible long-count calendar.

HISTORICAL RECORDS

While other Mesoamerican peoples *(p144)* had writing systems, none was as complete or sophisticated as that of the Maya. They used about 800 different hieroglyphs (or simply "glyphs"), some representing whole words, others phonetic sounds. Maya books (codices) were created by writing on both sides of a thin sheet of bark, which was then folded like a concertina. Only four codices have survived, and their study led to major advances in dicipherment in the mid-20th century.

In the Tzolkin or Sacred Round, 20 day names were combined with 13 numbers to give a year of 260 individually named days.

ASTRONOMY

The Maya had a knowledge of astronomy that was very advanced for their time. They observed and predicted the phases of the moon, equinoxes, and solstices, as well as solar and lunar eclipses. They knew that the Morning and Evening Star were the same planet, Venus, and calculated its "year" to 584 days, within a fraction of the true figure (583.92 days). Remarkably, they achieved all this without the use of lenses for observing distant objects, instruments for calculating angles, or clocks to measure the passing of time.

ENDURING ARTWORKS

Of all Mesoamerican civilizations, the Maya produced the most enduring works of art, in the greatest quantity. Maya art is distinguished by its naturalistic approach which makes it more accessible to the modern eye. Particularly striking are the Maya's portraits of themselves – as seen especially in the wall paintings of Bonampak *(p248)* and the carved bas-reliefs of Palenque *(p246)* – which give us an understanding of their way of life, methods of warfare, costumes, customs, and beliefs.

← The El Caracol observatory at Chichén Itzá

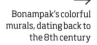
→ Bonampak's colorful murals, dating back to the 8th century

THE MAYA CALENDAR

The Maya observed the 52-year "Calendar Round." This resulted from two calendar cycles, the Haab and the Tzolkin, which acted simultaneously but independently. For periods longer than 52 years, the Maya used a separate system called the Long Count.

Glyph gives name of the month

13 day numbers

The Haab consisted of 365 days organized into 18 months of 20 days – with 5 unlucky days added at the end.

20 named days

Dots and bars give the day of the month

↑ Illustration of the 52-year "Calendar Round" system

The date here has two names which interlock: 4 Ahaw (from the Tzolkin cycle) and 8 Kumk'u (from the Haab cycle). Because of the different lengths of the cycles, it would take 52 years for this combination to come around again.

❽

Chetumal

⬛G5 **⬛Quintana Roo** **✈🚌**
**ℹ Centro de Convenciones
Anexo A, corner of Blvd
Bahia and Ignacio
Comonfort; (983) 835 08 60**

Founded on the estuary of the
Río Hondo in 1898, Chetumal
is now the capital of Quintana
Roo state. It is situated near
the frontier with Belize, and is
a typical border town. There is
a large naval base and a duty-
free zone, with stores selling
cut-rate luxury items from all
over the world. Visitors from
Belize and Guatemala come
here for shopping, giving the
city an exciting atmosphere.
Most of the original wooden
and tin-roofed buildings were
destroyed in a hurricane in the
1950s, and the town has been
rebuilt around wide avenues,
some of which still end in
undergrowth. Chetumal's
spacious **Museo de la Cultura
Maya** explores the Maya world,
including astronomy, daily life,
and Maya codices. Many of the
exhibits are replicas, but there
are good explanatory panels
and interactive screens.

Situated 25 miles (40 km)
northwest of Chetumal, is the
village of Bacalar. There is a
natural pool here, over 200 ft
(60 m) deep. Named Cenote
Azul for its vivid blue color, it
is perfect for a swim.

Museo de la Cultura Maya
♻🏛 **⬛Corner of Avenida
Héroes and Cristobal Colón
☎(983) 832 68 38** **🕐9am–
7pm Tue–Sat**

---

❾

Campeche

⬛F4 **⬛Campeche** **✈🚌**
**ℹ Avenida Ruiz Cortines;
www.campeche.travel**

The Spanish settlement of
Campeche was built on the site
of a former Maya fishing village
in about 1540. In colonial times
it was the most important

INSIDER TIP
Belize Bound

Water taxis connect
Chetumal with Caye
Caulker and San Pedro
in Belize. You'll need to
pass immigration and
customs, but low rates
and beautiful vistas
make up for that *(www.
belizewatertaxi.com).*

port on the Yucatán Peninsula.
Campeche's prosperity made it
a target for attacks by pirates.
As a consequence, thick walls
were built around the town.
These were strengthened by
eight *baluartes* (bastions),
seven of which have been
put to other uses. The largest
of them, in the middle of the
stretch of wall facing the sea,
is the **Baluarte de la Soledad**.
It is now a museum displaying
an important collection of
Maya stelae, many of which
were found at the Maya burial
ground on the island of Jaina,
25 miles (40 km) north of
Campeche. The Baluarte de
Santiago, at the northwestern
corner of the walls, has been
transformed into a walled
botanical garden containing

> **Chetumal's spacious
> Museo de la Cultura
> Maya explores
> the Maya world,
> including astronomy,
> daily life, and
> Maya codices.**

over 200 species of subtropical plants. On the landward side of the walls, the Baluarte de San Pedro sells a small selection of regional handicrafts.

Two gateways in the walls – the Sea Gate and the Land Gate – give access to the old part of the city. Between them runs Calle 59, on which stand several restored, single-story colonial-era houses, painted in bright blues, pinks, and ochers. One of the finest buildings is the **Casa de Teniente del Rey** (King's Lieutenant's House), the former residence of the Spanish king's military representative in the Yucatán. Transformed into offices, the house has a splendid courtyard, which can be visited.

The focal point of the old part of Campeche is the main square, the Parque Principal, which has elegant arcades and an elaborate, modern bandstand. Tours of the city in open-sided trams

start from here. Facing the square is **El Palacio Centro Cultural**, a museum that explores Campeche's history. Nearby is the cathedral, one of the first churches built on the Yucatán mainland, although much of the present building was constructed later, in the Baroque style. Behind it, on Calle 10, stands the Mansión Carvajal, now government offices. This building is a fine example of 19th-century Spanish-Moorish architecture. Another attractive building in the city center is the ExTemplo de San José, a former Jesuit church, with an elaborate facade of blue and yellow tiles. It is now used as a cultural center and craft market.

Campeche's defenses were completed by adding two forts on hills outside the city, both now housing museums. Situated to the north is the **Museo Histórico Reducto San José El Alto**, with exhibits on colonial military history. To the south of the city is the **Fuerte de San Miguel**, begun in 1771 and protected by a moat crossed by a drawbridge. Inside the fort is the Museo Arqueológico, whose

exhibits include distinctive jade masks from Calakmul (*p309*) and ceramic figurines from the island of Jaina.

Baluarte de la Soledad

Calle 8 Circuito Baluartes (seaward side) (981) 816 91 36 8am-5pm Tue-Sun

Casa de Teniente del Rey

Calle 59 40, between Calles 14 & 16 (981) 816 91 11 8:30-5pm daily

El Palacio Centro Cultural

Parque Principal (981) 816 77 41 10am-7pm Tue-Sun

Museo Histórico Reducto San José El Alto

Avenida Morazan (981) 816 91 11 8am-5pm Tue-Sun

Fuerte de San Miguel

Avenida Escénica (981) 816 91 36 8:30am-5pm Tue-Sun

EAT

La Palapa del Tío Fito
Lively open-air restaurant along the seafront; a popular spot for seafood and cocktails.

F4 Avenida Resurgimiento s/n, Campeche facebook. com/lapalapadeltiofito

$$$

La Pigua
Here you'll find some of the best fish and seafood in the city. Meaty crab claws are among the specialties.

F4 Miguel Alemán 179A, Campeche lapigua.com.mx

$$$

↑ Independence Plaza, notable for the beautiful cathedral, in old Campeche

The Puuc Route

F4 **Starts from Mex 261, 12 miles (20 km) SE of Uxmal, Yucatán** **8am–5pm daily**

Forming a low ridge across the western part of the Yucatán, about 62 miles (100 km) south of Mérida, the Puuc hills provide a welcome relief from the flat monotony of the rest of the peninsula. Despite a lack of water, they offered a strong defensive position for the ancient Maya people, as well as good soil for farming.

Several Maya settlements have been discovered in the region. All are believed to have reached their peaks from about AD 600 to 900 and they share the striking style of architecture and ornamentation that has become known as the Puuc style. This style is marked by a facade which has plain walls at the base and detailed stone mosaic masks (often depicting gods) on its upper sections.

Some settlements are linked to each other and to their contemporary site of Uxmal (p284) by *sacbeob*, or "white roads," which were mainly used for ceremonial purposes.

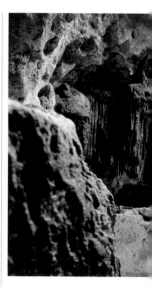

GREAT VIEW
From the Hilltop

Just a short drive from Kabáh on the Puuc Route is the small town of Santa Elena, where the large hilltop church – which looks more like a fortress than a place of worship - provides a wonderful vantage point from where to survey the incredible surrounding region.

The Puuc Route runs across four Maya sites, starting with Kabah. The main building here is the Codz Poop. The facade of this palace is decorated with more than 250 masks representing the rain god Chac (p287), with his distinctive hooked nose. Kabah was the closest settlement to the important Maya city of Uxmal. A single, undecorated arch straddles the entrance road.

Of all the Puuc sites, Sayil, around 6 miles (10 km) south of Kabah, is the one that provides most evidence of how the Maya in this area lived. Around the edge of the site, many of the ordinary dwellings have been excavated, as have the homes of the settlement's ruling elite, located in the central area. It is hard to envisage today, but the excavations suggest that Sayil was once populated by more than 8,000 people, with a similar number living in small, outlying communities surrounding the city. The huge three-tiered palace of Sayil's rulers is a splendid example of the rich Puuc style.

Sayil has no accessible supply of surface water, but several *chultunes*, large man-made cisterns for storing water, have been found at the site.

About 5 miles (8 km) east is Xlapak. The best-preserved building here is the palace, which has Chac masks above its entrances. Details such as a frieze of columns stand out on other buildings, but much of this site has yet to be cleared.

The last settlement on the Puuc Route is Labná, 3 miles (5 km) northeast of Xlapak. Among several spectacular structures here, the Arch is the best known. Originally part of a building between two courtyards, it is adorned with Chac

The Arch, a Maya highlight along the Puuc Route, at the settlement of Labná

EXPERIENCE The Yucatán Peninsula

A visitor inside the Loltún cave system and *(inset)* detail of a wall painting

masks and representations of thatched Maya huts. Nearby is a structure with a high crest above its facade. Known as El Mirador (The Observatory), it may have been a temple.

At the other end of the site is the main two-story palace, which has a frieze of masks and latticework. On one corner of the palace is a carving of a serpent with a human head in its jaws.

Another impressive structure is the Temple of Columns, which has a frieze around it, decorated with small columns.

⓫
Celestún

🅰F4 🅰Yucatán 🅘Palacio Municipal, Calle 62, Mérida; www.yucatan.travel

The small fishing village of Celestún is situated on a spit of land almost entirely separated from the mainland. Several kilometers of palm-fringed

beaches line the coast to the west of Celestún, but it is the flamingos on the estuary to the east that attract most of the visitors. Boats can be hired to get closer to the birds, which include pelicans and various waders, as well as flamingos. However, strict environmental laws prohibit anyone from disturbing the birds, so it is a good idea to bring a pair of binoculars with you so that you can see their natural behavior from afar.

Other excursions on board small launches are available, depending on weather conditions. These include visits to the *bosque petrificado*, a forest of petrified wood. This surreal, desolate place, located on the Isla de Pájaros to the south of Celestún, was created by prolonged salinization.

Several kilometers of palm-fringed beaches line the coast to the west of Celestún, but it is the flamingos on the estuary to the east that attract most of the visitors.

⓬
Grutas de Loltún

🅰G4 🅰Off Mex 180, 12 miles (20 km) SW of Maní, Yucatán 🅞Daily

The breathtaking Loltún Grottoes form the longest cave system in the Yucatán. The earliest remains discovered here are bison, mammoth, and other animal bones, suggesting that Loltún was inhabited soon after the last Ice Age. The caves contain fascinating wall paintings from various periods of occupation. The natural features of the caves are also striking, with impressive stalagmites and stalactites that give them the name Loltún, meaning "stone flowers."

Tours are compulsory, so book a guide from Mérida *(p290)* to explore the caves.

Visitors taking the challenging climb to the top of a pyramid at the archaelogical site of Cobá

 13

Cobá

G4 **29 miles (47 km) NW of Tulum, Quintana Roo** **983) 837 24 11** **8am-5pm daily**

Built around a group of lakes, Cobá is one of the most interesting archaeological sites in the Yucatán Peninsula. The city stood at the center of a network of *sacbeob* (meaning "white roads"): straight processional routes paved with limestone that connected Maya buildings. Up to 40,000 people are thought to have lived at this huge site, due to the local abundance of water. Only a small proportion has been excavated.

There are three key clusters of buildings. Be prepared for long walks between them, or rent a bike. Near the entrance of the site is the Cobá Group. The main building in this group is a pyramid called La Iglesia (the Church), because local people regard it as a shrine.

A trail beginning on the other side of Lago Macanxoc leads to the Macanxoc Group, where a collection of stelae carved by the Maya as historical records can be seen. Just north is the Nohoch Mul Group. Standing at 138 ft (42 m), Nohoch Mul is the highest pyramid in the Yucatán. It's a hard climb to the temple, but once reached there is an incomparable view of the lakes and jungle below.

14

Dzibilchaltún

F4 **Off Mex 261, 9 miles (15 km) N of Mérida, Yucatán** **(999) 944 00 43** **8am-5pm daily**

Dzibilchaltún was one of the most important centers in pre-Hispanic Yucatán, and one of the earliest to be built. However, it was explored only in the 1940s, making it one of the latest to be rediscovered.

The site is arranged concentrically. A *sacbe*, or "white road," leads from the central plaza to the impressive Temple of the Seven Dolls. This building is named after the tiny clay dolls found buried in front of its altar. Several of the dolls have deformities, and are thought to be associated with rituals. Replicas are displayed in the ultramodern and well laid-out museum.

Other noteworthy exhibits include the stelae and sculptures found in the gardens leading up to the museum, ceramic figures, wooden altarpieces from the colonial era, and an attractive display on the pirates who plagued the seas around the Yucatán coast in the 16th and 17th centuries. Interactive screens and audiovisual commentaries provide information about the ancient Maya world view, the Maya today, and the history of the henequen industry.

Dzibilchaltún's cenote, a natural turquoise pool that is covered with lilies floating on the surface, is more than 130 ft (40 m) deep. It provides a refreshing place for a swim after visiting the other sights. Many artifacts have been recovered from its depths.

→ Izamal's imposing Convento de San Antonio de Padua, built by Spanish Franciscan monks

Modern Izamal is a fascinating combination of Maya remains and Spanish Colonial buildings. There are around 20 Classic Maya structures still standing.

Izamal

G4 ▢Yucatán
▢ *i* Palacio Municipal, Calle 62, Mérida; www. yucatan.travel

Once as important a site as Chichén Itzá, Izamal is believed to have been founded around AD 300. The original village grew into an influential city-state and, by AD 800, it was governing the surrounding region. Modern Izamal is a fascinating combination of Maya remains and Spanish Colonial buildings. There are around 20 Classic Maya structures still standing. Chief among these is the pyramid K'inich K'ak' Mo', named after the ruler "Great-Sun Fire Macaw." It is one of the largest pyramids in the Yucatán.

The importance of Izamal had declined by the time the Spanish arrived in the mid-16th century, but it retained enough religious influence for the Franciscan monks to construct the spectacular Convento de San Antonio de Padua here. They demolished a Maya temple and built the church on its massive platform base, giving it an elevated position. The huge atrium contains some early Franciscan frescoes.

The church acquired even more importance when Bishop Diego de Landa installed in it a statue of the Virgen de la Inmaculada, which he had brought from Guatemala. This was immediately attributed with miraculous powers by the local Maya population, and in 1949 the Virgin was adopted as the patron saint of the Yucatán. A small museum housed inside the church commemorates Pope John Paul II's visit to Izamal in 1993, the International Year of Indigenous People, when he pledged the Catholic Church's support for the indigenous Maya. Adjacent to the church are two pretty arcaded squares. Here, and in the surrounding streets of

low Spanish Colonial houses, most of the buildings' facades are painted a glowing ocher color. This led to Izamal being nicknamed La Ciudad Amarilla, literally "The Yellow City."

Today, the town is known as a center for arts and crafts, with wood-carving, papiermâché and jewelry particular specialties. Many local artisans have shops or studios that are open to the public and there's a small museum on the main square that showcases crafts from across Mexico, including the Yucatán.

STAY

Casa Hamaca

Set in a tranquil garden, this charming B&B has eight attractive rooms, a communal terrace, and a small swimming pool. The owners also offer tips to explore the region.

🅐G4 🅐Calle 49 No 202-A, Valladolid 🆆casa hamaca.com

💲💲💲

Genesis Eco-Oasis

This eco-lodge is a delightful place to get away from it all, with simple but comfortable rooms. There is a lovely garden, a pool, and a vegetarian restaurant.

🅐G4 🅐Ek Balam, 17 miles (28 km) N of Valladolid 🆆genesis retreat.com

💲💲💲

Valladolid

🅐G4 🅐Yucatán 🚌 🆋Palacio Municipal, Parque Principal, Calle 40 No 200; www. valladolid.gob.mx

Lying almost exactly halfway between Mérida and Cancún, Valladolid is the third largest city on the Yucatán Peninsula. It was founded by the Spanish on an earlier Maya settlement known as Zaci, and quickly became an important religious center. In 1552 the Franciscans built the Yucatán's first ecclesiastical buildings here, the Iglesia de San Bernardino de Siena and the adjoining Ex-Convento de Sisal. These have been restored, revealing original frescoes behind two side altars in the church.

The *zócalo* (main square) is the focal point, and often the liveliest part, of this quiet and attractive city. Maya women sell *huipiles* (embroidered dresses) around its perimeter, and in the northeast corner small, inexpensive restaurants serve tasty local dishes and fruit juices late into the night. Overlooking the square is the cathedral, with its elegant facade, and the colonial-era hotel El Mesón del Marqués. Also on the square is the Palacio Municipal (City Hall). In the first-floor hallway are painted panels showing the history of the town from Maya times, and portraits of military leaders from Valladolid who helped initiate the revolution (p62).

West of town is the **Cenote de Dzitnup**, a natural well, apparently unearthed by a pig in the 1950s. Visitors can climb down the steep steps to the underground pool, where a hole in the roof and electric lighting illuminate the dramatic setting. You can also swim here among the fish in the blue water.

Located a bit farther west are the **Grutas de Balankanché**, huge caves that were discovered in 1959. Maya artifacts found here suggest that this was a place of worship as early as 300 BC, dedicated to the rain god Chac. Guides point out some of the Maya objects that remain in situ, which include miniature corn-grinding stones and decorated incense burners. There is also a small but informative museum on site.

↑ Admiring the stalactites and turquoise water in the Cenote de Dzitnup, Valladolid

Cenote de Dzitnup

 🔲 4 miles (7 km) W of Valladolid ⏱ 8am–7pm daily

Grutas de Balankanché

🔲 Off Mex 180, 22 miles (35 km) W of Valladolid ⏱ 8am–5pm daily

---

⑰

Maní

🔺 G4 🔲 Yucatán ℹ️ Palacio Municipal, Calle 62, Mérida; www.yucatan.travel

The town of Maní is the best base from which to discover an array of Catholic sites dating back to the mid-16th century, when Catholic priests, particularly Franciscan friars, came from Spain to convert the Maya population of the Yucatán. They constructed a network of huge, fortress-like churches and monasteries, often on the sites of earlier Maya temples. The most imposing of these is the Iglesia de San Miguel Arcángel, which dominates the town of Maní. It was constructed by around 6,000 enslaved people on ground that was already holy to the Maya – a cenote

(natural well) is visible under the front of the church.

The *Ruta de los Conventos* (Convent Route) connects other Franciscan churches in the towns around Maní. The one in Oxkutzcab, 6 miles (10 km) to the south, has a lovely Baroque altarpiece. The Iglesia de San Pedro Apóstol in Teabo, east of Maní, was begun in 1694, and traces of Franciscan murals can still be seen in its powder-blue interior. To the north, Teco's church houses a huge red and blue wooden altarpiece and a beautiful wooden cross with the last hours of Christ's life painted on it.

Located between Tekit and Tecoh is **Mayapán**, which became the political and cultural Maya capital in the north of the peninsula after the fall of Chichén Itzá. Abandoned in the mid-15th century, Mayapán's most remarkable surviving feature is the pyramid of Kukulcan, which is built on nine levels and topped with a temple.

Mayapán

🔲 37 miles (60 km) N of Maní 📞 (999) 944 40 68 ⏱ 8am–5pm daily

⑱

Río Lagartos Biosphere Reserve

🔺 G4 🔲 Mex 295, 65 miles (104 km) N of Valladolid, Yucatán ⏱ Daily

The UNESCO-listed nature reserve of Río Lagartos occupies brackish lagoons on the north coast of the peninsula. It is known as a birdwatchers' paradise and is home to huge colonies of flamingos that breed here in the summer. Between April and June, the flamingos' nests are protected, but at other times of the year, boat trips to view these elegant birds can be arranged in Río Lagartos village. Occasionally, snakes and turtles can also be spotted here.

260
—
The number of bird species you can see in the Río Lagartos nature reserve.

Progreso

 F4 Yucatán Calle 80, between Calles 25 & 27; (969) 103 01 61

Situated on the north Yucatán coast, Progreso was once an important port. With the construction of the railroad linking the port to Mérida in the 1880s, the town experienced a boom that is hard to imagine now as one approaches the relaxed, low-lying town past mangrove swamps.

Although Progreso shares Mexico's Yucatán Peninsula with Cancún (p282), it is less developed and glamorous. But it does have what is probably the longest concrete pier in the world – 4 miles (6.5 km) long – which is often bustling with people, and live mariachi bands play music here. Near its landward end is an attractive 19th-century lighthouse.

Crystal-clear water rolls gently onto the beautiful white sandy beach. Running alongside, the paved boardwalk is pleasant to stroll, and there are many good seafood restaurants. Cruise liners stop in Progreso, and there are a number of ocean-front resorts, making the town popular with people from the north looking for a warmer winter.

Río Bec Sites

20 G5 Mex 186, 75 miles (120 km) W of Chetumal, Campeche 8am–5pm daily

A group of stylistically similar Maya sites, situated in the lowlands west of Chetumal, are known collectively as the Río Bec sites. Many are hidden by jungle, but three of them, Xpujil, Becán, and Chicanná, are near enough to the main road (Mex 186) to be accessible. These three can be visited on a day-trip from Chetumal, or en route to the city from Palenque (p244) or Villahermosa (p273).

The Río Bec style, which the sites share, was dominant between AD 600 and 900. The style is characterized by elongated platforms and buildings, flanked by slender towers with rounded corners. These towers are "fake" temple-pyramids – the steps are too steep to be used, and the structures seem to have no inner chamber and no special function apart from decoration. Representations of Itzamná, the creation god responsible for life and death, are the main ornamentation.

From Chetumal, the first site is Xpujil, clearly visible from the road. Here, 17 building groups surround a central

square, but the most striking structure is the main temple, whose three towers rise over 50 ft (15 m) from a low platform. These pointed towers soar enigmatically above the surrounding jungle.

Farther west, a track north of the main road leads to Becán. The site is thought to have been the principal Maya center in the Río Bec region. The substantial number of non-local artifacts found during excavations suggests it was an important trading center linking the two sides of the peninsula. Unusually, the main buildings here were surrounded by a trench and moat (now dry) that is up to 16 ft (5 m) deep and 52 ft (16 m) wide, and about 1.5 miles (2 km) in circumference. Various Río Bec towers can be seen here, but Becán is also noted for the unusual rooms found inside Structure VIII. These chambers had no means of light or ventilation and may have been used for religious rituals that required darkness and isolation.

Chicanná, 2 miles (3 km) farther west, and south of the main road, has the most

Tables and chairs set under palapas on the soft white sands at Progreso

The three Río Bec towers rising above the principal temple at Xpujil

> A group of stylistically similar Maya sites, situated in the lowlands west of Chetumal, are known collectively as the Río Bec sites.

extraordinary architecture of the three sites. Its name means "house of the serpent's mouth," which refers to Structure II, whose facade is a snake's head formed by an intricate mosaic of stone. This zoomorphic shape represents the god Itzamná, while the snake's mouth forms the doorway. Structure XX, set apart from the main plaza, is a two-level building that echoes the design of Structure II. Its sides are decorated with masks of Chac, the rain god (p287).

A few detours off the main highway will reward you with quieter archaeological sites. With less crowds, the crumbling ruins appear even more impressive and mysterious as they are reclaimed by the vines and trees around them.

The first two diversions take you west from Chetumal along Mex 186, and then north on Quintana Roo Francisco Villa-Graciano Sánchez. Here, fields give way to jungle, the setting for the Maya site of Kohunlich and its Temple of Masks, dedicated to the Maya sun god. The steps of this 6th-century pyramid are flanked with

masks facing the setting sun. Around 18 miles (29 km) north of Kohunlich lie the equally impressive ruins of Dzibanché.

Further west near the village of Conhuás, a minor road branches to the south to Calakmul, one of the most important Maya cities in the Classic period. The 165-ft (50-m) high pyramid here is the largest in Mexico. Around a hundred stelae remain on site, but the jade masks found in the tombs are now on display in Campeche (p300). Just west of Conhuás is the site of Balamkú, discovered

---

🔍 HIDDEN GEM
Secret Ruins

Although close to the major archaeological site Tulum (p288), the Maya ruins of Chunyaxché (also known as Muyil) receive few visitors. On the edge of Sian Ka'an, shrouded by jungle, there are some 100 crumbling temples, pyramids, and other structures to explore.

---

by chance in 1990. Its most striking feature is a 55-ft (17-m) long stucco frieze on the building known as the House of the Four Kings. The frieze is thought to represent the relationship between Maya royalty and the cosmos.

---

21 Ⓜ

Sian Ka'an Biosphere Reserve

🅰 G4 🏛 Quintana Roo

Comprising over 1,700 sq miles (4,500 sq km) of low jungle and marshlands, and 69 miles (110 km) of coral reef, Sian Ka'an has a range of natural habitats that make it an important conservation area. It is run by a government agency and is not primarily geared toward tourism – indeed, the poor roads within the preserve deter all but the most intrepid. However, the Amigos de Sian Ka'an (Friends of Sian Ka'an) run night tours for visitors, which focus on the crocodiles that inhabit the mangrove swamps (www. amigosdesiankaan.org). Lucky visitors may also see the flocks of local and migrating birds in the marshlands around Boca Paila, in the northern part of the preserve – including the rare Jabirú stork – or the elusive turtles and manatees that live in the waters off the coast.

NEED TO KNOW

A trolley passing the main square in Campeche

BEFORE
YOU GO

Forward planning is essential to any successful trip. Be prepared for all eventualities by considering the following points before you travel.

AT A GLANCE

CURRENCY
Mexican Peso
($/Mex$)

AVERAGE DAILY SPEND

SAVE
$900

SPEND
$1200

SPLURGE
$1900

BOTTLED WATER
$15

COFFEE
$35

BEER
$25

DINNER FOR TWO
$500

ESSENTIAL PHRASES

Hello	Hola
Goodbye	Adiós
Please	Por favor
Thank you	Gracias
Do you speak English?	Habla usted Inglés?
I don't understand	No entiendo

ELECTRICITY SUPPLY
Standard voltage is 110 volts. Power sockets are type A and B, fitting two- or three-pronged plugs.

Passports and Visas

Citizens of the US, Canada, the UK, Ireland, Israel, Australia, New Zealand, Japan, and most EU countries do not need visas to enter Mexico as tourists for less than 180 days. Other Europeans can stay for 90 days.

All visitors need a valid passport and a tourist card (or **FMM** – *Forma Migratoria Múltiple*). You will likely be offered one on the plane before landing in Mexico, but the authorities encourage visitors to fill in the FMM online in advance. The law requires you to carry your FMM at all times. It also has to be handed in on leaving the country.

Visitors entering by land are also required to pay a *erecho de no inmigrante* (nonimmigrant visa) entry fee for stays over seven days.
FMM
🅦 mexicotouristcard.com

Travel Safety Advice

Visitors can get up-to-date travel safety information from the UK Foreign and Commonwealth Office, US State Department, and the Australian Department of Foreign Affairs and Trade.
AUS
🅦 smartraveller.gov.au
UK
🅦 gov.uk/foreign-travel-advice
USA
🅦 travel.state.gov

Customs Information

Visitors over the age of 18 have a duty-free allowance of 3 liters of spirits, 6 liters of wine, 25 cigars, and 20 packs of cigarettes or 300 grams of tobacco. If carrying prescription drugs, bring the original prescription. Archaeological artifacts may not be taken out of Mexico.

Insurance

It is important to take out insurance covering health problems, accidents, trip cancellation and interruption, and theft or loss of valuables.

Vaccinations

No specific vaccinations are required to enter Mexico, but all travelers are advised to seek immunization against hepatitis A, typhoid, tetanus, diphtheria, hepatitis B and rabies. Malaria is present in some rural parts of Mexico, so ask your doctor about antimalarial medicines.

Money

Major credit and debit cards are accepted almost everywhere. ATM machines are widely available, though most charge a small fee. Changing US dollars is easy, though other foreign currencies can be tough outside the big cities and major banks. Always carry small amounts of cash around in both coins and small denomination bills, for tips and minor purchases. Beware that shops, taxis, and buses are often unable to give change for larger denomination notes.

Booking Accommodations

A number of online hotel booking services provide lists of available quality lodgings all around the country. Reasonably priced, comfortable apartments are also available for rent all over the country via agencies such as Homeaway, Airbnb, and VRBO.

In some hotels, guests may be asked to sign a blank credit card slip on arrival. Many will change or accept foreign currency, but not always at the best rate. Some budget hotels are cash only.

The normal 16 percent IVA tax is supplemented with a 2 percent lodging tax. These are not always included in the advertised rate.

Travelers with Specific Needs

Many of Mexico's big resorts are accessible – especially Cancún, where you can organise tours and transportation through **Cancún Accesible**.

However, rural areas are not as well equipped, and public transportation can be difficult to negotiate, especially for those with reduced mobility. Check online resources such as the Society for Accessible Travel & Hospitality (**SATH**), **México Accesible**, and the **Accessible Tourism in Mexico City** brochure for detailed advice.
Accessible Tourism in Mexico City
w turismo.cdmx.gob.mx/turismo-accesible

Cancún Accesible
w cancunaccesible.com
México Accesible
w accesiblemexico.com
SATH
w sath.org

Language

The official language is Spanish. In major tourist areas, many locals will speak some English, but a basic knowledge of Spanish is a great advantage to anyone traveling off the beaten track.

There are also some 62 indigenous groups in Mexico, and each has its own language. In remote villages some people may not speak Spanish, although there are usually a few bilingual locals.

Closures

Even when times are posted at museums, tourist offices, and shops, they are not always adhered to. Many places will close for a couple of hours in the early afternoon, usually from 1pm to 3pm. A lot of museums and galleries have reduced entry fees – or are free – on Sunday, and most are closed on Monday. Some museums close for lunch, but archaeological sites are open all day. Banks are generally open Monday to Friday from 9:30am to 5pm, often with shorter hours for currency exchange.

PUBLIC HOLIDAYS	
Jan 1	New Year's Day
Early Feb	Constitution Day
Mar 21	Birthday of Benito Juárez
Mar/Apr	Easter Thursday
Mar/Apr	Good Friday
May 1	Labor Day
May 5	Cinco de Mayo
Sep 16	Independence Day
Mid Oct	Day of the Race
Nov 20	Revolution Day
Dec 12	Festival of the Virgin of Guadalupe
Dec 24	Christmas Eve
Dec 25	Christmas Day

GETTING
AROUND

Whether you are visiting for a short city break or rural retreat, discover how best to reach your destination and travel like a pro.

AT A GLANCE

PUBLIC TRANSPORTATION

LOS CABOS

$12.50

Single bus journey

CANCÚN

$10

Single bus journey

MEXICO CITY

$5

Single bus or subway journey

TOP TIP
Have the exact fare ready when using cash, as change isn't always available.

SPEED LIMIT

MAJOR HIGHWAYS

110 km/h (68 mph)

TWO-LANE HIGHWAYS

90 km/h (56 mph)

URBAN AREAS

60 km/h (37 mph)

RESIDENTIAL AREAS

10 km/h (6 mph)

Arriving by Air

Mexico's largest international airports are Mexico City, Cancún, Guadalajara, Monterrey, Tijuana, Los Cabos, Puerto Vallarta, Mérida, Del Bajío, and Culiacán. Other major tourist entry points are found in Mazatlán, Oaxaca, Acapulco, and Cozumel.

The country has a well-developed domestic flight network, and fares are often very reasonable. Aeroméxico is the country's largest airline, and it serves most national destinations as well as many international ones. Interjet, Volaris, and VivaAerobús are also popular low-cost carriers that serve airports throughout the country, and some international destinations.

Crossing the Mexican Land Border

When entering into Mexico by bus or on foot, pick up the FMM (p312) at Immigration, as these are not handed out automatically.

The area bordering the US – particularly Ciudad Juárez, and also Tijuana – covers some of the biggest hot spots in Mexico's drugs war. Extra caution should be exercised when crossing this area, especially by car.

If heading to Baja California, San Diego–Tijuana is the most popular crossing; get there early or expect to queue for up to 3 hours. Alternatively, try one of the quieter crossings, such as Tecate or Calexico–Mexicali.

Crossings in and out of Central American countries can be hectic; having the correct fees and documentation at hand will make the process easier.

Chetumal is the main crossing into Belize, with buses running to Belize City, and ferries available for Caye Caulker and San Pedro.

There are three conventional crossings into Guatemala: Ciudad Cuauhtémoc–La Mesilla, El Carmen–Talismán, and Ciudad Hidalgo–Tecún Umán. The Río Usumacinta crossing is an interesting adventure involving a 30-minute motorboat ride. In Mexico, head to Corozal in eastern Chiapas and visit Immigration, then take a boat to the border town of Bethel, Guatemala.

GETTING TO AND FROM THE AIRPORT

Airport	Distance to city	Taxi fare	Transportation	Journey time
Mexico City (MEX)	9 miles (15 km)	$300	Metro	50 mins
Cancún (CUN)	12 miles (20 km)	$600-900	Bus	25 mins
Guadalajara (GDL)	10 miles (16 km)	$300	Bus	30 mins
Monterrey (MTY)	17 miles (27 km)	$350-400	Bus	45 mins
Tijuana (TIJ)	4 miles (7 km)	$220-250	Bus	20 mins
Los Cabos (SJD)	20 miles (32 km)	$1250-2000	Bus	1hr
Puerto Vallarta (PVR)	4 miles (7 km)	$340-560	Bus	15-20 mins
Mazatlán (MZT)	12 miles (20 km)	$450-620	Bus	30-40 mins
Oaxaca (OAX)	10 miles (16 km)	$320-450	Bus	30-40 mins
Acapulco (ACA)	19 miles (30 km)	$400-600	Bus	40 mins

BUS JOURNEY PLANNER

This map is a handy reference for traveling between Mexico's main cities by public transportation, plotting the main bus routes according to journey time. The times given reflect the fastest and most direct routes available.

Mexico City to Veracruz	6-7 hrs		**Mexico City to Puerto Vallarta**	12 hrs
Mexico City to Acapulco	5-6 hrs		**Mexico City to Zacatecas**	8-9 hrs
Mexico City to Oaxaca City	6-7 hrs		**Oaxaca to San Cristobal**	10-12 hrs
Mexico City to Tijuana	36 hrs		**San Cristobal to Palenque**	5-6 hrs
Mexico City to Guadalajara	6-8 hrs		**Palenque to Cancún**	11-12 hrs
Mexico City to Monterrey	11-12 hrs		**Tijuana to La Paz**	22-24 hrs

Train Travel

Mexico's train lines are used for freight and, beyond the suburban rail services in Mexico City, there are no passenger rail lines. There are just two notable tourist train services: **Tequila Express** in Jalisco offers a fun day-trip to a tequila-producing hacienda, and the **Chihuahua al Pacífico Railroad** (nicknamed "El Chepe") runs through the Copper Canyon.

Chihuahua al Pacífico Railroad
w chepe.mx
Tequila Express
w tequilaexpress.com.mx

Long-Distance Bus Travel

Buses are the best and most economical form of public transportation between the cities and towns in Mexico. While journey times are longer than domestic air travel, buses are significantly cheaper while still being extremely comfortable.

Bus are operated by different companies across Mexico, but there are three standard types of intercity bus: luxury, first-class, and second-class services. For long-distance travel, luxury or first-class is recommended. These services are more reliable, more comfortable, safer, and less likely to break down. Top-of-the-range luxury *(de lujo)* buses offer direct intercity services, with air-conditioning, fully reclining seats, refreshments, video screens, and on-board toilets, although fares are between 30 and 50 per cent more than first-class tickets. First-class *(primera)* buses are air-conditioned, with semi-reclining seats, video, and a toilet. On shorter trips, less reliable second-class buses may be the only option.

The following are some useful bus companies operating long-distance services:

ADO
w ado.com.mx
ETN Turistar
w etn.com.mx
Omnibus
w odm.com.mx
Senda
w gruposenda.com
Tufesa
w tufesa.com.mx

Public Transportation in Mexico City

Traffic congestion in Mexico City means that driving is not practical. Walking is the easiest way to negotiate the center of the city, but when traveling farther afield in this vast metropolis, some form of transportation will be necessary.

The extensive **Metro** and **Metrobús** systems cover most of the city. In the south, an electric train connects the subway at Tasqueña to Embarcadero in Xochimilco. Taxis are inexpensive, and *peseros* (collective taxis) are even cheaper.

Note that traffic and public transportation are busiest during rush hours (6:30–9am and 4–7pm on weekdays).

Metro
w metro.cdmx.gob.mx
Metrobús
w metrobus.cdmx.gob.mx

Driving

Traveling by car at your own pace is a practical and flexible way to explore most areas of Mexico, but there are exceptions: Mexico City (due to congestion), and the states of Colima, Guerrero, Michoacán, Sinaloa, and Tamaulipas (due to high levels of drug violence). Driving elsewhere is generally safe, but motorists need to take some precautions. Robberies do occur, and it is advisable not to drive at night, and to avoid overnight street parking. In Mexico City, drive with the doors locked and the windows rolled up. Plan your trip in advance, take a good road map, and know where your stops are likely to be. Hitchhiking is not recommended.

Driving to Mexico

Regulations for bringing cars into Mexico are very strict. Obtain a *permiso de importación temporal* (temporary import permit) from Banjercito banks at border crossings, various Mexican consulates in the United States, or online from the **Banjercito** website. Online applications can be made up to 60 days or a minimum of seven days prior to arrival. Expect to be charged a fee of around US$60 for the six-month, multiple-entry permit, plus a deposit of US$200–400 depending on the year of your car. Several other original documents are also needed, and these should all be photocopied twice. These include an authorized immigration form (**FMM**) or visa, a valid driver's license (US, Canadian, British, Australian, and New Zealand licenses are valid), a passport, vehicle registration papers, and a credit card (Visa, MasterCard, or American Express) in the same name as the car registration papers. It is rare for rental firms to allow their vehicles over the border, but if you manage to find one who will comply you'll also need to provide written proof of their permission.

Note that US car insurance does not cover driving south of the border, so separate coverage must be arranged.

Banjercito
w gob.mx/banjercito
FMM
w mexicotouristcard.com

Car Rental

International car rental companies, such as Hertz and Budget, have offices in main airports and large towns, but local companies may offer cheaper deals. When pre-booking, make sure the price incorporates the 16 percent sales tax, and full insurance. It is important that the insurance includes theft and collision damage waiver. Some policies provide only nominal coverage (liability insurance is the minimal legal requirement), and you may need to pay for additional insurance cover.

To rent a car in Mexico you must be 21 or over (25 for some agencies) and have held a driver's license for at least one year. The rental must be paid for with a major credit card. Most rental companies offer GPS (SatNav) for an additional daily fee, and child seats with advance notice. Free unlimited mileage is usually included, but leaving the car in a different city than the one in which you rent it may incur a substantial drop-off fee.

Mopeds and motorbikes can usually be rented in resorts. Before setting out, make sure that the vehicle is in good condition and that your insurance cover is adequate. Also check that your personal travel insurance covers motorbike accidents.

Rules of the Road

Mexicans drive on the right-hand side of the road, and distances are measured in kilometers rather than miles. Most traffic regulations and warnings are represented by internationally recognized symbols and signs, but some signs are unique to Mexico. The wearing of seat belts is compulsory. Traffic must stop completely at *Alto* (halt) signs. Slow down when approaching villages, where there are often speed bumps (*topes*). Beware that these can be very high, and are not always marked.

Take extreme care at rail crossings, both in cities and in the open country, as there is often no system to warn that a train is coming, and accidents can occur.

Avoid driving at night as there is increased risk of robbery and animals on the roads, and it is harder to spot obstacles like potholes, which are often unmarked.

Toll roads

There are three main kinds of highway in Mexico: four-lane *super carreteras*, ordinary *cuota* (toll) roads, and *libre* (free) roads.

The cost of the tolls on the *super carreteras* is much higher than the ordinary *cuota* roads. As a result, there is less traffic, no trucks, and few buses. Beware that there aren't many service stations on the *super carreteras*.

Cuota highways range from fast, four-lane roads, to those that are little better than *libre*

roads. Tolls are charged according to distance and the number of axles on the vehicle. If there is a choice of toll payment booth, opt for the lane marked *autos*.

Parking

Parking is permitted where you see a sign with a black E (for *estacionamiento*) in a red circle. The same E with a diagonal line through it means no parking. A white E on a blue background indicates a parking lot.

Parking may be difficult in big cities, so when planning your day, make sure to factor in time to find a parking space.

Cycling

Bicycles are a universal means of transportation in Mexico, and bikes can be rented in most resorts.

Cycling is not recommended in Mexico City due to poor quality roads and the volume of traffic – although a network of dedicated bike lanes is being developed. Bosque de Chapultepec is one exception, as the park has good cycling lanes; you can hire bicycles from the nearby Museo de Antropología via the **Ecobici** bike-sharing scheme.

Ecocolors and **Bike Mexico** provide excellent guided bike tours. For mountain biking, the most popular location is Copper Canyon.

Ecobici
w ecobici.cdmx.gob.mx
Ecocolors
w ecotravelmexico.com
Bike Mexico
w bike-mexico.com

Boats and Ferries

Passenger and car ferries leaving from Santa Rosalía and La Paz connect the Baja California peninsula to Guaymas, Topolobampo, and Mazatlán on the Pacific mainland. Two standards of cabin are offered – a *turista* with bunkbeds and a washbasin, or a more expensive *especial*, which has an entire suite of rooms. Schedules change often and should always be confirmed before travel.

On the Caribbean coast around the Riviera Maya, ferries leave from Puerto Morelos (car ferry) and Playa del Carmen (passenger only) to the island of Cozumel. Passenger ferries from Cancún to Isla Mujeres depart from Puerto Juárez, Playa Tortugas, El Embarcadero, and Playa Caracol. Car ferries from Punta Sam also travel to Isla Mujeres.

Cancún, Playa del Carmen, Punta Sam, and Puerto Morelos
w ultramarferry.com
Santa Rosalía and La Paz
w bajaferries.com.mx

PRACTICAL
INFORMATION

A little local know-how goes a long way in Mexico. Here you will find all the essential advice and information you will need during your stay.

AT A GLANCE

EMERGENCY NUMBERS

GENERAL EMERGENCY

911

TIME ZONE
Mexico spans three time zones: CST, MST, and PT. Daylight Savings Time (DST) is from the first Sunday in April to the last Sunday in October – however, in a few US border cities DST begins the second Sunday in March and ends on the first Sunday in November to match the US.

TAP WATER
Outside major resort hotels, drink purified or bottled water only.

TIPPING

Waiter	10-15 percent
Hotel Porter	$10-20 a bag
Taxi Driver	Not expected

All tips should be given in cash rather than added to the credit card bill. At major resort hotels, additional tips are expected: $20-50 night for housekeeping and $50-100 for the concierge.

Personal Security

Mexico has a reputation for a high incidence of crime, but the overwhelming majority of foreign visitors have a trouble-free experience. Tourist areas are generally very safe, and Mexico City is no more dangerous than most major cities. Beware of pickpockets (especially on public transportation in Mexico City), leave valuables in a hotel safe, and keep cash concealed.

Areas affected by violence associated with organized crime should be avoided. Check your government's travel advisory for an up-to-date assessment of the situation (p312).

Natural Hazards

Parts of the Mexico are prone to natural disasters: earthquakes, flooding, hurricanes (June through November), and though unlikely, volcanic eruptions. With the exception of earthquakes, which are notoriously hard to predict, local authorities and media outlets should provide plenty of warning for these type of events, most of which are, in any case, seasonal.

Hazard Warnings
🆆 gob.mx/cenapred

Health

Some tropical diseases are present in Mexico, but are rare and can be avoided by getting vaccinated prior to departure (p313).

The sun's rays are very strong in Mexico and dehydration can lead to sun stroke, so always carry bottled water, sunscreen, and a hat when visiting archaeological sites, the beach, or any exposed places.

Mosquitoes are rife in low-lying regions; DEET is the strongest insect repellent, but those with sensitive skin may prefer organic alternatives. Dengue fever is a viral illness spread by mosquitoes. The best protection is to use plenty of insect repellent, cover up well when outside, and sleep under mosquito nets. Mexico City's high altitude and air pollution can aggravate respiratory problems like asthma; seek medical advice before traveling.

Smoking, Alcohol, and Drugs

You must be 18 to drink or purchase alcohol. It is illegal to walk the streets with an open container of alcohol.

You must also be 18 to smoke in Mexico. Hotel and resorts are legally required to provide smoke-free rooms and areas. Smoking is completely prohibited indoors in schools and in federal government facilities.

Mexico has decriminalized the possession of up to 5 grams of cannabis or 500 mg of cocaine, but you may still be detained by police for carrying this much – taking any amount across international borders is illegal. Being caught in possession of larger amounts of any drug will likely result in serious jail time.

ID

Except for the FMM (*p312*), carrying ID is not required by law, but it is advisable to carry copies of your passport when traveling by between cities by bus, near any Mexican border, or if driving a car – since there are frequent police checkpoints.

Local Customs

When visiting churches, make sure you are dressed respectfully,, avoiding shorts and short skirts. Observe signs that forbid photography. Some indigenous people also do not like to be photographed, so always ask first.

LGBT+ Safety

Homosexuality is tolerated in Mexico, but public displays of affection are generally frowned upon. Discrimination on the basis of sexual orientation has been officially outlawed but there is still a degree of prejudice, especially in smaller, rural communities.

Mobile Phones and Wi-Fi

To use your cell phone in Mexico, you will need a roaming-enabled quad-band handset – consult your service provider for tariffs. Calls can be expensive for both caller and recipient, so consider purchasing a Mexican SIM card or phone once you've arrived. (You can also make calls for free on some apps such as Whatsapp and Skype, but this will depend on having a stable Internet connection.)

Local calls are inexpensive and can be made from pay phones. Internal long-distance calls are best made with a phonecard (sold at newsstands and usable in public phones).

High-speed Internet is generally widely available throughout Mexico, especially in the cities. Increasingly, cities are providing free Wi-Fi in public spaces, and many cafés, restaurants, and businesses offer free Wi-Fi.

Post

The main post offices (*oficinas de correos*) are open from 8am to 8pm on weekdays, and from 8am to 3pm on Saturdays. Smaller post offices usually have shorter opening hours.

Taxes

Prices usually include 16 percent sales tax, or IVA (*Impuesto al Valor Agregado*). If a price is given as *más IVA* (plus sales tax) it means that 16 percent will be added to the bill.

Discount Cards

Some Mexican cities have started operating tourist discount cards, such as the **Go City** program in Cancún. ISIC student cards are accepted at some sights.
Go City
w gocity.com

INDEX

N

PHRASE BOOK

Mexican Spanish is essentially the same as the Castilian spoken in Spain, although there are some differences in vocabulary and pronunciation. The most noticeable are the use of *ustedes* (the plural version of "you") in both informal and formal situations, and the pronunciation of the soft "c" and the letter "z" as "s" rather than "th."

Mexicans use *carro* (instead of *coche*) for a car, and often call buses and trucks *camiones*. Words of indigenous origin are common. A word for market used only in Mexico is *tianguis*, for example, although *mercado* is also employed.

Mexicans tend to be fairly formal, and it is good manners to use *usted* (rather than *tú*) for "you," unless you know the person well. Always say *buenos días* or *buenas tardes* when boarding a taxi, and address both male taxi drivers and waiters as *señor*.

If you wish to decline goods from street vendors, a polite shake of the head and a *muchas gracias* will usually suffice. Adding *muy amable* (very kind) will help to take the edge off the refusal. A term to be handled with care is *madre* (mother), as much bad language in Mexico is based on variants of this word. When referring to someone's mother, use *tu mama* (your mother), or the formal version *su señora madre*, just to be safe.

IN AN EMERGENCY

Help!	¡Socorro!	soh-**koh**-roh
Stop!	¡Pare!	pah-reh
Call a doctor!	¡Llame a un médico!	yah-meh ah oon meh-dee-koh
Call an ambulance!	¡Llame una ambulancia!	yah-meh ah oonah ahm-boo-lahn-see-ah
Call the fire department!	¡Llame a los bomberos!	yah-meh ah lohs bohm-beh-rohs
Where is the nearest telephone?	¿Dónde está el teléfono más cercano?	dohn-deh ehs-tah ehl teh-leh-foh-noh mahs sehr-kah-noh
Where is the nearest hospital?	¿Dónde está el hospital más cercano?	dohn-deh ehs-tah ehl ohs-pee-tahl mahs sehr-kah-noh
policeman	el policía	ehl poh-lee-**see**-ah
Could you help me?	¿Me podría ayudar?	meh poh-**dree**-yah ah-yoo-**dahr**
I've/we've been mugged	Me/nos asaltaron	meh/nohs ah-sahl-**tahr**-ohn
They stole my ...	Me robaron el/la...	meh roh-**bahr**-ohn ehl/lah

COMMUNICATION ESSENTIALS

Yes	Sí	see
No	No	noh
Please	Por favor	pohr fah-**vohr**
Thank you	Gracias	grah-see-ahs
Excuse me	Perdone	pehr-**doh**-neh
Hello	Hola	oh-lah
Good morning	Buenos días	bweh-nohs **dee**-ahs
Good afternoon (from noon)	Buenas tardes	bweh-nahs **tahr**-dehs
Good night	Buenas noches	bweh-nahs noh-chehs
Bye (casual)	Hasta luego	ah-stah loo-weh-goh
Goodbye	Adiós	ah-dee-ohs
See you later	Hasta luego	ah-stah loo-weh-goh
Morning	La mañana	lah mah-**nyah**-nah
Afternoon/ early evening	La tarde	lah tahr-deh
Night	La noche	lah noh-cheh
Yesterday	Ayer	ah-yehr
Today	Hoy	oy
Tomorrow	Mañana	mah-**nyah**-nah
Here	Aquí	ah-kee
There	Allí	ah-yee
What?	¿Qué?	keh

When?	¿Cuándo?	kwahn-doh
Why?	¿Por qué?	pohr-keh
Where?	¿Dónde?	dohn-deh
How are you?	¿Cómo está usted?	koh-moh ehs-tah oos-tehd
Very well, thank you	Muy bien, gracias	mwee bee-ehn grah-see-ahs
Pleased to meet you	Mucho gusto	moo-choh goo-stoh
See you soon	Hasta pronto	ahs-tah **prohn**-toh
I'm sorry	Lo siento	loh see-**ehn**-toh

USEFUL PHRASES

That's fine	Está bien	ehs-tah bee-ehn
Great/fantastic!	¡Qué bien!	keh bee-ehn
Where is/are ...?	¿Dónde está/están ...?	dohn-deh ehs-tah/ehs-tahn
How far is it to ...?	¿Cuántos metros/ kilómetros hay de aquí a ...?	kwahn-tohs meh-trohs/kee-loh-meh-trohs eye deh ah-kee ah
Which way is it to ...?	¿Por dónde se va a ...?	pohr dohn-deh seh vah ah
Do you speak English?	¿Habla inglés?	ah-blah een-glehs
I don't understand	No comprendo	noh kohm-prehn-doh
Could you speak more slowly, please?	¿Puede hablar más despacio, por favor?	pweh-deh ah-blahr mahs dehs-pah-see-oh pohr fah-vohr
I want	Quiero	kee-yehr-oh
I would like	Quisiera/ Me gustaría	kee-see-yehr-ah meh goo-stah-**ree**-ah
We want	Queremos	keh-reh-mohs
Do you have change (for 50 pesos)?	¿Tiene cambio (de cincuenta pesos)?	tee-eh-neh kahm-bee-yoh deh seen-kwehn-tah peh-sohs
(It's) very kind of you	Muy amable	mwee ah-mah-bleh
There is/there are	Hay	eye
Do you have/is there/are there?	¿Hay?	eye
Is there any water?	¿Hay agua?	eye ah-gwah
It's broken	Está roto/a	ehs-tah roh-toh/tah
Is it far/near?	¿Está lejos/cerca?	ehs-tah leh-hohs/**sehr**-kah
Take care/be careful!	¡Ten cuidado!	tehn koo-ee-dah-doh
We are late	Estamos atrasados	ehs-tah-mohs ah-trah-**sah**-dohs
We are early	Estamos adelantados	ehs-tah-mohs ah-deh-lahn-**tah**-dohs
OK, all right	De acuerdo	deh ah-**kwehr**-doh
Yes, of course	Claro que sí	klah-roh keh see
Of course!/with pleasure	¡Cómo no!/con mucho gusto	koh-moh noh/ kohn moo-choh **goo**-stoh
Let's go	Vámonos	vah-moh-nohs

USEFUL WORDS

big	grande	grahn-deh
small	pequeño/a	peh-keh-nyoh/nyah
hot	caliente	kah-lee-**ehn**-the
cold	frío/a	free-oh/ah
good	bueno/a	bweh-noh/nah
bad	malo/a	mah-loh/lah
enough	suficiente	soo-fee-see-**ehn**-teh
well	bien	bee-ehn
open	abierto/a	ah-bee-ehr-toh/tah
closed	cerrado/a	sehr-rah-doh/dah
full	lleno/a	yeh-noh/nah
empty	vacío/a	vah-**see**-oh/ah
left	izquierda	ees-key-ehr-dah
right	derecha	deh-reh-chah
(keep) straight ahead	(siga) derecho	(see-gah) deh-**reh**-choh
near	cerca	sehr-kah

far	lejos	leh-*hohs*
up	arriba	ah-*ree-bah*
down	abajo	ah-*bah-hoh*
early	temprano	tehm-*prah-noh*
late	tarde	tahr-*deh*
now/very soon	ahora/ahorita	ah-*ohr-*ah/ah-ohr-ee-*tah*
more	más	mahs
less	menos	meh-*nohs*
very	muy	mwee
a little	(un) poco	oon poh-*koh*
very little	muy poco	mwee poh-*koh*
(much) more	(mucho) más	(moo-choh) mahs
too much	demasiado	deh-mah-see-ah-*doh*
too late	demasiado tarde	deh-mah-see-ah-*doh* tahr-*deh*
farther on/ahead	más adelante	mahs ah-deh-lahn-*teh*
farther back	más atras	mahs ah-trahs
opposite	frente a	frehn-teh ah
below/above	abajo/arriba	ah-*bah-hoh*/ah-*ree-bah*
first, second, third	primero/a segundo/a tercero/a	pree-*meh-roh/ah* seh-*goon-doh/ah* tehr-*sehr-oh/ah*
floor (of a building)	el piso	ehl pee-*soh*
ground floor	la planta baja	lah plahn-tah bah-*hah*
entrance	entrada	ehn-*trah-dah*
exit	salida	sah-lee-*dah*
elevator	el ascensor	ehl ah-sehn-*sohr*
toilets	baños/sanitarios	bah-*nyohs*/sah-nee-tah-*ree-ohs*
women's	de damas	deh dah-*mahs*
men's	de caballeros	deh kah-bah-yeh-*rohs*
sanitary napkins	toallas sanitarias/ higiénicas	toh-ah-yahs sah-nee-tah-*ree-yahs*/hee-hyeh-nee-kahs
tampons	tampones	tahm-*poh-nehs*
condoms	condones	kohn-doh-nehs
toilet paper	papel higiénico	pah-pehl hee-hyen-ee-koh
(non-)smoking area	área de (no) fumar	ah-*ree-ah* deh (noh) foo-mahr
camera	la cámara	lah kah-*mah-rah*
batteries	las pilas	lahs pee-*lahs*
passport	el pasaporte	ehl pah-sah-pohr-*teh*
visa	el visado	ehl vee-*sah-doh*

HEALTH

English	Spanish	Pronunciation
I feel ill	Me siento mal	meh see-*ehn-toh* mahl
I have a headache	Me duele la cabeza	meh doo-*eh-leh* lah kah-*beh-sah*
I have a stomach- ache	Me duele el estómago	meh doo-*eh-leh* ehl ehs-*toh-mah-goh*
I need to rest	Necesito descansar	neh-seh-*see-toh* dehs-kahn-*sahr*
The child is/the children are sick	El niño está/los niños están enfermo(s)	ehl*nee-nyoh* ehs-*tah*/lohs nee-*nyos* ehs-*tahn* ehn-*fehr-moh(s)*
We need a doctor	Necesitamos un médico	neh-seh-see-*tah-mohs* oon meh-dee-koh
thermometer	el termómetro	ehl tehr-*moh-meh-troh*
drug store medicine	la farmacia la medicina/ el remedio	lah fahr-*mah-see-ah* lah meh-dee-*see-nah*/ehl reh-*meh-dee-oh*
pills	las pastillas/ píldoras	lahs pahs-*tee-yahs*/lahs peel-*doh-rahs*

POST OFFICES AND BANKS

Where can I change money?	¿Dónde puedo cambiar dinero?	dohn-deh pweh-doh kahm-bee-ahr dee-neh-roh
What is the dollar rate?	¿A cómo está el dólar?	ah koh-moh ehs-tah ehl doh-lahr
How much is the postage to...?	¿Cuánto cuesta enviar una carta a...?	kwahn-toh kweh-stah ehn-vee-yahr oo-nah kahr-tah ah
and for a post- card?	¿y una postal?	ee oo-nah pohs-tahl
I need stamps	Necesito estampillas	neh-seh-*see-toh* ehs-tahm-*pee-yahs*
cashier	cajero	kah-*heh-roh*
ATM	cajero automático	kah-*heh-roh* ahw-toh-*mah-tee-koh*
withdraw money	sacar dinero	sah-kahr dee-neh-roh

SHOPPING

How much does this cost?	¿Cuánto cuesta esto?	kwahn-toh kwehs-tah ehs-toh
I would like ...	Me gustaría ...	meh goos-tah-ree-ah
Do you have?	¿Tienen?	tee-yeh-nehn
I'm just looking, thank you	Sólo estoy mirando, gracias	soh-loh ehs-toy mee-rahn-doh grah-see-ahs
What time do you open?	¿A qué hora abren?	ah keh oh-rah ah-brehn
What time do you close?	¿A qué hora cierran?	ah keh oh-rah see-ehr-rahn
Do you take credit cards? traveler's checks?	¿Aceptan tarjetas de crédito/ cheques de viajero?	ahk-sehp-tahn tahr-heh-tahs deh kreh-dee-toh/ cheh-kehs deh vee-ah-heh-roh
I am looking for...	Estoy buscando...	ehs-tohy boos-kahn-doh
Is that your best price?	¿Es su mejor precio?	ehs soo meh-hohr preh-see-oh
discount	un descuento	oon dehs-koo-ehn-toh
clothes	la ropa	lah roh-pah
this one	éste	ehs-the
that one	ése	eh-she
expensive	caro	kahr-oh
cheap	barato	bah-rah-toh
size, clothes	talla	tah-yah
size, shoes	número	noo-mehr-oh
white	blanco	blahn-koh
black	negro	neh-groh
red	rojo	roh-hoh
yellow	amarillo	ah-mah-ree-yoh
green	verde	vehr-deh
blue	azul	ah-sool
antique store	la tienda de antigüedades	lah tee-ehn-dah deh ahn-tee-gweh-dah-dehs
bakery	la panadería	lah pah-nah-deh-ree-ah
bank	el banco	ehl bahn-koh
bookstore	la librería	lah lee-breh-ree-ah
butcher's	la carnicería	lahkahr-nee-seh-ree-ah
cake store	la pastelería	lah pahs-teh-leh-ree-ah
department store	la tienda de departamentos	lah tee-ehn-dah deh deh-pahr-tah-mehn-tohs
fish store	la pescadería	lah pehs-kah-deh-ree-ah
greengrocer's	la frutería	lah froo-teh-ree-ah
grocer's	la tienda de abarrotes	lah tee-yehn-dah deh ah-bah-roh-tehs
hairdresser's	la peluquería	lah peh-loo-keh-ree-ah
jeweler's	la joyería	lah hoh-yeh-ree-yah
market	el tianguis/ mercado	ehl tee-ahn-goo-ees/mehr-kah-doh
newsstand	el puesto de periódicos	ehl poo-es-toh deh pe-rio-dee-kohs
post office	la oficina de correos	lah oh-fee-see-nah deh kohr-reh-ohs
shoe store	la zapatería	lah sah-pah-teh-ree-ah

| supermarket | el supermercado | ehl soo-pehr-mehr-**kah**-doh |
| travel agency | la agencia de viajes | lah ah-**hehn**-see-ah deh vee-**ah**-hehs |

SIGHTSEEING

art gallery	galería de arte	ehl moo-**seh**-oh deh ahr-teh
beach	la playa	lah plah-yah
cathedral	la catedral	lah kah-teh-drahl
church	la iglesia/ la basílica	lah ee-**gleh**-see-ah/ lah bah-**see**-lee-kah
garden	el jardín	ehl hahr-**deen**
library	la biblioteca	lah bee-blee-oh-**teh**-kah
museum	el museo	ehl moo-**seh**-oh
pyramid	la pirámide	lah pee-**rah**-meed
ruins	las ruinas	lahs roo-**ee**-nahs
tourist information office	la oficina de turismo	lah oh-fee-**see**-nah deh too-**rees**-moh
town hall	el palacio municipal	ehl pah-**lah**-see-oh moo-nee-see-**pahl**
closed for holidays	cerrado por vacaciones	sehr-**rah**-doh pohr vah-kah-see-**oh**-nehs
ticket	la entrada	lah ehn-**trah**-dah
how much is the entrance fee?	¿Cuánto vale la entrada?	**kwahn**-toh vah-leh lah ehn-**trah**-dah
guide (person)	el/la guía	ehl/lah **gee**-ah
guide (book)	la guía	lah **gee**-ah
guided tour	una visita guiada	oo-nah vee-**see**-tah gee-**ah**-dah
map	el mapa	ehl **mah**-pah
city map	el plano de la ciudad	ehl **plah**-noh deh lah see-oo-**dahd**

TRANSPORTATION

When does the... leave?	¿A qué hora sale el...?	ah keh oh-rah sah-leh ehl
Where is the bus stop?	¿Dónde está la parada de autobuses?	**dohn**-deh ehs-tah lah pah-**rah**-dah deh ow-toh-**boo**-sehs
Is there a bus/train to...?	¿Hay un camión/ tren a...?	eye oon kah-mee-**ohn**/trehn ah
the next bus/train	el próximo camión/tren	ehl **prohx**-ee-moh kah-mee-**ohn**/trehn
bus station	la central camionera/ de autobuses	lah sehn-**trahl** kah-mee-ohn-**ehr**-ah/deh aw-toh-**boo**-sehs
train station	la estación de trenes	lah ehs-tah-see-**ohn** deh **treh**-nehs
subway/metro	el metro	ehl **meh**-troh
platform	el andén	ehl ahn-**dehn**
ticket office	la taquilla	lah tah-**kee**-yah
round-trip ticket	un boleto de ida y vuelta	oon boh-**leh**-toh deh ee-**dah** ee voo-**ehl**-tah
one-way ticket	un boleto de ida solamente	oon boh-**leh**-toh deh ee-dah sol-lah-**mehn**-teh
airport	el aeropuerto	ehl ah-ehr-oh-poo-**ehr**-toh
customs	la aduana	lah ah-doo-**ah**-nah
departure lounge	sala de embarque	sah-lah deh ehm-**bahr**-keh
boarding pass	pase de abordar	pah-seh deh ah-**bohr**-dahr
taxi stand/rank	sitio de taxis	see-tee-oh deh **tahk**-sees
car rental	renta de automóviles	rehn-tah deh aw-toh-**moh**-vee-lehs
motorcycle	la moto (cicleta)	lah moh-toh (see-**kleh**-tah)
mileage	el kilometraje	ehl kee-loh-meh-**trah**-he
bicycle	la bicicleta	lah bee-see-**kleh**-tah

daily/weekly rate	la tarifa diaria/ semanal	lah tah-**ree**-fah dee-ah-**ree**-ah/seh-mah-**nahl**
insurance	los seguros	lohs seh-**goo**-rohs
gas station	la gasolinería	lah gah-soh-leen-er-**ee**-ah
garage	el taller mecánico	ehl tah-**yehr** meh-**kahn**-ee-koh
I have a flat tire	Se me ponchó la llanta	seh meh pohn-**shoh** lah yahn-tah

STAYING IN A HOTEL

Do you have a vacant room?	¿Tienen una habitación libre?	tee-**eh**-nehn oo-nah ah-bee-tah-see-**ohn** lee-breh
double room	habitación doble	ah-bee-tah-see-**ohn** doh-bleh
with a double bed	con cama matrimonial	kohn **kah**-mah mah-tree-moh-nee-ahl
twin room	habitación con dos camas	ah-bee-tah-see-**ohn** kohn dohs **kah**-mahs
single room	habitación sencilla	ah-bee-tah-see-**ohn** sehn-**see**-yah
room with a bath	habitación con baño	ah-bee-tah-see-**ohn** kohn bah-nyoh
shower	la ducha	lah **doo**-chah
Do you have a room with a view (of the sea)?	¿Hay alguna habitación con vista (al mar)?	eye ahl-**goo**-nah ah-bee-tah-see-**ohn** kohn vees-tah (ahl mahr)
I have a reservation	Tengo una habitación reservada	tehn-goh oo-nah ah-bee-tah-see-**ohn** reh-sehr-**vah**-dah
The ... is not working	No funciona el/la...	noh foon-see-oh-nah ehl/lah
I need a wake-up call at ... o'clock	Necesito que me despierten a las ...	neh-seh-**see**-toh keh meh dehs-pee-**ehr**-tehn ah lahs
Where is the dining-room/bar?	¿Dónde está el restaurante/ el bar?	**dohn**-deh ehs-tah ehl rehs-toh-**rahn**-teh/ehl/bahr
hot/cold water	agua caliente/ fría	ah-goo-ah kah-lee-**ehn**-teh/free-ah
soap	el jabón	ehl hah-**bohn**
towel	la toalla	lah toh-**ah**-yah
key	la llave	lah yah-veh

EATING OUT

Have you got a table for ...	¿Tienen una mesa para ...?	tee-**eh**-nehn oo-nah meh-sahpah-rah
I want to reserve a table	Quiero reservar una mesa	kee-eh-roh reh-sehr-**vahr** oo-nah meh-sah
The bill, please	La cuenta, por favor	lah **kwehn**-tah pohr fah-vohr
I am a vegetarian	Soy vegetariano/a	soy veh-heh-tah-ree-**ah**-no/na
I am a vegan	Soy vegano/a	soy veh-**gah**-no/na-
waiter/waitress	mesero/a	meh-**seh**-roh/rah
menu	la carta	lah kahr-tah
fixed-price menu	menú del día/comida corrida	meh-noo dehl dee-ah/koh-mee-dah koh-ree-dah
wine list	la carta de vinos	lah kahr-tah deh vee-nohs
glass	un vaso	oon vah-soh
bottle	una botella	oo-nah boh-**teh**-yah
knife	un cuchillo	oon koo-chee-yoh
fork	un tenedor	oon teh-neh-dohr
spoon	una cuchara	oo-nah koo-**chah**-rah
breakfast	el desayuno	ehl deh-sah-**yoo**-noh
lunch	la comida	lah koh-**mee**-dah
dinner	la cena	lah **seh**-nah
main course	el plato fuerte	ehl **plah**-toh foo-**ehr**-teh
starters	las entradas	lahs ehn-**trah**-das
dish of the day	el plato del día	ehl **plah**-toh dehl dee-ah

rare	termino rojo	tehr-*mee*-noh *roh*-hoh
medium	termino medio	tehr-*mee*-noh **meh**-*dee*-oh
well done	bien cocido	bee-*ehn koh*-**see**-doh
Could you heat it up for me?	¿Me lo podría calentar?	meh loh pohd-**ree**-ah kah-lehn-**tahr**
chair	la silla	lah **see**-*yah*
napkin	la servilleta	lah sehr-vee-**yeh**-*tah*
tip	la propina	lah proh-**pee**-*nah*
Is service included?	¿El servicio está incluido?	ehl sehr-**vee**-*see*-oh ehs-**tah** *een-skloo*-**ee**-*doh*
Do you have a light?	¿Tiene fuego?	tee-*eh*-*nee foo*-**eh**-*goh*
ashtray	cenicero	seh-nee-**seh**-*roh*
cigarettes	los cigarros	lohs see-**gah**-*rohs*

MENU DECODER

el aceite	*ah*-**see**-**eh**-*teh*	*oil*
las aceitunas	*ah-seh*-**toon**-*ahs*	*olives*
el agua mineral	*ah-gwa mee-neh*-**rahl**	*mineral water*
sin gas/con gas	*seen gas/kohn gas*	*still/sparkling*
el ajo	**ah**-*hoh*	*garlic*
el arroz	*ahr*-**rohs**	*rice*
el azúcar	*ah*-**soo**-*kahr*	*sugar*
la banana	*bah-nah-nah*	*banana*
una bebida	*beh*-**bee**-*dah*	*drink*
el café	*kah*-**feh**	*coffee*
la carne	**kahr**-*neh*	*meat*
la cebolla	*seh*-**boh**-*yah*	*onion*
la cerveza	*sehr*-**veh**-*sah*	*beer*
el cerdo	**sehr**-*doh*	*pork*
el chocolate	*choh-koh*-**lah**-*teh*	*chocolate*
la ensalada	*ehn*-**sah**-**lah**-*dah*	*salad*
la fruta	**froo**-*tah*	*fruit*
el helado	*eh*-**lah**-*doh*	*ice cream*
el huevo	*oo*-**eh**-*voh*	*egg*
el jugo	*ehh***hoo**-*goh*	*juice*
la langosta	*lahn*-**gohs**-*tah*	*lobster*
la leche	**leh**-*cheh*	*milk*
la mantequilla	*mahn-teh*-**kee**-*yah*	*butter*
la manzana	*mahn*-**sah**-*nah*	*apple*
los mariscos	*mah*-**rees**-*kohs*	*seafood*
la naranja	*nah*-**rahn**-*hah*	*orange*
el pan	**pahn**	*bread*
las papas	**pah**-*pahs*	*potatoes*
las papas a la francesa	**pah**-*pahs ah lah frahn*-**seh**-*sah*	*French fries*
las papas fritas	**pah**-*pahs* **free**-*tahs*	*potato chips*
el pastel	*pahs*-**tehl**	*cake*
el pescado	*pehs*-**kah**-*doh*	*fish*
picante	*pee*-**kahn**-*teh*	*spicy*
la pimienta	*pee-mee*-**yehn**-*tah*	*pepper*
el pollo	**poh**-*yoh*	*chicken*
el postre	**pohs**-*treh*	*dessert*
el queso	**keh**-*soh*	*cheese*
el refresco	*reh*-**frehs**-*koh*	*soft drink/soda*
la sal	**sahl**	*salt*
la salsa	**sahl**-*sah*	*sauce*
la sopa	**soh**-*pah*	*soup*
el té	**teh**	*herb tea (usually camomile)*
el té negro	**teh** *neh*-**groh**	*tea*
la torta	**tohr**-*tah*	*sandwich*
las tostadas	*tohs*-**tah**-*dahs*	*toast*
el vinagre	*vee*-**nah**-*greh*	*vinegar*
el vino blanco	*vee*-**noh** **blahn**-*koh*	*white wine*
el vino tinto	*vee*-**noh** **teen**-*toh*	*red wine*

NUMBERS

0	cero	**seh**-*roh*
1	uno	**oo**-*noh*
2	dos	*dohs*
3	tres	*trehs*
4	cuatro	**kwa**-*troh*
5	cinco	**seen**-*koh*
6	seis	*says*
7	siete	**see**-*eh-teh*
8	ocho	**oh**-*choh*
9	nueve	**nweh**-*veh*
10	diez	*dee*-**ehs**
11	once	**ohn**-*seh*
12	doce	**doh**-*seh*

13	trece	*treh*-*seh*
14	catorce	*kah*-**tohr**-*seh*
15	quince	**keen**-*seh*
16	dieciséis	*dee-eh-see*-**seh**-**ees**
17	diecisiete	*dee-eh-see-see*-**eh**-*teh*
18	dieciocho	*dee-eh-see*-**oh**-*choh*
19	diecinueve	*dee-eh-see*-**nweh**-*veh*
20	veinte	**veh**-*een-teh*
21	veintiuno	*veh-een-tee*-**oo**-*noh*
22	veintidós	*veh-een-tee*-**dohs**
30	treinta	**treh**-*een-tah*
31	treinta y uno	*treh-een-tah ee* **oo**-*noh*
40	cuarenta	*kwah*-**rehn**-*tah*
50	cincuenta	*seen*-**kwehn**-*tah*
60	sesenta	*seh*-**sehn**-*tah*
70	setenta	*seh*-**tehn**-*tah*
80	ochenta	*oh*-**chehn**-*tah*
90	noventa	*noh*-**vehn**-*tah*
100	cien	*see*-**ehn**
101	ciento uno	*see*-**ehn**-*toh oo*-*noh*
102	ciento dos	*see*-**ehn**-*toh dohs*
200	doscientos	*dohs-see*-**ehn**-*tohs*
500	quinientos	*khee-nee*-**ehn**-*tohs*
700	setecientos	*seh-teh-see*-**ehn**-*tohs*
900	novecientos	*noh-veh-see*-**ehn**-*tohs*
1,000	mil	*meel*
1,001	mil uno	*meel oo*-*noh*

TIME

one minute	un minuto	**oon** *mee*-**noo**-*toh*
one hour	una hora	*oo*-*nah* **oh**-*rah*
half an hour	media hora	*meh*-**dee**-*ah* **oh**-*rah*
half past one	la una y media	*lah* **oo**-*nah ee* **meh**-*dee-ah*
quarter past one	la una y cuarto	*lah* **oo**-*nah ee* **kwahr**-*toh*
ten past one	la una y diez	*lah* **oo**-*nah ee* *dee-ehs*
quarter to two	cuarto para las dos	**kwahr**-*toh pah-rah lahs* **dohs**
ten to two	diez para las dos	*dee-ehs pah-rah lahs* **dohs**
Monday	lunes	**loo**-*nehs*
Tuesday	martes	**mahr**-*tehs*
Wednesday	miércoles	*mee-ehr-koh*-**lehs**
Thursday	jueves	*hoo*-**weh**-*vehs*
Friday	viernes	*vee*-**ehr**-*nehs*
Saturday	sábado	**sah**-*bah-doh*
Sunday	domingo	*doh*-**meen**-*goh*
January	enero	*eh*-**neh**-*roh*
February	febrero	*feh*-**breh**-*roh*
March	marzo	**mahr**-*soh*
April	abril	*ah*-**breel**
May	mayo	**mah**-*yoh*
June	junio	**hoo**-*nee-oh*
July	julio	**hoo**-*lee-oh*
August	agosto	*ah*-**gohs**-*toh*
September	septiembre	*sehp-tee*-**ehm**-*breh*
October	octubre	*ohk*-**too**-*breh*
November	noviembre	*noh-vee*-**ehm**-*breh*
December	diciembre	*dee-see*-**ehm**-*breh*
Two days ago	Hace dos días	*hah*-*seh* **dohs** *dee*-*ahs*
In two day's time	En dos días	*ehn* **dohs** *dee*-*ahs*
May 1	El primero de mayo	*ehl pree*-**meh**-*roh deh* **mah**-*yoh*

ACKNOWLEDGMENTS

The publisher would like to thank the following for their kind permission to reproduce their photographs:

Key: a-above; b-below/bottom; c-centre; f-far; l-left; r-right; t-top

123RF.com: Belikova 90bl; Yulia Belousova 20tl, 230-1; Freda Bouskoutas 121br; Anton Ivanov 116-7b; Andrea Izzotti 170t; Loes Kieboom 10ca; Joanne Weston 281crb.

akg-images: Bildarchiv Steffens 145crb.

Alamy Stock Photo: Aclosund Historic 59br; Aflo Co. Ltd. / AM Corporation 263br; agefotostock / Jerónimo Alba 76bl, / Cem Canbay 302bl, / J.D. Dallet 61clb, / Sara Janini 272-3t; / Laurent Marolleau 247tr, / Richard Maschmeyer 284bl, / Leonardo Díaz Romero 146bl, / Toño Labra 157bl, 159tr, 211cra, 240bl, / Douglas Williams 91t; AGF Srl / Charles Mahaux 150bl, 266bl; Tatiana Aksenova 63cb; Rubens Alarcon 195tr; Jerónimo Alba 37cl; Dorothy Alexander 37br; Luis Emilio Villegas Amador 156t; Al Argueta 50tr, 183br; Rafael Ben-Ari 38-9b; Bildagentur-online / Schoening 79tr; Robert Briggs 272bl; Chad Case 24tr; Cavan / Aurora Photos / Ethan Welty 28bl; Jui-Chi Chan 196-7t; Creative Touch Imaging Ltd. 221c; David Crossland 42tl; Bob Daemmrich 63tr; Danita Delimont / Brent Bergherm 28crb; Danita Delimont, Agent / Russell Gordon 47clb, 238crb, / Charles Sleicher 285tl; Keith Dannemiller 54clb; Simon Dannhauer 306-7t; Bill Davis 71t, 126; Bill Davis / Museo de Arte Popular -AAMAP / *Vochol* - Crystal Beads Vw Beetle by Bautista And Ortbautista And Ortíz Families 36bl; dbimages / Amanda Ahn 132tl, / Allen Brown 206t, / dbtravel 197br, / Roy Johnson 289tr; Kinn Deacon 27tr; Design Pics Inc / Axiom / Richard Maschmeyer 295tl, / Destinations / Richard Cummins 25tr, / Destinations / Stuart Westmorland 52bl; directphoto.bz 47br; Reinhard Dirscherl 31tr; Douglas Peebles Photography / *Mural at Museo Alhondiga de Ganaditas, Guanajuato* by Jose Chavez Morado © DACS 2020 198tl; dpa picture alliance / Jesús Alvarado 54cr; Daniel Gustavo Apodaca Duron 178-9t; John Elk III 285tc; Richard Ellis 53br, 214-5b, 219tl, 274tr; Esdelval 217br; Everett Collection Inc / CSU Archives 117cra; Eye Ubiquitous / Nick Bonetti / *Sunday Afternoon in Alameda Park* by Diego Rivera © Banco de México Diego Rivera Frida Kahlo Museums Trust, Mexico, D.F. / DACS 2020 88b; Eye Ubiquitous / Nick Bonetti 202br, 205br, 263t; Michele Falzone 45br; Tiago Fernandez 238-9t; FineArt 117tr; Robert Fried 205cla; Eddy Galeotti 30tl; Scott Goodno 151tr; Paul Christian Gordon 119cl; Diego Grandi 83bc; Granger Historical Picture Archive, NYC 59tr, 62t, 62crb,117cb; Leigh Green 168bl; Jeff Greenberg 107tr; Jeffrey Isaac Greenberg 5 87br; Luis Gutierrez / NortePhoto.com 179br, 185t, 187br; Pedro Gutierrez 8clb; ML Harris 236bl; Andrew Hasson 128crb; Have Camera Will Travel | Central & South America 77tc; hemis.fr / Leroy Francis 220b, / Franck Guiziou 182cl, / José Nicolas 105br, / Paul Seux / Museo de Arte Moderno / *Las Dos Fridas* by Frida Kahlo © Banco de México Diego Rivera Frida Kahlo Museums Trust, Mexico, D.F. / DACS 2020 108tl; Hi-Story 62cr; David Hilbert 140br; Simone Hogan 33cla; Keith Homan 53cra; Dave G. Houser 179clb; IanDagnall Computing 57tr; Image Professionals GmbH / Franz Marc Frei / *La Giganta* by Jose Luis Cuevas © DACS 2020 86br;

imageBROKER / Oliver Gerhard 41br, / Knut Hildebrandt 238bc, / Stefan Kiefer 46b, / Horst Mahr 248b, / Martin Siepmann 223tr, / Vision 21 32bl, 42cra; Independent Picture Service / A.A.M. Van der Heyden 57cla; Anton Ivanov 120-1t, 123br, 241t; JeffG 133crb; Jon Arnold Images Ltd 145tr, / John Coletti 60tr, 82-3t, / *stained glass in Chapultepec Castle* Dr. Atl; aka Gerardo Murillo © DACS 2020 108-9b; Bjanka Kadic 36-7t, 101tr,117tl, 118t, 125tr, / Diego Rivera's studio, House - Studio Museum of Diego Rivera and Frida Kahlo, San Angel, Mexico City © Banco de México Diego Rivera Frida Kahlo Museums Trust, Mexico, D.F. / DACS 2020 119bl; Chon Kit Leong 80br; Lifestyle pictures 63br; Melvyn Longhurst 77ca, 285br, 294cl; Craig Lovell / Eagle Visions Photography 47tr; Elijah Lovkoff 12t, 123tl; M&N 63tl; M.Sobreira 101crb; Alain Machet (4) 246bl; © Marco / ASK Images 54cl; Marshall Ikonography 302-3t; Richard Maschmeyer 255br; Angus McComiskey 22bl, 289br; Mehdi33300 234-5t; Cathyrose Melloan 227tl; Margaret Metcalfe 83crb; Robert Meyers 28t; John Mitchell 46tl, 110cl, 156cr, 170bc, 269b; J.Enrique Molina 145fbr, 241cra, 248cl; Mostardi Photography 295ca; National Geographic Image Collection / Richard Nowitz 212tl; Nature Picture Library / Jack Dykinga 34cla; Niday Picture Library 60clb; Ai Nishino 236tr; Luc Novovitch 181br; Frank Nowikowski / *stained glass* by Leopoldo Flores 160t; Brian Overcast 28cr, 58cla, 63cra, 141cra, 145cra, 210bl, 212-3b, 215tr, 229br, 238clb, 255t, 270bl; David Parker 85br; Pascopix 204-5t; Stefano Paterna 308-9t; PhotoBliss 145br; Pictorial Press Ltd 60br; The Picture Art Collection 60tl, 221cb (La Catrina); Marek Poplawski 188-9b; Prisma Archivo 57br, 58br, 61br, 235tr; Radius Images 22t; Alberto Sibaja Ramírez 55tr; Bernardo Ramonfaur 49crb, 59clb; Stefano Ravera 287tr; Robertharding / Wendy Connett 51tr, / Christian Kober 40-1t, 48bl, 158-9b, 208br, / Kim Walker 237t; Emiliano Rodriguez 143cra; Marcelo Rodriguez 216t; Eduardo Fuster Salamero 144-5b; Chico Sanchez 142cl; Schoening 292bl, 292-3b, 293tl; David Shaw 264cr; Mirosław Skórka 265bl; Witold Skrypczak 171b; Jonny Snowden 21t, 276-7; Jan Sochor 55clb, 221ca, 239br; Kumar Sriskandan 286tr; Lee Karen Stow 49bl; Egmont Strigl 143t; Keren Su / China Span 54cra; Hiroko Tanaka 90br; Darren Tierney 280-1b; TMC images 253tr; Travelpix 104br; Jane Tregelles 282t; Nathan and Elaine Vaessen 184bl, 310-1; Lucas Vallecillos 11cr, 12clb, 33br, 43cl, 84b, 89tl, 120bl, 130b, 199b, 219tr; Ivan Vdovin 186t; John Warburton-Lee Photography / David Bank 70, 112-3; Judy Waytiuk 287cr; Jim West 48-9t; Xinhua / Rong Hao 26tl; Zoonar GmbH / Konstantin Kalishko 297cl; Bosiljka Zutich 283clb; Александар Тодоровић 55crb.

Bridgeman Images: 58-9t.

Depositphotos Inc: Naticastilling 109cl.

Dreamstime.com: Adeliepenguin 51cla; Adfoto 238cra; Atosan 68c, 72-3; Florian Blümm 55cra; Boggy 225b; Byelikova 13br, 162bl; Kobby Dagan 32-3t; Igor Dymov 270-1b; Eddygaleotti 86tl, 244-5t; Marc Elicagaray 152clb; Esdelval 208t; Alexandre Fagundes De Fagundes 93br; Frenta 287b; Gerasimovvv 290-1b; Diego Grandi 95br, 106b; Sven Hansche 31tl; Tim Hester 34cr; Pablo Hidalgo 283br; Vlad Ispas 41cl; Javarman 30tr, 275b; Denis Kabanov 169t; Liliya

Main Contributors Kana Awoyemi,
Huw Hennessy, Stephen Keeling, Shafik Meghji,
Nick Caistor, Maria Doulton, Petra Fischer,
Eduardo Gleason, Phil Gunson, Alan Knight,
Felicity Laughton, Richard Nichols, Chloë Sayer

Senior Editor Alison McGill

Senior Designers Sarah Snelling, Ben Hinks

Project Editor Robin Moul

Project Art Editor Van Anh Le

Designers Bharti Karakoti, William Robinson,
Ankita Sharma, Stuti Tiwari Bhatia,
Vinita Venugopal, Nell Wood

Factcheckers Huw Hennessy, Feike de Jong

Editors Emma Gibbs, Zoë Rutland, Jackie Staddon,
Laure Gysemans, Lucy Sara-Kelly, Yvonne Thouroude

Proofreader Samantha Cook

Indexer Helen Peters

Senior Picture Researcher Ellen Root

Picture Research Naomi Bristow,
Sumita Khatwani, Vagisha Pushp,
Rituraj Singh, Åsa Westerlund

Illustrators José Luis de Andrés de Colsa,
Gary Cross, Richard Draper, Javier Gómez Morata
(Acanto Arquitectura y Urbanismo S.L.), Isidoro
González-Adalid Cabezas (Acanto Arquitectura
y Urbanismo S.L.), Stephen Guapay, Paul Guest,
Claire Littlejohn, John Woodcock

Senior Cartographic Editor Casper Morris

Cartography Ashutosh Ranjan Bharti,
Simonetta Giori, Zafar ul Islam Khan

Jacket Designers Bess Daly, Sarah Snelling

Jacket Picture Research Susie Watters

Senior DTP Designer Jason Little

DTP Designer Rohit Rojal

Technical Prepress Manager Tom Morse

Image Retouching Steve Crozier

MIX
Paper from
responsible sources
FSC™ C018179
www.fsc.org